THE INNOVATION PLAYBOOK

A REVOLUTION IN BUSINESS EXCELLENCE

Nicholas J. Webb

WILEY

John Wiley & Sons, Inc.

Published by John Wiley & Sons, Inc., Hoboken, New Jersey.
Published simultaneously in Canada.

For general information on our other products and services or for technical support, please contact our Customer Care Department within the United States at (800) 762-2974, outside the United States at (317) 572-3993 or fax (317) 572-4002.

Wiley also publishes its books in a variety of electronic formats. Some content that appears in print may not be available in electronic books. For more information about Wiley products, visit our web site at www.wiley.com.

Library of Congress Cataloging-in-Publication Data:

Webb, Nicholas J., 1958–
    The innovation playbook : a revolution in business excellence / Nicholas J. Webb.
        p. cm.
    Includes index.
    ISBN 978-0-470-63796-8 (cloth); ISBN 978-0-470-91687-2 (ebk);
ISBN 978-0-470-91688-9 (ebk); ISBN 978-0-470-91689-6 (ebk)
    1. Technological innovations—Economic aspects. I. Title.
    HC79.T4W43 2011
    658.4′063—dc22

                                                                    2010021342

Printed in the United States of America

10 9 8 7 6 5 4 3 2

I would like to dedicate this book to my amazing family: my beautiful wife Michelle, my daughters Taylor, Madison, and Paige, and my son Chase. I would also like to acknowledge the ongoing support of my identical twin brother, Charles Arthur Webb.

Contents

Foreword

Everyone talks about innovation. As companies, it's our under-pinning of success and growth. As consumers we demand it—and with increasing speed. As innovators, we thrive on the prospect of launching something game-changing.

But delivering on that need, demand, and passion with consistency and true benefit is what spells the difference between a one-time wonder and a company positioned for long-term success.

How do you ensure that you have a pipeline of eurekas? A steady supply of business propositions strong and relevant enough to capture the attention, imaginations, hearts, and intent-to-buy of your key audiences? And how do you ensure that they come quickly enough, since the window for market-leadership success, even for the most revolutionary innovations, continues to grow shorter as the world grows more interconnected.

It's a delicate balance and an interesting interplay of *managed creativity*.

As outlined in the pages that follow, winning the innovation game calls for a series of highly choreographed elements that must play out with symphonic precision and elegance, firmly directed and fueled by passionate talent.

At Procter & Gamble, we've seen the extraordinary benefits—to the company and to our customers—of delivering in-market innovations that support our mission of touching and improving lives. Some of our most notable innovations have been:

- First disposable razor
- First synthetic detergent
- First fluoride toothpaste proven to fight tooth decay
- First commercial disposable diaper
- First fast-acting treatment for osteoporosis
- First in-home teeth whitening system

We've also seen the challenges, throughout our 173-year history, of keeping those ideas coming and, most critically, of ensuring that they are relevant.

One of our core learnings has been the need to remain connected to our customers—and to appreciate that you are never connected enough. When we've stepped back to evaluate the failure of an innovation or a new market introduction, the root cause has almost always been no understanding of what people really want and need. We often thought we knew. We tried to show them. And in the end, they showed us.

What those experiences also taught us is that a game-changer has to do more than deliver on today's need. It also must deliver on tomorrow's. We learned that once you understand the need, you must pull out all stops to find a solution, package it in a way that captures heads and hearts, and deliver on the value equation. Plus get it to market fast. Because if you're working on it, chances are very high someone else either already is or will be very soon.

Nicholas Webb, in *The Innovation Playbook,* offers core elements that all of us can incorporate and learn from to help build success.

At P&G, we've been working on our orchestra for some time. We've built a team of experts in consumer research, R&D, and marketing. We've made innovation part of everyone's job, regardless of what their job is. We try to ensure that our culture supports playing to win, but at the same time we must manage failure as part of the race. We also build innovation partnerships, through our Connect+Develop process, with experts, companies, and innovators outside P&G all over the world. And we try to have everyone connected so that ideas flow, grow, and improve. We appreciate that this must be an orchestra of precision. We have hit some sour notes, and we're still learning. We always will be.

But we also keenly appreciate why we continue to practice, and how sweet the melodic sound of success can be. As our Chief Technology Officer Bruce Brown likes to say: "The answer to the challenges we face is always the same. The answer is innovation."

Chris Thoen
Director, External Innovation & Knowledge Management,
Global Business Development,
The Procter & Gamble Company

Acknowledgments

This book would not have been possible without the help of Peter Sanders, Jennifer Dean and Stephen Orsatti. I would also like to especially thank the amazing team at Brightidea, including Matthew Greeley the CEO of Brightidea, Paul Tran, Director of Strategic Initiatives and Marketing Manager, Stefanie Mainwaring. I would like to thank Ken Grossman at Sierra Nevada. Also, the team at Snap-on Tools. Lisa Underkoffler, the Principal Product Manager at Acrobat .com. Dr. Geoffrey Moore for his kind permission to allow us to share some of his amazing work. Ann Marie Dumais, senior vice president of new product introductions at Nielsen Company. One of the best patent attorneys in the country Robert M. Siminski. I also would like to thank Jim Austin, Director of Life Sciences, Decision Strategies International, Inc. Terry Fadem, Managing Director, Corporate Alliances, University of Pennsylvania School of Medicine Paul J. H. Schoemaker, Research Director, Mack Center for Technological Innovation at The Wharton School for allowing me to share their amazing work in the area of scenario planning. Last but certainly not least, I would like to thank Hewlett-Packard Corporation for allowing us the opportunity to share their HP garage material. I would especially like to thank Silvi Steigerwald Innovation Strategist HP Software & Solutions and Art Beckman Innovation Program Lead HP Software & Solutions.

Introduction

The innovation headlines speak for themselves.

- For almost 90 percent of CEOs, generating organic growth through innovation has become essential for success in their industry. (Source: Boston Consulting Group.)
- Of more than 900 CEOs surveyed, less than half are satisfied with the financial returns on their investments in innovation. (Boston Consulting Group.)
- The global innovation success average, across all geographies and all industries, is only 4 percent. (Dolphin Group, *BusinessWeek*.)
- Businesses today have no shortage of ideas; rather, they lack the ability to determine their value in a systematic, timely, and cost-effective way. (Microsoft white paper: Innovation Process Management.)
- According to a global survey published by the Boston Consulting Group, 74 percent of companies contacted planned to increase spending on innovation and 90 percent of them consider innovation "essential for success" in their industries. However, less than half were satisfied with the financial returns on their investments in innovation.
- Improving competitive advantage, increased revenue growth, and faster innovation are among the top 10 issues for CIOs. (Gartner Group CIO Survey.)
- The failure rate of innovation is huge, or you could say the success rate—4 percent—is pathetic. (Larry Keeley, Doblin Inc.)

Are we, as stewards of our own capitalistic future and fate, doing what we need to do to stay on top of the competitive heap? Or are we locked in an inexorable race to the bottom?

Still Crazy about Innovation—After All These Years

Over the past 20 years I've had the privilege of working as a CEO for several successful medical device companies and now as a Certified Management Consultant in the area of innovation management. I've also had a career as a successful inventor with over 35 US patents. I have invented products, started, run and sold companies, and turned my experiences into value for many others in the corporate and university research spaces who have sought to do the same. So I believe that my innovation industry vantage point is somewhat different than that of the average person. Different how, you ask? Different because I see the realities and practicalities of all stages of business, from sitting across from a buyer, to bringing a product to market, to promoting a new invention.

I also understand from my discipline as a management consultant, the realities—good and bad—of the innovation process within organizations. What is interesting to me, and is also the major thesis of *The Innovation Playbook*, is the fact that great organizations develop great technologies, and as we've seen there is a lot of evidence of that.

Now for some people that proclamation may seem too simplistic. But it's true. We must also look at the other side of the coin—what about the organizations that can't develop new things? Those companies that go down in flames despite their best efforts? Or spend millions on R&D, only to bring a minor tweak to market or to end up buying technology through expensive licenses—or worse, end up doing nothing at all?

Don't Buy "The Diet"

In fact, the best way to look at the innovation space is considering that it's very much like dieting. It seems every week there is a new book on innovation, and likewise, there's a new book on dieting. And what is that book? It's the latest tool. The South Beach Diet. The Grapefruit Diet. The Beverly Hills diet. And on and on.

What is the usual result of these diets? Weight gain. The bottom line is most diets don't work. Why don't they work? Because they are taking a fractional approach while embarking on a global challenge. We don't get skinny or become thinner as a result of using fractional tools that focus only on fatness. In fact, the biggest cause of obesity in America is the focus on fatness. According to a recent Harris poll, 80 percent of Americans are overweight.

So what does this have to do with innovation? Weight loss focuses on fatness, and innovation focuses on risk. And, to paraphrase the great behavioral psychologist Dr. Dennis Waitley, we move towards the thing we think about most often.

Could it be that innovation is a philosophy? A culture? A philosophy and culture focused on delivering insanely cool products to valued customers, instead of process orientation designed to address the internal needs of risk management?

I believe the answer is absolutely yes. Organizations year-by-year, month-by-month, continue to buy more innovation-diet books that involve more bureaucracy, more risk mitigation, and ultimately greater failure. Studies are suggesting that almost 95 percent of consumer products fail, yet most companies have tried desperately to control that—ironically—by using risk management systems. Why? Because of a certain focus—the focus on risk, just like the fat focus phenomenon.

It's All about the Customer

In researching this book, I was surprised to learn there are more than 170 different so-called new product development or innovation management systems. The reason there are so many systems is that most systems don't work. The message of this book is that great companies develop great technologies, and those great companies don't focus on risk. They focus on customers instead. More specifically, they focus on the *net value* they *deliver* to their customers. That's where success lives.

But more than focusing on customer net value, great organizations understand that great innovation is systemic. It's *cultural*. Innovation has to do with the organizational climate, and organizational *focus*. It has to do with the people a company hires, the way it treats employees, the way it lives within the global and local community. I've found through my research that the best companies in innovation are championed by the best people. These people create systems that reward smart risk and their ultimate focus on a daily basis is on delivering systematic customer value.

Why am I so critical of the Grapefruit Diet approach to innovation management? It's not just that the Grapefruit Diet approach doesn't work—and believe me, it doesn't. In fact, most approaches designed to increase access to external innovation and speed time to market and improve commercialization are wrong. The ones that are right are only right for some companies because, like weight loss, in order to have a successful innovation system, you need to begin with a great philosophy, which is like a holistic philosophy of health for an individual.

. . . Really, Net Customer Value

When it comes to innovation, we need to have a holistic philosophy of net customer value. I'll spend a good bit of time in this book describing what I mean by that—especially in Chapters 6 and 7. Then we'll look at some specific tools that can be deployed in today's fast moving, flexible environment in a prescribed way in order to address the issues that face current organizations. These tools will help you get things done by combining the best of your internal resources and those on the outside in the industry at large.

The first problem and a major pitfall in innovation today is the use of a cookie-cutter approach towards improving innovation. Some companies are excellent at accessing external innovation, yet extremely bad at taking those technologies to market. Some companies have a very good new product development function, but are very bad at deploying it. I could go on and on. The problem is that innovation requires a broad array of skill sets. But those skill sets can be easily built in as long as the right philosophy—and culture—of innovation exists.

In fact, years of being in the innovation business have made it clear to me that achieving superstardom in the innovation space is a matter of three things, and these things must be taken in balance: a customer focus and an effective process that keeps innovation moving along, all supported by a healthy innovation-focused culture. I'll get back to the superstar idea in a minute.

"There's No More Room to Suck"

In researching this book we found some of the greatest companies delivering some of the greatest products and technologies to the market had no new product development system at all. I'm not suggesting that systems are always bad, but to suggest that they are always going to add to customer value is obviously dead wrong. Again, the Grapefruit Diet says "just eat grapefruit" and "don't worry about fitness," "don't worry about a balanced diet," "don't worry about a holistic approach towards wellness"—just eat grapefruit and everything will be okay.

That's what's being propagated in the innovation space, and it's bad. It's bad for two reasons: First, it's a fractional solution distracting us from the focus of creating customer net value. Second, quite simply, there is no more room to suck. By that I mean if you're bad, everyone knows you're bad. In days past you could create a mediocre product and, frankly, the community you served didn't have a great means to communicate with one another, certainly not in real time. But the Internet is the great equalizer. It provides a tremendous opportunity to propagate positive viral marketing but at the same time, unfortunately, it provides an opportunity for real time, derogatory feedback for people who are unhappy with your service. The importance of being great and delivering true customer value has never been greater. Throughout the book you'll be shown the importance of digital media and their impact on the role of innovation.

Another important component in the world of innovation is speed. The world has speeded up to the point where, frankly, it's hard for most CEOs and most organizations to keep up. But the ability to keep up with what's going on and deploying solutions is the difference between success and failure.

Speed does rule the day. If your organization does not have fast-track methodologies that deliver technologies and products to market before your competition, you will put your business in great jeopardy. Speed does rule the day, and again, we'll talk about this more as we go through case studies that show how speed was the secret weapon that delivered technologies before the competitors were able to.

When the economy is good and competition is slight, it's easy to be involved in—consumed by—process orientation, where company teams get together, pontificate, test, and evaluate every process out there. But unfortunately, there is no more opportunity to allow process orientation to rule the day within your company. Process orientation has become an infectious disease within most organizations.

Becoming an Innovation Superstar

Indeed, there's a certain *je ne sais quoi* that separates true excellence from all the rest. You've probably heard about it in Tom Peters' book, *In Search of Excellence*. You've probably also heard about it from

Jim Collins in his book, *Good to Great*. "It" is found in attention to customers, attention to customer service, attention to details, and attention to execution.

But if you take a broader view of the excellence story, it all boils down to innovation. Product innovations. Service innovations. Innovations that bring quality. Innovations in employee satisfaction, which brings all of the above. Most people think only of "technology" or "product" when they think of innovation. Innovation is clearly not limited to product or technology, or the next bright shiny object to come rolling off the assembly line. Innovation is broader, deeper, and more visceral than that. In fact, I believe all that makes the Peters' and Collins' companies great is really, bottom line, innovation, and behind that, innovative thinking and culture.

And it doesn't stop there. Innovation is really about customers. What customers want, but also what they need or don't even know they want. Henry Ford once said: "If I had asked the market what they wanted, they would have said a faster horse." True innovators are so close to their customers they know what they need—and how to deliver exceptional value to satisfy that need—even more than the customers do.

So with these ideas in mind, here are a couple of core definitions.

- *Innovation* is about being truly connected to customer needs and lifestyles, so that you can deduce their needs and apply technologies and ideas to their solution.
- *Innovation Superstars* are connected to their customers; furthermore they have the right balance of process and culture to *consistently* deliver excellent customer value quickly and thus to stay ahead of the competition and achieve leading market share in their industries.

Much of the rest of *The Innovation Playbook* examines the moving parts that support these definitions.

Why Apple Shines

You'll hear about Apple over and over again in innovation books. And I'll refer to Apple too, but won't dwell on their already visible successes. Apple is a perennial superstar, not because the company lets their customer tell them what they need, but because they understand the needs so well and deliver really cool stuff to meet them. Apple has a culture of innovation second to none, which allows it not just to lead—but to control—its market, in a way few companies have ever been able to pull off. In fact, Apple is number one on *BusinessWeek's* annual innovative company rankings, and it moved up 15 places to reach number 56 in the Fortune 500—an impressive, but hardly a surprising, move.

Apple isn't recreating the wheel with each new product. What makes a company like Apple innovative isn't that it creates something completely new each time, but that it is able to create designs, devices and functionality so that their products are popular with consumers and successful financially.

Obviously, not everyone can match Apple's success. But if you can just match Apple's mind-set, you're well on your way. That's really what *The Innovation Playbook* is all about.

Plays in *The Innovation Playbook*

The Innovation Playbook is organized in two parts. Part I: *What's Wrong with Innovation Today* highlights the importance of innovation in today's world and explains why so many of today's organizations can't get it done.

> Chapter 1: *The New Economy: Different for Good* examines why innovation is the key to survival in today's fast-paced business world.
>
> Chapter 2: *The Wheels Keep Falling Off* highlights the many reasons thrown around to describe why innovation doesn't work in today's organizations. I distill that long list of reasons down to ten "Nick's Picks" to explain why innovation doesn't work and to begin to describe what to do about it.
>
> Chapter 3: *The Danger of Safety* is a full frontal attack on one of the great ills in the innovation world today—the obsession with risk and risk management.
>
> Chapter 4: *What's Mything in Innovation Today* explores four other common myths about what innovators and innovative organizations should do.
>
> While Part I concerns itself with the ills and ailments in the innovation space today, Part II, *Innovating Your Way to*

Business Excellence, lays out in six chapters the Nick Webb solution to achieving excellence in your business or organization through innovation.

Chapter 5: *Anatomy of an Innovation Superstar*. Here I jump right in with a description of the magic combination of customer focus, process, and culture that separates true innovation superstars from the rest of the pack.

Chapter 6: *Creating Net Customer Value* takes apart the crucial concept of net customer value, including my "value strata" set of standards of excellence; then I'll describe how, as an organization, to go about achieving it.

Chapter 7: *Carpet Time* tells you how to get close to your customers and to establish the "conduits of connectivity" necessary to really understand net customer value.

Chapter 8: *The Real Open Innovation Framework*. In this chapter I lay out a framework and a toolbox I call "Real Open." It is used to find new ideas from external and internal sources, filter those ideas, and move them through the development process at utmost speed. These tools are set up to be adapted to the specific needs of any given organization; it is emphatically not a one-size-fits-all solution, unlike so many others out there.

Chapter 9: *Creating a (Digital) Innovation Culture*. Here I describe the key cultural components in an organization that support good innovation, and give some tips for how to get there, with particular emphasis on using today's digital media tools to support innovation.

Chapter 10: *Dancing with the Innovation Superstars*. Finally, I give some case examples of companies that have made it and how they did so. Then I describe how *you* can become a superstar using the Certified Innovation Superstar certification and training program.

There you have it—I'll leave it to you to read the Playbook, get down on the field and practice, and kick some real business butt! Remember, no pain, no gain, but let me tell you from experience—the rewards for making it all happen are simply amazing.

PART

I

WHAT'S WRONG WITH INNOVATION TODAY

CHAPTER 1

The New Economy: Different for Good

Most of the time, when you think about the term innovation, you think in terms of significant breakthroughs in technology—nanotechnology, biotechnology, energy, and so on. But the truth of the matter is that innovation is really about creating ways of delivering meaningful *net customer value*. And especially in today's challenging and competitive economic times, net customer value really rules (or should rule) the innovation universe.

Okay, you ask—what is net customer value? It's a fair question, and I'll come back to this concept again and again throughout *The Innovation Playbook*. Net customer value refers to the benefit customers receive from a product—real and perceived—relative to its cost. It's a hard thing to measure, but, like good architecture or good wine, you'll know it when you see it (or drink it).

Problem: It isn't so easy to see customer value (or taste it), right? Part of the reason net customer value is hard to quantify or measure, and part of what makes it such an important thing to understand for a business is that it's a multisensory experience. The best way to explain is by example.

A Better Beer, a Better Burger

One of the greatest restaurants on the planet, in my opinion, is a West Coast hamburger eatery—a fast food restaurant, if you will—called In-N-Out Burger. Now, In-N-Out Burger knows really special things about innovation. They know innovation really is about touching people. What does that mean? Touching people is about the fact that we are multisensory beings. We have a sense of smell. We have a sense of vision. We taste things. We feel things. It's about the combination of those senses that creates a visceral determination about that experience. In-N-Out Burger is a perfect example of a company that understands this concept.

The Eyes, the Ears, the Nose Have It

To illustrate, In-N-Out Burger has specially designed exhaust fans that send out the smell of its mouth-watering fare in multiple directions for several blocks. Anyone on the West Coast knows if you drive anywhere near an In-N-Out Burger, you'll quickly pick up the scent of delicious food, which is no accident! They not only want you to *see* the restaurant but also *feel* it from a sensory point of view. But they also know that, in order for you to want to eat something there, the restaurant also has to be visually inviting.

So they created a simple, clean, and ultra-fresh environment that really indicates the quality and cleanliness of the food. They pay a lot of attention to the appearance of the restaurants, actually employing full time people to clean and pick up trash on the grounds. This might not seem like such a big deal, but if you want to eat something, it had better be visually inviting, so they create a simple, clean, and ultra-fresh environment that really communicates the quality and cleanliness of the food.

The fact that, when you're at an In-N-Out Burger, you don't see any trash on the ground may not seem like a big deal, but unfortunately, many other restaurants don't see that as a big deal either. Obviously, as consumers of food, we have a lot of options. When we inhale something that's clean, when we inhale something that smells great, we know that is part of an overall experience we, as multi-sensory beings, are going to enjoy.

But In-N-Out Burger goes far beyond that. For example, when you pull up to the restaurant drive-thru you'll see that the speaker is the size of a manhole cover. Why is that important? Most drive-thru restaurants have really small speakers, so communication between a customer service person and the customer is extremely tenuous and cryptic. This results in mistakes and increased pressure on the customer who must yell into the speaker, and stress and fatigue for the employees.

Such attention to detail shows In-N-Out Burger understands a very basic concept for the business: In order to get accurate orders and communicate properly back to customers, they needed a large speaker. I remember when early In-N-Out Burgers had something akin to a megaphone mounted on a pole—even this provided a tremendous benefit and would be considered an innovation.

But it continues to even get better. When you go to the restaurant and start to place an order, you have an intelligent and articulate person taking the order. They're able to communicate clearly what you're ordering and verify that they got it right in a super-friendly way that adds to the feeling of a good customer experience.

It continues from there. As you navigate the drive-thru, there's a gigantic plate glass window. Now that's not there so the employees can look out at the cars—it's so you can look into the kitchen—for three important reasons. First, they want you to see the cleanliness of the kitchen and their staff. The staff comes in impeccably clean, and if their clothing becomes soiled on the job, they have to change immediately. The second thing you see is a clean eating area. Picked up, wiped down, no food left lying around.

Magical Theater

Thirdly and finally, there's one other magical theme in the theater, and it is performed every day in every In-N-Out Burger across the country. They have one of their employees, behind this gigantic plate glass window, producing french fries by hand. None of that frozen food service stuff—they actually press freshly peeled potatoes through a french fry press by hand. Now why's that important? Because you know for a fact that those french fries were just made. They came from fresh potatoes. That is a tremendously important value perception for you. That the environment is clean is also an extremely important value perception.

Now when you get to the pick-up window to collect your box, you're greeted by another clean, well-dressed, intelligent, articulate, smiling employee. "Let me make sure you're order is right. Have a great day." They make sure you have enough napkins and the right condiments and straws for the kids. You feel as though they really care and that they're paying attention to detail.

But the essential magic really is, not surprisingly, that they have created a simple, delicious hamburger. They produce great products. Their hamburgers are good. Their french fries are good. Their milk shakes are good. They realize that they have to produce all of these things right to create the perfect customer scenario—which they rightly recognize as being the perfect scenario for success. A great environment, a clean environment, a quality environment, and a tasty environment are all necessary elements of the total experience—all are prerequisites—to get you to come back.

In-N-Out Burger is, in my opinion, a perfect example of a wonderful innovator. They understand that their omni-directional fans will deliver an appealing aroma that is very pleasing. They create, externally and internally, a visually clean and pleasing environment. They also know you can hear them and they can hear you through an amazingly simple but ingenious intercom system (in how many other drive-thru fast food places have you seen such a thing?) that insures a wonderful communication dialog that is not stressful. (Like you might expect from a waiter in a fine restaurant.)

One Plus One Is Three

They know that when you pull up to the window, you're continuing to build on what I call the *service cycle*. They know that you're adding more and more ingredients to your overall opinion of them, as you take in things visually, as you smell, as you listen and talk, as you pay and eat, as you observe. This is all part of what innovation is about—the ability to look, the ability to feel, the ability to sense an environment in a way that adds real value to the customer.

In-N-Out Burger is a perfect example of masterful innovation and, as a result, they're one of the most successful restaurant chains on the West Coast. But there's far more to the story than innovation as it pertains to the creation and implementation of ideas and technologies. Like most of our examples, In-N-Out Burger pays their employees more than most restaurant chains—particularly fast food chains. They also treat and train their employees extremely well.

Remember, great companies develop great technologies. Great companies also add value every step of the way, from employees to their community to their valued customer. While the innovations may seem to be simple, "gee-I-should-have-thought-of-that" ideas, In-N-Out Burger is definitely a world-class innovator.

Would You Like Something to Drink?

It's interesting to me to see how many resources go into trying to create and replicate these processes and systems when it really has to begin with creating a great company. Another great example is a company called Sierra Nevada Brewing Company, located in Chico, California and founded by a gentleman named Ken Grossman. Here's a guy who loved beer, and he loved it so much that his goal was to create the best product in the world. The truth of the matter is—as hard as that challenge is, the real challenge is to try to *scale up* that commitment.

So many companies have lost their competitive edge in the process of trying to go from a hand-crafted, customer-connected product to one that really has to be McDonald-ized and distributed worldwide. But Grossman's commitment continued. So he hired great people, and he treated them extremely well, and he continued to grow his business with one principal goal: Make the best beer in the world. In the meantime, he made it a point to honor everyone he touched, from his local community to his global community, including his employees, and especially his valued customers.

What's interesting about Sierra Nevada is that they're now the sixth largest brewery in the country. As a beer connoisseur myself, I have to say their beer is absolutely exceptional. If you know and love beer, you will love Sierra Nevada. If you're not a gourmet beer person, you too will love Sierra Nevada.

Great Companies Care

In fact, several large brewers across the country have tried to do what I call McDonald-izing the process of what Grossman has done—make lots and lots of products but maintain an ongoing commitment to developing new products and staying connected to the customer. Sierra Nevada, for example, has made a commitment to being a sustainable and globally environmentally conscious company because of Grossman's commitment, like that of all great companies, to be a good global and local citizen.

As a result, his brewery has the second largest solar array of any company in the state of California—second only to Google—producing some 80 percent of the brewery's electricity requirements. Not only does this ultimately help his bottom line, but it also shows his commitment to sustainability and community. But if you work there—if you're lucky enough to work at Sierra Nevada—it gets even better.

Like all companies I talk about in this book, they're great to their employees, because great companies care about their employees as much as they care about their customers and their global and local communities. If you work there, part of your compensation package is—you guessed it—a massage. You also get, with every paycheck, something they call a "beer buck." Each beer buck allows you to get a case of the exquisite beer they produce.

When you take the tour of Sierra Nevada Brewery, you see something that seems to be lost at so many companies—an amazing sense of pride. I can only describe that, consistent with all of the great companies we talk about in this book, there's such a pride in what Grossman does. You see it in the cleanliness of his operation. You see it in the efficiency and just the passion of every employee he has working there. They absolutely love working for him, they absolutely love working for Sierra Nevada, they're proud of their brand, and, not surprisingly, they love beer.

They also have a great restaurant called the Sierra Nevada Tap Room. It has tasty food, and often, even in a small town (albeit a college town) like Chico, you have to wait hours to get in. But wait many people will, because it is such a great experience. Grossman understands that, and the food and the entire restaurant experience is emblematic of his pride and his commitment to being multisensory.

From the design of his bottles to the variety of beers he produces, Grossman has earned his success. From the very select and conscientious way he distributes his beer to his commitment to the global and local community and to his beloved employees, again, that's how Grossman has earned success. I would say Grossman is another example of someone who has become bulletproof by doing the right thing for all people in his sphere of influence.

The Darkest Hour

Sierra Nevada and In-N-Out may be making it on the basis of understanding—and delivering—net customer value. But there's no doubt that business conditions during the "Great Recession" were a huge wake-up call for virtually every business and organization in the country—in the world, for that matter. The severity of the recession and its effects on employment, corporate profits, and general business morale hardly bear additional coverage here.

But the way I see it, the most recent downturn was really a symptom of economic maladies that had been building up for a long time. As Warren Buffett put it so well: "When the tide goes out, you see who's been swimming naked." And we sure saw a lot of naked swimmers: Eastman Kodak, Blockbuster, Circuit City (which I'll talk more about below), GM, and Chrysler, just to name a few, and not to mention entire industries like the U.S. financial services industry.

Yes, there were colossal failures and near-failures. Sure, at the time of this writing, Eastman Kodak and Blockbuster are trying to hang on, but their business models have essentially been reduced to shreds by, in the first case, a failure to keep up with technological changes, and in the second, a failed business model. But outside these big names, there are signs of failure everywhere in businesses large and small, and even entities in the public sector. What happened? How did these organizations lose their way, often knowing full well that better technologies and more competitive business models were emerging and, frankly, knowing that customers wanted something else?

Will the Great Pumpkin Return?

What's different about these failing companies that make them fail? What lessons are there to learn? I believe companies that continue their R&D spending during downturns will be better positioned to grow when the economy comes back. I also believe economic downturns force a better focus in R&D efforts—at least for those companies that get it.

But I also believe that a great many companies fail to get it, doing R&D for R&D's sake, or worse, letting R&D efforts languish in order to reduce short term expenses. These companies in particular are vulnerable because they're relying solely on the resurgence of the economy—the next "up" cycle—to bring them back. I call this the "Great Pumpkin Syndrome"—one may recall the images of Peanuts' Linus waiting in the pumpkin patch for the Great Pumpkin that never came. I believe those organizations that simply wait for the return of an economic Great Pumpkin will find themselves similarly waiting in vain by the pumpkin patch while others around them succeed and prosper.

Do Recessions Kill R&D Spending?

One might justifiably wonder what the economic downturn did to R&D expenses at U.S. and global corporations. Companies, of course, used the downturn as a reason to cut spending in a lot of areas, including R&D. As the economy climbs out of the recession, the next question is: "Will corporations that did cut R&D restore it?"

At the time of this writing, the facts are still arriving. Statistics published by the Battelle Memorial Institute indicate that U.S. research and development spending decreased in 2009, but it is expected to rebound in 2010 with the economy. According to their report, overall U.S. R&D spending is expected to rise 1.7 percent in 2010 to $395.9 billion after accounting for inflation. In the industrial sector, 2009 R&D spending in the United States actually fell 4.8 percent to $275.3 billion from $289.1 billion in 2008, but is expected to rise to $283 billion. Globally, R&D spending is expected to increase 4 percent to $1.16 trillion from 2009's $1.11 trillion and 2008's $1.12 trillion.

The real news may lie in the behavior of specific corporations and economic sectors. In the first nine months of 2009, Microsoft Corp. and International Business Machines Corp. cut R&D spending by 5.7 percent and 9.3 percent, respectively, while Apple increased R&D spending by 19 percent. Pfizer Inc. and Johnson & Johnson each cut their R&D spending by more than 10 percent. But there was a big surge in R&D among certain drug and biotech companies. According to a table published by *BusinessWeek*, Merck & Co., Gilead Sciences., Biogen Idec, and Monsanto increased theirs by more than 10 percent—in some cases, by as much as 30 percent. I'd not only say these companies are keeping a clear eye on the future, but they're probably also getting their research done at a reduced cost. Not a bad idea, in my view.

Not Your Father's Economy

One thing that we all must realize, in the wake of the Great Recession, is that the economy—and the role of innovation in the economy—have both changed, and changed for good. The biggest change is really in change itself: Everything changes faster.

What do I mean by this? The cycles of change, the ups and downs, are getting swifter, and may hit with little warning. Economic and business boom-bust cycles themselves are getting shorter. But more than that, technology and product cycles—the length of time a technology lasts in the marketplace—are getting shorter. Customer preference cycles are getting shorter—new things go out of style more quickly. So the key questions are: How are companies adapting to this? How should they be adapting to this? Should they spend more on R&D? Should they spend it more wisely? Should they spend it faster? We'll examine those questions, but first, a little more on the ups and downs today's businesses face.

A Faster Roller Coaster

Not so long ago—in the twentieth century and before—boom-to-bust business cycles may have been 20 years long, or longer. Although the cycles in those days were quite pronounced, with the Great Depression representing the granddaddy of them all, they were less frequent. They were pronounced because there was little that central banks, governments, or business leaders could do about them. Moreover, important safeguards like banking and securities laws hadn't yet been put into place. So people—and businesses—were literally wiped out in those days without ever knowing what hit them.

Today's business cycles are more frequent, generally shorter, and generally turn faster. More potent economic management through monetary and fiscal policy tends to reverse the cycle more quickly. But the biggest change over the years is the change in the *speed* of business—the rapidity in which business decisions are made and products and services are developed and sold. The pace of information about those products, as well as the economy as a whole, has become so much more rapid that entire sectors of the economy can change on a dime, in much the same way in which the latest military conflict or supply change can change the energy industry.

Technology and Product Cycles

Put simply, new technologies of yesteryear last longer than their counterparts of today.

Railroads, the great new technology of the nineteenth century, had a huge impact on business and commerce nearly everywhere. Their dominance as a transportation technology lasted more than 100 years. Fast forward to radio. As a major communication and advertising medium, its dominance ran for 40 years until eclipsed by TV. Fast forward to PCs and their key components. Seen a 3 1/2-inch floppy disc lately? Then there's VHS video. Dial-up Internet service.

The Internet itself—how long do products last these days before they must change or evolve?

The obvious answer: not very long. In almost all industries—even industries where the *product* doesn't change (like coal mining) but the *process* does—companies must deal with change, and rapid change at that. Not only does the speed of business make change happen faster within the enterprise, but the quantity and facility of rapid communications between customers and businesses have also played a role. The Internet has increased customer awareness, expanded feedback, and provided a medium for customers to share experiences *with each other*—all serving to level the playing field among large corporations and much smaller companies in many aspects of their business. The Internet has also increased pricing transparency, enabling customers to make price comparisons at a speed that was unheard of 30 years ago.

There are two upshots. First, combining the availability of product information, price information, and peer review of many key products, customers have become far more conscious of the net customer value they might expect to receive from a purchase. Second, competitors can copy or imitate even the most breakthrough technologies very rapidly. Trendy or market-leading products risk becoming obsolete almost instantly, and as the world becomes a global marketplace, competitive pressure is both wider and faster.

This isn't an economics book, but it's clear that innovation must respond to this environment. And it may not be enough to respond. True innovation success—and I'll argue this point in good times or bad—means that successful organizations must drive the environment. The good ones will pace the change, not just respond to it, in good times and bad.

Creative Destruction

The process of natural business and technological evolution and destruction was appropriately labeled "creative destruction" by economist Joseph Schumpeter. The forces of creative destruction, especially during economic downturns, tend to speed the passing of older, less efficient businesses and technologies (especially without the intervention of policymakers, as exemplified by U.S. automakers). The dot-com bust hastened the demise of legacy phone switching technologies, independent bookstores, and the Oldsmobile, not to mention thousands of Internet applications that probably served little to no economic purpose. As a result, corporate investments, which aren't so safe to begin with, become even riskier in a crisis if they are producing legacy products and services vulnerable to change.

These forces can be obvious or subtle, and technology evolutions are easy to confuse with business cycles; indeed, many fall to that temptation. Many thought the interurban railway—or rail travel in general—would come back after the Great Depression; in fact, it began a slow and inevitable decline because of the automobile. Now, it's the automobile itself that's in question; some wonder whether demand for SUVs or even traditional gasoline-powered cars will ever resume previous levels—or will future demand shift permanently toward hybrids, alternative energy, and smaller cars? Similarly, many are now wondering whether the standalone PC will survive the advent of cloud computing, and in what form. PC sales may decline because of the business cycle; every time they do, people wonder whether the change is temporary or more permanent. The wealth sustaining investor must make these calls, remembering Joseph Schumpeter's "creative destruction" occurs more rapidly these days and often with little advance warning.

Likewise, the solid stars of the last decade, best exemplified by Microsoft with its near monopoly and gigantic cash margins from low production costs, seemed unassailable, and investors treated it so. But now with Linux and Ubuntu community-enhanced freeware threatening its operating system monopoly, cloud applications and free alternatives like StarOffice threatening its Office applications, and Mozilla and Google knocking at the Internet browser door, the Microsoft fortress doesn't look so formidable.

On the other hand, Apple is running on all cylinders today, although it already endured one decline. But now the company has realized otherworldly success from the digital music business. That said, this level of success is hard to project even two to three years down the road as digital music and smartphone competitors sharpen their offerings. To be sure, no business or business model is safe. One might even question the long term viability of electric utilities in these times. What if solar panels got simple and cheap, so you could buy them and install them simply in just one day, replacing two-thirds of your electricity purchase from your electric utility? That would signal huge and disruptive change for the electric utility business.

Solid and regular cash generators like Coca-Cola and Procter & Gamble have had their ups and downs and have endured competitive threats, but nothing is guaranteed even there. Technology isn't the only thing that changes—consumer tastes change, too, and Coke has been forced recently to introduce whole lines of new products to stay in front of the shift towards healthier drinks. As a result, any investor in any business, or any investment dependent on a business, must take these risks into consideration. Those who thought, for instance, that the industrial demand for silver would be forever supported by the photography industry were in for a surprise.

The Great Recession: A Tipping Point

Arguably, the recent Great Recession was a tipping point for many companies already on the brink, and/or who had already fallen behind their technology cycle. A company on a short financial leash, with no new innovations coming to market, will simply be forced to watch while more nimble and forward-looking competitors eat its lunch. Some companies, unable to cope with change or deliver innovation, simply go into bunker-down mode, cutting costs and hoping for the best. I can think of no better example than consumer electronics retailer Circuit City.

Short Circuit

Circuit City filed for bankruptcy in November 2008. I think Circuit City is a great example of what can go wrong when you take your finger off the customer service pulse, and moreover, depart from the principles of using innovation to deliver net customer value. That's where the real war is waged, in the area of net customer value.

Let's take a closer look at Circuit City's failures to innovate in customer service. Circuit City was originally formed in the 1940s as a television retailer. Like many other consumer electronic retailers, it went through several changes as it attempted to chase the changes—the rapid changes—in the consumer electronics industry. The problem at Circuit City was simple: It completely and totally lost its connection to its customer. Beyond that, it had no platform to innovate and create the changes that were necessary in order to adapt.

One of the biggest concerns a customer would have going into a Circuit City was the lack of knowledge among its salespeople.

That lack of knowledge was actually fatal. Once this genie of less knowledgeable and trustworthy salespeople was out of the bottle, there was no getting it back in.

What they should have done was create certified computer specialists, certified audiovisual specialists, certified car audio specialists, you name it, with a level of training sufficient to give confidence to the customer. But they didn't get that. They thought they were in the box-of-electronics for $X amount business—and they were dead wrong. In fact, if you were to put "Circuit City customer complaints" into a search engine, you'd find thousands—*millions*—of complaints about this organization's lack of service.

But—it got worse. As it often does, the worse it got, the worse it got. Because they were so disconnected from the problem, without a core ability to invent solutions for their customers, in a highly competitive industry with razor-thin margins to begin with, they started to run into financial problems. Customers simply were not persuaded that employees at Circuit City could direct them to the right products or right solutions—losing ground even to the relatively distant and impersonal Internet sales channel.

So what did they do? In March of 2007, in the face of falling business trends, they fired all of the higher-paid employees and kept all the lower hourly paid employees, assuming reduction of costs would save the day. Employees who knew something about the products were gone, replaced by less motivated employees who knew nothing about the products (It should be noted that that same year their CEO made $7 million in compensation.)

The worse it got, the worse it got.

Parenthetically, I should add that cost cutting, the apparent strategy here, is seldom a strategy. Strategies should be about delivering customer value, not just about more internally focused efforts to reduce cost. In most situations, if cost cutting is warranted at all, it should be a tactic to achieve a focused customer strategy of delivering better value. But I digress. . . .

So, back to the Circuit City story. Their actions were clearly focused on internal concerns, not their customers. They could have created informational kiosks to give customers valuable information about the products. They could have created a "certified specialist" program in every department to make sure they had the efficacy to communicate with customers to help them get what they were looking for. They could have had pamphlets or tip sheets to help their customers. They could have developed strategic partnerships with their vendors to assure they were seen by their customers as experts in consumer electronics.

They did none of that. And to my knowledge, they implemented no other innovation solutions that would have created amazing solutions that would have allowed them to save the day.

In a down economy, down companies are out. In a down economy, great companies survive. Why? Because they deliver great customer value, and they create *devotees*, not just customers.

Customer Value *Is* Business Value

Today, we tend to revere most companies based on numbers—revenues, profits, head count, inventory turnover, fixed costs, debt levels. There's a rationale to that. But the sharp analyst, looking for value in a company, will focus on value delivered to its customers—knowing full well that when a company delivers value to its customers—the cause—the other numbers fall into line—the effect. Good financial performance is a result of good market and customer performance—not an end in and of itself. We may be using the wrong indicators to determine who's going to win and who's going to fail. Think about it.

Beginning of the End, or End of the Beginning?

As we move forward, it will become obvious that companies should not be judged based only on their financials, but also on their innovations. I like to describe it this way: We should be looking at the breadth and depth of every company's innovations. That is, are they just about products? Or services, processes, employee practices, environmental practices, and so forth? At the end of the day, it's what a company is doing to invent new solutions regularly for its customers, either directly or indirectly.

The book *Good to Great* (Jim Collins, HarperBusiness, 2001) is a great example of a book that looks at companies based on what I believe can be the wrong success drivers—or at least, they fail to tell enough of the story. Collins postulates that "great" companies focus on the things they're good at, avoiding mindless diversification. That may be true, but it doesn't go far enough in my opinion.

For me, "great" happens when that focus is on the success drivers of innovation and customer value. By Collins's definition, a company that made great buggy whips might be considered a great company—again, for me it goes deeper. The fact that Collins cited Circuit City, with Fannie Mae, Wells Fargo, GE, and others supplies further evidence that business excellence may be driven by something else quite unseen—at least until now.

There is a major thing that happens in a down economy with corporations. It is what former Intel CEO and author Andrew S. Grove refers to in his excellent book *Only the Paranoid Survive* as a *strategic inflection point*—in other words, a fork in the road. This fork in the road begs the question: "Do we continue to innovate?" or do we focus on cost reduction, and get into what I call the "bunker-down syndrome"—in the hope that we can stop spending money so that if we're in the fallout shelter, eventually all of the economic adversities that are happening will simply go away.

History has shown us that going into bunker-down mode is the beginning of the end for most companies. The question that's most commonly asked of me by clients is: "Should we increase or should we decrease our research and development spending?" And the answer I usually give is: "How much money are you spending on R&D?" True, it violates the simple protocol of not answering a question with a question, but that aside, they don't understand what the question means.

The point, of course, and the explanation I give is again in the form of a question: "Are you really good at spending that money, and do the successes justify the investment?" If you're making a return on the R&D dollars spent, then of course it makes sense to spend the money, perhaps spend even *more* money. Why? Because, for the most part, a dip in the business cycle does not mean a permanent change in customer interests, beliefs, or need for product or service value. According to a recent Nielsen report appropriately titled "What's the Role of Innovation in a Slow Economy?" (December 2008), there is no reason to believe consumers aren't still attracted to new innovations even in a down economy. The first sentence says it all: "Based on data from the U.S. and U.K. over the past 20 to 30 years, consumers' purchase interest and value perceptions for new products do not change significantly with changes in the economic climate." (To read the full report, see http://cn.en.acnielsen.com/site/documents/Innovation_en.pdf.)

Can Bad News Really Be Good News?

So we know for a fact that in business-to-consumer, business-to-business—really, all industries—customers are looking for new solutions. In fact, for many businesses the best opportunity might be in a down economy, where there is a stronger imperative to create innovations that really deliver value and serve customer needs. A good example is the advent of frozen foods during the Great Depression and the infrastructure to distribute them; the advent of board games like Monopoly serves as another example. Both delivered customer value at a time when such value was dictated by the bad times.

Here's the basic question companies need to ask themselves. Can we take advantage of the current economic environment to create new innovations to help our customers address the challenges *they* are experiencing in a down economy? Or do we pull the lever of the bunker-down syndrome where the focus changes to reducing our own cost, including the cost of delivering meaningful new innovation to our customers that will benefit them in this down economy?

The answer lies in appraisal of two things about your business: First, what are the right new products to innovate to help customers the most in tough times; and second, can those innovations be delivered efficiently? Does the R&D function work efficiently and effectively to produce these products, or is it a money pit that, even if it could hit the mark for the customer, would cost too much and/or take too much time to get a product to market? Is the real problem that your R&D function is operating at a fraction of its efficiency? This is what you as a manager of a business must figure out, and Part I of this book is largely devoted to helping you make that appraisal.

Failure is Not an Option

I believe the answer to the question: "Why do companies fail?" is pretty straightforward. First of all, to answer that question, we have to go back and redefine the term "innovation."

Innovation is such a generic term that it doesn't really mean anything to many companies any more. In fact, many of the least innovative companies in the world use the term "innovation" in their tag line, and they're under the impression that putting the words "leaders in industrial innovation" or some such *by itself* makes them top-notch innovators.

And so again, why do companies fail in a down economy, and what is the role of innovation? Well, true innovation, in my view, is first and foremost a phenomenally strong and accurate connection to what your customers want. The world famous business guru Peter Drucker said that there were three questions you need to answer about your business: (1) What is my business? (2) Who are my customers? and (3) What do my customers value?

I would argue that Drucker's definition is really one of innovation. What is my business? You need to know what you do. What your core values and efficacies are. You need to know who your customers are—really know who they are—not just from a demographic analysis, but who they are in terms of *what they really care about*. Knowing who your customers are and what they value *is* innovation.

The Difference Between Invention and Innovation

Many people, without thinking, use the two words interchangeably and, I would argue, inappropriately. When one thinks of an invention, one thinks of a shiny whizbang new product based on some sexy new technology to do something new or do something better. A handheld GPS device is an *invention*. An innovation is a higher level, more conceptual success that *may be* developed around an invention, but is something that really serves a customer need and delivers customer value in excess of what it costs, that is, *net customer value*. A GPS device that uses a well-designed global GPS system to deliver the right information customers need when they need it at a reasonable price is an *innovation*.

As an exercise, take a few minutes to look at products or services around you to determine whether they are inventions or innovations. A stand-alone iPod might be an invention (a very good one) but an iPod bundled with iTunes as a complete digital music platform? That's an innovation. An In-N-Out Burger, fries and milkshake, on the other hand, would hardly be considered an invention, right? But the way it's delivered? Even without an invention, In-N-Out is a clear example of an innovation.

Most companies don't know the answer to the third question: "What do my customers value?" Why? The main reason is this: The people who have the greatest authority—and make all the decisions about what a business delivers to its customers—have the least amount of customer contact. Conversely, the people in an organization who have the greatest amount of customer contact almost always have the least amount of control over what is delivered to the customer. Even worse, companies rarely provide a regular venue to allow high customer contact people to be able to communicate ideas to the people who do have authority to make decisions.

Innovations—and businesses—fail in this economy due to the lack of customer contact. Circuit City is but one example—do we really think the managers who made the decision to fire all the expert level employees were fully aware of the needs of their customers?

Thriving on Chaos

So back to the basic (implied) question: Are bad times necessarily the death of innovation? Do bad business conditions seal the fate of bad businesses, destroying any chance that they might innovate their way to prosperity? Do bad times eliminate the funding and focus necessary to innovate? Should firms be expected to cut back on innovation during bad times?

I would argue that good businesses thrive during times of economic turmoil. Sure, there are painful choices to be made. But if you look at the course of history, some of the best businesses—and business ideas—have started their trajectory during bad times.

GE started during the panic of 1873, Disney started during the recession of 1923–24, HP began during the Great Depression, and Bill Gates and Paul Allen founded Microsoft during the recession of 1975. Several companies benefited from aggressive marketing at a time when their rivals were all cutting back. A good example is Kellogg besting C.W. Post during the Depression. Customers didn't stop spending during that time; most just looked for better deals. The companies providing those better deals came out stronger after the economy began picking up. And, consumer loyalty remained after the fact.

Some companies find that economic downturns provide better markets for innovations already made, because it brings their value proposition closer to the true needs of the customer. Here's a great example—the story of Clarence Birdseye, the innovator of store-bought frozen foods.

In the early 1920s, Clarence Birdseye invented a new freezing system for fish products, called a "double belt" freezer, where cold brine chilled stainless steel belts carried fish in packages, freezing it almost instantly. His company, General Seafood Corporation, operated out of Gloucester, Massachusetts, and he got a U.S. patent for his invention. He got additional patents for mechanical improvements to reduce the size of ice crystals formed on the product, and in 1927 he expanded the process to freeze meat, poultry, and what became his trademark: vegetables.

Birdseye did quite well, and in fact was able to sell his company, equipment and patents for the tidy sum of $22 million in 1929—to Goldman Sachs and the Postum Company. Postum eventually became General Foods, which in turn founded the Birds Eye Frozen Food Company as a subsidiary. It was a clever and successful innovation in the late 1920s, but it became an even better one in the Depression-ravaged 1930s. Frozen food products were seen as a good and less expensive alternative to fresh foods, especially out of season or outside their native geography. Simultaneous development of frozen refrigerated transport and home food storage obviously helped. As these technologies evolved, the company conducted customer tests and experiments on numerous frozen food products, which took off well. Given the economic and technology environment of the times. Today, Birds Eye Foods remains a leading frozen-food brand.

Innovate or Get Out

The Birds Eye example makes clear that continued innovation helps build on success, especially when the environment is right and other technologies are evolving simultaneously. It also highlights the potential folly of stopping—or selling out—too soon.

The example offers further evidence that companies should continue to pursue innovations not just during good times or during bad times, but at all times. An innovation that might be ahead of its market in good times may suddenly find itself dead center for a market in bad times; typically the interest in these innovations persists once good times return, because people make the adjustments and come to expect the value delivered even when times are better.

Many businesses that do well in tough times do well because they continue advertising and marketing as though the public still had money to spend. They didn't wait for the product demand to rise again; they created that demand even during tough times. Those companies who diminished or cut advertising altogether lost existing customers to more aggressive competitors and, in many cases, lost investors no longer interested in participating in invisible companies.

Success in these instances—really in all of business—requires a strong and relentless customer focus, an awareness of the external environment, a commitment to the long term, and avoidance of barriers to success. The next two chapters explore some of those barriers to success—and what to do about them.

Chapter Takeaways

- Innovation is not just about products or technologies; it is about the entire customer experience. Companies like In-N-Out Burger show us that even small details like cleanliness, aroma, and pleasant greetings matter.
- Bad times should be perceived as good times for innovation. Those that avoid the temptation to cut back are often rewarded, those that do cut back often seal their fate.
- The current business climate of rapid change and short business cycles strengthens the case for innovation more than ever. Companies must keep up with—or lead—the change, and those that continue to innovate through the short cycles will be rewarded more quickly.
- An *invention* is a new process or technology, while an *innovation* is something that really serves a customer need in a new way. An innovation may or may not include an invention.

CHAPTER 2

The Wheels Keep Falling Off

Innovation is plagued with failure. But to try to target the real reason—and I mean, the real reason an innovation fails—for that I'd like to give an example.

It's two o'clock in the morning. The infomercial starts with: "How would you like to lose weight?" Then the infomercial goes on to tell you that it's not your fault you're overweight; the *real* reason you weigh more than you should is a hormonal imbalance, and if you simply take this pill once a day, you'll "achieve your weight goals that you've tried to achieve for a lifetime."

So why does that TV infomercial *work?* First of all, 80 percent of Americans are overweight, and virtually all overweight people don't want to be overweight. But most are not willing to look at their lives—their behaviors and their focus—as a reason for obesity. As a result, they're looking for what I call "a fractional solution to a global or holistic problem." In other words, a panacea. On top of that, they want the solution to require no effort, and no analysis. This last characteristic is the secret of all weight loss programs.

In that context, we should look at the common pitch to solving your innovation problems. It isn't hard to imagine the infomercial pitch here: "It's not your fault. You just need a new system. Once this new system is installed, you'll be able to be more customer connected and you'll be able to deliver more successful products, right?"

Wrong.

The truth of the matter is that it requires effort, self-analysis, and it must be—*holistic*. Dieting will not make you healthy. Physical fitness—alone—will not make you healthy. Your organization is a holistic being that must be made healthy through a holistic approach. It is a holistic approach that must address your unique weaknesses and your unique strengths. That's where *prescribed* innovation comes into play, which I'll describe shortly.

Before I share with you one of my favorite lists by a fellow innovation consultant, Mitchell Ditkoff of Idea Creations, Inc., I would like to tell you that there are two things that guarantee successful innovation. The first is *enterprise-wide innovation*. The second is prescribed innovation.

Enterprise-wide innovation suggests that you must invent at all levels in your organization—from customer service to supply chain to accounting to human resources—as well as product innovation. All aspects of your company are about delivering meaningful net customer value, and you must do it holistically. You can't necessarily fix all of your innovation problems through your Research & Development department.

Prescribed innovation means that innovation must be based on a hard and sober analysis of what works in your organization, as well as what doesn't work. It entails a unique and custom approach aimed at strengthening your weaknesses and building on your strengths.

One last note before we go into the shopping list of what's wrong: Remember what organizations are made up of—people. These people have habits, and they have beliefs. What psychologists have taught us is that there is but one way to change bad habits. Bad habits are changed only through what is referred to as "meaningful consequence."

In my practice, I've found that people don't come to us until they've tried every grapefruit diet and every magic pill. It isn't until innovation has stopped, competition is killing them, and the organization has started to fail that they develop the lucidity to recognize that things have to change.

Let's look at what the majority of people identify as the most common problems.

56 Reasons Why

I'll make an educated guess that most readers of *The Innovation Playbook* have read at least a few other books, magazine articles, web sites, blogs—you name it—on innovation. How to do it, how not to do it, why it works, why it doesn't, and a variety of other related topics. As a reader of this genre of management books, or as an audience to the industry's leading consultants, either way, you've probably seen a lot of lists—lists of reasons why innovations succeed, and probably more often, lists of why innovations fail.

As an example, Idea Creations Inc., a well-known innovation consultant, famously published a list of the "56 Reasons Why Innovations Fail" in June 2010. I actually thought they got a lot of it right, and with their permission, here's the list. (For more, see: http://www.ideachampions.com/weblogs/archives/2010/06/55_reasons_why.shtml.)

1. "Innovation" framed as an initiative, not the normal way of doing business.
2. Absence of a clear definition of what innovation really means.
3. Innovation not linked to company's existing vision or strategy.
4. No sense of urgency.
5. Workforce is suffering from "initiative fatigue."
6. CEO does not fully embrace the effort.
7. No compelling vision or reason to innovate.
8. Senior team not aligned.
9. Key players don't have time to focus on innovation.
10. Innovation champions are not empowered.
11. Decision making processes are nonexistent or fuzzy.
12. Lack of trust.
13. Risk-adverse culture.
14. Overemphasis on cost cutting or incremental improvement.
15. Workforce ruled by past assumptions and old mental models.
16. No process in place for funding new projects.
17. Not enough pilot programs in motion.
18. Senior team not walking the talk.
19. No company-wide process for managing ideas.
20. Too many turf wars. Too many silos.
21. Analysis paralysis.
22. Reluctance to cannibalize existing products and services.
23. NIH (not invented here) syndrome.
24. Funky channels of communication.
25. No intrinsic motivation to innovate.
26. Unclear gates for evaluating progress.
27. Mind numbing bureaucracy.
28. Unclear idea pitching processes.
29. Lack of clearly defined innovation metrics.
30. No accountability for results.
31. No way to celebrate quick wins.

32. Poorly facilitated meetings.
33. No training to unleash individual or team creativity.
34. Voodoo evaluation of ideas.
35. Inadequate sharing of best practices.
36. Lack of teamwork and collaboration.
37. Unclear strategy for sustaining the effort.
38. Innovation teams meet too infrequently.
39. Middle managers not on board.
40. Ineffective rollout of the effort to the workforce.
41. Lack of tools and techniques to help people generate new ideas.
42. Innovation initiative perceived as another "flavor of the month."
43. Individuals don't understand how to be a part of the effort.
44. Diverse inputs or conflicting opinions not honored.
45. Imbalance of left-brain and right brain thinking.
46. Low morale.
47. Over-reliance on technology.
48. Failure to secure sustained funding.
49. Unrealistic time frames.
50. Failure to consider issues associated with scaling up.
51. Inability to attract talent to risky new ventures.
52. Failure to consider commercialization issues.
53. No rewards or recognition program in place.
54. No processes in place to get fast feedback.
55. No real sense of what your customers want or need.
56. Company hiring process screens out potential innovators.

Now, I find that there's nothing wrong with this list. In many cases, you probably feel that these bullets are right on target in describing your own organization and your own innovation processes. You probably wouldn't be wrong for having those feelings; they're pretty common in today's corporate world. But we need to dig a little deeper to find the true causes of innovation failure, and to find solid ground for traction to get out of the quagmire.

Climate Change Is Important

I do think most of the reasons on this list are real and important. But I believe many of these reasons are really symptoms of greater underlying problems, that is, greater problems of focus and leadership inherent in an organization, just like the daily meteorological phenomena called weather are really driven by climate. Weather describes dynamic conditions that can change day-to-day, challenging and often defying prediction and control. Climate, on the other hand, is constant; it is the physical environment in which weather phenomena occur; thus it's the thing that's really important to understand. As it's important to know, for instance, whether we want to or don't want to live in a particular geography.

A fundamental difference between physical climate and organizational climate comes to mind almost immediately, however. No matter how hard we try (save for the highly incremental efforts to reduce global warming) we cannot change physical climate. Organizational climate, on the other hand, can be changed. It's slow, and it takes the right leadership, and it takes a holistic and systemic focus. But it can be changed, and I've seen it change, but not as often as I'd like.

One example of climate change and its effects can be found in electronics retailer Best Buy. The retailer was facing stiff competition (soon to become less stiff with the exit of Circuit City) and employee turnover rates exceeding 100 percent annually. The company, as most in retail tend to do, had very strict requirements about employee attendance and hours, all the way up through the management ranks. In 2007 the company decided to let people have some choices as to how they achieve goals, and allowed 60 percent of its headquarter staff to work on flex hours, as an example. It was a huge cultural change; and later measures indicated employee productivity increased by 35 percent in areas affected by this and other changes.

Unfortunately, I find more examples of climate change working in the other direction; employee-focused companies bow to the competitive pressures of Main Street competition and Wall Street short-term financial requirements. They take the sorts of things Best Buy put into place away from their people. They centralize decision making and trim staff, overloading the remaining workers. They reward cost cutting behavior over true innovating behavior. American industry—and particularly the high tech industry—is loaded with examples of negative climate change. Ask yourself: Is the climate in your organization getting better or worse? Better or worse for innovation?

Why Is Customer Needs #55?

If you've been reading along—that is, my Introduction and Chapter 1—you probably guessed one of the places where I think this list—and many of the other lists published by others in the industry—fail. You'll notice that the "C" word—customers—doesn't show up until No. 55 on the 56-item list. It's there, I'll grant that. But why does "No real sense of what your customers want or need" rank so low on their list? I don't have a good answer to that.

But it does reinforce my lesson of looking outside in, that is, defining your products and your business using customer needs—net customer value—as a starting point. If you fix reasons 1 through 54, and you still aren't focused on customers, your innovation efforts will be off-track from the very start. Your organization may innovate efficiently, but your innovations will miss in the marketplace, and you'll gain little traction for all your efforts to fix reasons 1–54. I'm not criticizing Idea Creations' list specifically, because I see this upside-down priority almost everywhere; it seems to be systemic in current thinking about the innovation space. Of course, a major theme of *The Innovation Playbook* is getting to right-side-up with customer focus and thinking, *then* (and only then) getting your processes and organizational culture to execute.

Number 55, Indeed

In a recent study of more than 630 U.S. and U.K. executives done by Accenture, it was found that more than half (57 percent) of respondents said the most frequent reason for new product or service launch failures was their inability to meet customer needs. Most also cited a lack of new or unique customer-perceived value.

See: http://newsroom.accenture.com/article_display.cfm?article_id=4901.

Getting to Ten

Fifty-six reasons are nice and may well encircle the problem. But the truth is probably simpler, and I find that working with such long lists doesn't help much. Where do you start? How do you separate the symptoms from the causes? How do you focus on the things you need to change in order to address the fact that the wheels keep falling off?

Like most presenters, I find that breaking things down into three to seven major focal points really helps. I'd like to do that here, but the topic of innovation is so multifaceted that, when I tried to do this, frankly, I failed. So I'll compromise with the number ten—ten important reasons—mega-reasons if you will, why innovation fails.

Even keeping it at ten isn't as easy as it sounds. It's hard to understand the root causes of why so many corporations fail at identifying, filtering, developing, and ultimately commercializing successful, sustainable solutions for their valued customers. Part of the reason is that, for the most part, it's hard for companies to identify root causes, and it's hard for them to agree on root causes. The answers to the question: "What are the major causes of failure in innovation?" tend to be highly prejudiced.

What does that mean? If you ask the CFO of a corporation, "What is the cause of innovation failure?" you will likely receive a response that has something to do with the lack of financial planning. Conversely, if you talk to the director of research and development, and you ask, "What is the major cause of innovation failure?"—and I've asked hundreds that very question—typically they will tell you it's a lack of organizational commitment to the technology, or failures in engineering, marketing, or even manufacturing.

My point is that, beyond a prevalent focus on symptoms instead of problems, there is a tremendous amount of "blamestorming" going on in the area of innovation. Between "symptom-storming" and "blamestorming," when we look at the answers to the question, "Why do innovations fail?" we almost always get an incomplete or a prejudiced list that is not accurate, and in most cases, is un-actionable.

My goal in *The Innovation Playbook* is to investigate the reality, the facts, the *climate* around innovation, the facts and features of the organizational environment that cause most innovation failure. I call these "Nick's Picks," or "The Ten Great Innovation Killers." Without further ado, here they are.

Nick's Pick #1: The Wrong Focus

Picture this: In 1979, chances are you'd be reading your news in a printed newspaper or magazine. Today, you may well be reading your news on your computer, or perhaps your iPhone, BlackBerry, or iPad. It's hardly a surprise that the Internet—along with broadband, browsers, and HTML—would be among the top breakthrough innovations over the past few decades. What made the technology such an all-encompassing example of amazing innovation is this: It simply changed the world. It changed how information is delivered, how products are marketed and sold—and fundamentally, everyday communication.

It touched every industry and every corner of the public sector, from medicine to education to law enforcement and everything in between. Nearly every aspect of business or social relations today is touched by the Internet—not to mention the industries it created subsequently, like online auctions. And it did this on an international scale.

Beyond the Internet itself are its many offspring: laptop computers, and now, so-called "netbook" computers. These products took advantage of the new technology called the Internet. They mobilized people, they mobilized industry, and completely changed the nature of interaction. It isn't just about computers—there's a plethora of other devices, from digital music devices to cameras to cell phones and beyond, now even cars, flourishing upon the same interconnectivity.

A few health care industry innovations listed in the Top 30 Innovations of the Past 30 years, by Knowledge@Wharton and PBS's "Nightly Business Report," included DNA testing and sequencing, human genome mapping, Magnetic Resonance Imaging, and noninvasive laser and robotic surgery (laparoscopy). Why were these included? Not only are these innovations something new that creates new opportunities for growth and development, they also have huge problem-solving value. DNA has great promise to improve diagnoses and also enhances the pharmaceutical industry by spawning more effective drugs based on genetic factors that would have been impossible to determine without it.

Step back 30 years ago and you'll have the invention of Sony's The Walkman, which changed the way we listen to music. During its development Sony's Chairman Akio Morita did stop to ask, "Don't you think a stereo cassette player that you can listen to while walking around is a good idea?" He thought about what the customer would want. Initially, it didn't do so well. The media didn't expect it to take off, but they underestimated the power of the youth that would fall in love with the product. Even though it's now been replaced by iPods, mp3 players, and more, Sony still manufactures and sells the cassette-based Walkman players today.

If you miss these megatrends, you'll miss opportunities to innovate, and many organizations today find themselves behind the eight ball. We're starting to see Internet-connected digital cameras that can send pictures instantly (as many of us have done using cell phones)—but why wasn't Kodak at the forefront of this technology? We're starting to see Internet-based systems for providing security and managing house functions remotely, but why has this taken so long?

I think one of the main reasons is actually Nick's Pick No. 1: The Wrong Focus. Focus is at the top of my list because true innovation success must be driven by a continued and systemic focus on delivering true customer value. Most innovation experts refer to this as a "corporate culture of innovation." I believe that corporate culture is created from—or is a result of—a focus on delivering customer value.

Your success in the area of innovation is driven by your company's ability to manage a daily organizational focus that is truly bi-directional—where you're not just *delivering* great customer value, you're observing ways to *add* additional customer value. You'll always be successful if you do this, but no more clearly than when you're adapting to a new technology or megatrend like the Internet. How many Internet products and sites did we see go by the wayside because they didn't deliver meaningful net customer value?

Organizational focus is key. Because most organizations that fail in the area of innovation fail because they look at it from a departmental, or "siloed," approach. They look at it fractionally. They look at the speed of the Internet or the cool of the Internet or some other single feature of it that will solve all their problems. It doesn't. Just creating a web site for your customers doesn't mean you're creating great customer service. Again, it's like the Grapefruit Diet I first presented in the Introduction; it's applying one aspect of what should be a holistic innovation process and assuming that that is going to solve the problem.

From the CEO down, delivering customer value must be the centerpiece, as it is at Sierra Nevada Brewing Company, presented in the last chapter. They don't sit around and talk about processes and methods all day long, they talk about *beer*. They talk about delivering the absolute best product in the world. They talk about doing it in a way that honors everybody in their sphere of influence, and that's what makes the company magic.

A Blinding Flash of Pseudo-Value

Examples litter the product landscape. Did GM really create meaningful net customer value by adding trim to a Chevy Cavalier and calling it a Cadillac Cimarron? Did the financial institutions, prior to the recent bust, add real value with the various new financial "innovations" that weren't really innovations at all? Did these innovations, like the various new flavors of mortgage backed securities, really add value for their customers? One must never forget the importance of delivering not "pseudo," but real, value.

Nick's Pick #2: Lack of Sponsorship

The second of my Ten Innovation Killers is what I call Lack of Sponsorship. Hewlett-Packard understands the key to successful innovation is about securing sponsorship from the very team that brings the innovation to fruition. Without sponsorship, you'll never create the insanely cool products that will deliver meaningful net customer value.

Successful companies know that they need to secure innovation champions, who will take ownership and the responsibility for successful commercialization of products that need to succeed in the marketplace.

Sponsorship really equates to leadership, a topic we'll cover several times throughout the book. Sponsorship can take many forms, and it can occur at many levels in an organization. The most prominent, and often the most successful, sponsorship efforts are not always the most visible. But when they *are* visible, with news coverage in the public or trade media, it's usually a signal of something larger, in the direction of climate change as I mentioned earlier.

Prominent examples include Toyota's declared "Value Innovation Strategy," a program launched in 2005 to bring greater focus to product innovation in the wake of the Prius model's success. The company, to that point, had been more renowned as a manufacturing process innovator. The Value Innovation Strategy was at once a mantra and evidence of sponsorship for product innovation. It worked not only inside the organization as a wake-up call for more product innovation and to "see the big picture," it also opened the door to suppliers to participate in the innovation process beyond basic cost cutting tactics. Although some may place blame for Toyota's recent recall troubles on such expansion; in my mind it represents a clear break from a process-focused past.

BMW gives us another auto industry example. Each time the company begins developing a new car, the project's team members—about 200 to 300 staffers in engineering, design, production, marketing, purchasing, and finance—are relocated from their scattered locations to the automaker's Research and Innovation Center, called FIZ, for up to three years. The close proximity speeds communication, enables better communications, prevents unforeseen conflicts, and more—but it also sends a strong signal of innovation sponsorship straight from the offices of top management.

Nick's Pick #3: Process Driven to the Hilt

Another major problem—and it's my Number Three—is what I call Process Driven Innovation. I know this might hurt some people's feelings, but the truth of the matter is that successful innovation is *not* about the best process. I would argue that the current hyper-focus on the innovation process is, in fact, *killing* innovation. If you get no other message from reading *The Innovation Playbook*, I want you to leave with this one: Winning companies use processes to *build speed* and *improve customer value.*

Innovation losers, on the other hand, focus on internal needs and risk management that results in sub-incremental innovation—and often, a technology that is not customer or market relevant.

Nick's Pick #4: A Risk Centered Process

Number Four on my list is what I call A Risk Centered Process. I've reviewed dozens of lists of why innovations fail, and much to my surprise and chagrin, many of them said that there *weren't enough* risk management tools and systems in play! That is, to say the least, an interesting vantage point. From *my* vantage point, it is dead wrong.

The constant daily focus on managing risk at every level has actually *increased* the risk that a company will lose its competitiveness and market share. Obviously, the introduction of great innovations, and the launch of great products, is a good way to validate the innovation process. But the surefire way to avoid risk "drag" is to build and expand the *conduits of connectivity* to your customer to ensure, or at least increase the odds, that the products you deliver are meaningful and relevant. (Chapters 6 and 7 explain how to develop conduits of connectivity and customer insight overall.)

"Hyper" risk management kills innovation, reduces speed to market, and effectively eliminates breakthrough market innovations.

It also leads to what I frequently see as an obvious symptom: incrementalism.

Paint it Blue, Call it New

Incrementalism is probably one of the biggest problems—or symptoms—in the area of innovation today. Incremental innovation is not so much a problem in and of itself; rather, it is symptomatic of a greater problem—or greater problem(s)—most of which center on the common organizational fault of risk aversion.

When you look at great products—and I know this myself as an inventor—for instance, one of the greatest products I've invented is a so-called micro-silicone implant that's used to treat ocular surface disease. It just looks too crazy! But wait—the benefits were there. When I invented that product I remember it looking a bit ridiculous, something like a radiator hose—or maybe even a small insect at a distance. It also behaved like a radiator hose. You could push it along its axis to keep it from popping out of the eye, what we call clinically "inadvertent extrusion." It also could angulate anywhere within its axis so that when somebody rubbed their eyes we didn't have to worry about it coming out.

So here it was, something that looked absolutely crazy—and it wound up being a tremendously successful product. My point is that really great innovations can look crazy. And—really bad innovations can also look crazy. Great ideas and bad ideas both look crazy, and most people don't do anything with them. So what do we do instead? We paint it blue, and call it new.

Incrementalism may justify the R&D function, but it doesn't build meaningful value for the valued customer or for the organization. We'll talk about this a lot in the book, but eliminating incrementalism has a lot to do with dealing with its root causality—and that's risk aversion. If we're afraid to do something big to deliver impactful customer value, we make incremental improvements to the existing technology, and at the end of the day, that is a failure. Apple's initial success with the iPod is the antithesis of incrementalism, but whether or not they fall into the abyss of incrementalism—adding colors, adding megabytes—instead of delivering new value remains to be seen. Company after company has fallen into that trap.

Nick's Pick #5: Customer Be Damned

How would you like to take your kids to a playground where there's a gigantic sign that says: "No Running?" How would you like to take your kids to a playground that has a big antique railroad caboose that says: "Do Not Touch?" How would you like to take your kids to a natural history museum where, when they walk in, the "docents" are actually "don't-cents" and they yell at your kid for almost everything they do? The list goes on and on and on.

But such a natural history museum actually exists! It started with a great idea, to provide a wonderful and exciting environment for kids to learn about watersheds, sustainable communities, and natural habitats. What they wound up with was a severe change in their focus. Their focus went from serving a turnstile visitor to serving their granting source. They fired people in the museum to hire people as grant writers. They got rid of an approach that was customer centered, and changed to a self-centered and self-serving organization that is now all but finished.

The moral of the story here is going back to the Drucker navigators. Know what your business is. Know who your customers are. And most importantly, drive amazing innovation by knowing what your customers value—all in real time.

The natural evolutionary process of companies is to begin with an entrepreneurial spirit that is highly customer connected. As time marches on, corporations move through their evolutionary cycle, from entrepreneurship to organizational-centric models. This tends to take their gaze away from their customers and towards internal processes.

Companies have tried to deal with this issue by trying to reconnect with the customer through so-called "CRM," or customer relationship management systems. Unfortunately, the "McDonald-ization," or data pooling, of customer behavior has become the new focus in terms of observing customer needs. The problem is—it's all wrong. I believe the only way you can successfully identify what your customers care about, and so create great innovations, is to "innovate while walking about."

For an example, at one of the largest electronic retailers in the country, if you go in and try to get some answers to your most basic questions, the sales associates have no idea about the features, the advantages, the operation of the very products that they are selling. Despite the fact that customers are looking for a "consultative sale," that is, they're looking for someone to recommend, and make specific intelligent, educated comments about how and why they should purchase a given technology.

This large electronics retailer hasn't invested anything in the training or competence of their sales staff. But when you go to the register to check out, they'll ask you to go online to fill out a survey on the Internet to get a $10 gift certificate. This type of data pooling through typical customer relationship management grabs data that's dead wrong. A 10-year-old could walk onto the sales floor and realize what was wrong. They will never be able to secure meaningful data from these CRM methods that are poorly deployed. I'll address this issue again in Chapter 4.

Data pooling has its place, but the ultimate way to invent is to connect with your customer so you know what they actually care about.

Nick's Pick #6: No Resource Commitment

Number Six on my list is the No Resource Commitment. In order for a product to succeed, the model needs to have people, the product, and the plan. But not surprisingly, innovation also takes money. Organizations will often commit to a technology without providing enough resources for its ultimate success. The result is a lot invested in research and development that never translates into profit for the company because it was short-funded or had insufficient team members and/or time resources necessary to deliver the value to the customer.

Lack of resource commitment, again, is symptomatic of a lack of the right kind of leadership in the organization. When the CFO—typically a cost cutting champion—drives the business, look out. That was clearly the case at Ford Motor Company in the 1980s—a huge squeeze on costs produced such disasters as the Ford Fairmont. When a customer-driven, market-driven focus returned to the company, it produced the 1986 Taurus, and we saw not only a commitment to and focus on customers, but a clear move towards committing enough resources to get it right—not just on cutting costs.

Nick's Pick #7: Bail, Don't Fail

Number Seven is what I call Bail, Don't Fail. One thing that's really important for companies to understand is that innovation needs to have several off-ramps throughout the process where team members are comfortable "bailing" from the innovation because it doesn't meet the ultimate goal of delivering customer value.

As we go through the development process, functionality and other types of data surface that help us determine whether a technology is real. So I think the nomenclature of failing has been a very big innovation killer, and I'm suggesting that in this particular pitfall we change the vernacular—so we can look at bailing as a normal event, a healthy part of a natural innovation process, even rather than saying "fail early."

The term "fail early" has become very popular in the innovation space, but failing is not the right term. We need to learn to look at bailing from a project or product that isn't adding value for the customer as a learning experience, and we need to learn that "bailing early" isn't "failing early."

A good example is furnished by W.L. Gore & Associates in Newark, Delaware, makers of the waterproof fabric Gore-Tex. The company has a special reward for those individuals who spot projects that need to be killed before becoming a problem. When Brad Jones led Gore's Industrial Products Division, which makes sealants and filtration systems, he handed out "Sharp Shooter" trophies to managers when a project was killed for potential hazardous snags. Then the managers were asked to write up what they learned and if, looking back, they see anything that would have made the process even more efficient. Now, doesn't this "bail early" tactic stand in clear contrast to the typical corporate scenario, where employees try to drive projects to the wall, well past the folly stage, motivated by the need to save their own skins.

Nick's Pick #8: Not Really Open

Number Eight on my list is what I call "Not Really Open." So-called open innovation has become the latest innovation tool—the latest panacea—to save the day. And for good reason—open innovation, in the hands of the right organizations, can provide some real organizational value. The problem is that innovation—including open innovation—must be *systemic*. Chanting "open innovation" at your meetings will *not* create an open organization.

I'll give a quick example. Our company was charged with the task of licensing a painting technology that was developed by one of the country's leading universities. We presented it to one of the largest paint companies in the world. After 30 or 40 phone calls to try to get through to their Vice President of Business Development, finally out of sheer frustration, his secretary e-mailed us back and told us that under no circumstances could their Vice President of New Business Development be in touch with us about this new technology, because they were busy speaking at—you guessed it—an "open innovation" symposium!

So it dawned on me that even people who present themselves as experts in the field of open innovation do not have the systemic support systems in place to actually allow open innovation to occur—and for the most part, it's another piecemeal grapefruit diet.

Nick's Pick #9: Innovation Socialism

Number Nine on my list of Innovation Killers is what I call Innovation Socialism. Many organizations, especially research and university organizations, have become Innovation Socialists. What do I mean by that? Oftentimes, researchers are not rewarded for the successful commercialization of technology, and because many of these organizations are process centered, they're also not punished for—or even measured for—the lack of results.

So what are many of these organizations doing? The answer's simple: nothing. If you're not rewarded for commercialization success, and you're not held accountable for process orientation, as is often the case in large corporations and universities, nothing happens. You file patents—but patents aren't in and of themselves a measure of innovation success.

Instead, I believe in Innovation Capitalism. What is Innovation Capitalism? Short answer: You have innovation teams that are rewarded for innovation success by taking *smart risks*. You also make them accountable for processes that get in the way, that is, hinder the innovation process.

So ask yourself—is your organization Innovation Socialist? Or Innovation Capitalist in nature? Winning companies are always Innovation Capitalists.

Nick's Pick #10: Lack of Systemic Innovation

Last, but certainly not least—and I addressed this at the beginning of the chapter—is what I call the Lack of Systemic Innovation. *The Innovation Playbook* is about the ability to become true innovators, and the only way you can become true innovators is to make innovation a holistic part of your organization. Using innovation in your finance department, to streamline your customers' ability to pay; to give them easy and convenient ways to access accounting information; and creating front-end customer interface systems to make the experience of working with your business truly fast, friendly, and effective—that's innovative.

The fact is that great speakers and writers have talked about the process of creating value in the organization—but this process is only about 10 percent of product innovation. The overwhelming majority of what I'll call *organizational value* is in the area of innovation *outside of* product innovation. So systemic innovation rules the day. Every company we researched, and every business that we contacted that was doing great was a full time practitioner of systemic innovation; conversely, companies that were failing with mathematical certainty were fractional innovators.

At this point, the concept of systemic innovation may be a little fuzzy. That's understandable, but have no fear, Part II of *The Innovation Playbook* addresses it head on. Chapter 6 in particular addresses the many different ways to create net customer value in a systemic way; Chapters 9 and 10 address how to make systemic innovation part of your corporate culture.

Driving With the Rearview Mirror

About 12 years ago I worked as a consultant for one of the country's largest hospital bed manufacturers. They had a division that had a product that had both a hardware and a consumable to it; a razor-and-blade business model. What they would typically do in their daily business was look at historical sales and compare them to year-to-date. Their constant focus was on historical revenue numbers and historical performance—even though the procedure the product was used for was changing rapidly.

Unfortunately, there was, as there always is, a street price erosion of their technology. There was good old-fashioned competition, and based on the laws of supply and demand, there was continued erosion to the average selling price, or ASP, of the technology. So they continued to drive down the road, eyes constantly on the rearview mirror, making business decisions based almost entirely on historical data.

But it's worse than that. They were driving down the road at 100 miles per hour in a very dynamic market. They were driving while looking at the mirror assuming everything was based on historical financial performance from a time when they had little to no competition and when their medical procedures had a favorable reimbursement structure from third-party insurance payers. These things changed, they remained too focused on the bygone scenarios of the past, and it killed their business. Such rearview driving is a symptom of a lack of systemic thinking about innovation, and is rooted in many of the other causes, notably risk aversion, outlined in my Nick's Picks.

Aside from the reimbursement structure part, does this scenario sound a bit like General Motors?

It's Not Always about Money

One question that's interesting to ponder is: "What percent of business failures are directly or indirectly related to innovation? In other words, how often do businesses lose their way strictly out of their inability to effectively innovate?

If you take a look at an MBA thesis on business failure—I can remember a college professor telling me that 100 percent of the time they run out of money. Of course, it isn't that simple, but you could say that most of the time—90 percent of the time, anyway—they run out of money. But what's important is what happens *before* they run out of money.

I believe that companies run out of cash as a symptom of running out of innovation.

Innovation isn't just the ability to solve problems; it's the ability to use a variety of tools to make certain that you've done the right things to earn the money you need to run your business. I would argue that the overwhelming majority of business failures are associated with the inability to deliver meaningful net value.

Such failures can take many forms, each with symptoms that may be obvious or may be more subtle to most until it's too late. Often, these patterns of failure are observed by members of an organization who, unfortunately, have little power or influence to change them. It really takes a leader to, first, recognize the symptoms and, second, to put an organization back on course. In some organizations, the behavior patterns are so ingrained that it takes outsiders to change them, if they can be changed at all.

When Process Takes Over: What's Wrong with Innovation Management Systems?

It's important to switch gears a bit to consider innovation as a process. Too many companies focus on the process of innovation, not the result—customer net value. But, particularly in big organizations, like any other initiative, innovation cannot be done without at least some degree or form of structure. That said, process actually serves to get in the way and to ingrain old, bad habits in the organization and in the culture.

It's important to take a closer look at process, the lexicon of process, and the various ways well intentioned people put process into play—and how it stifles the innovation process. In analyzing innovation failure, excessive focus on process—internal focus—kills innovation over and over, often without the corporate victim having any real sense what's happening to them. With process, of course, come systems—the dozens of tools ranging from spreadsheets to elaborate custom innovation management software—used to manage innovation and new product development.

Process is such an important topic in understanding the root causes of innovation failure that it warrants its own chapter—Chapter 3.

When Leadership Fails

Another innovation failing I see over and over—and it's a broad and encompassing category that leads to many of the symptomatic failure causes in my Nick's Ten (as well as the Idea Companion 56 and other lists) is leadership. Lack of leadership, or more harmful, the wrong kind of leadership.

CEOs and other corporate executives serve many masters, I know that well. But too often they serve interests that are too internal, too short term—or frankly, too self-serving—to give innovation the daylight it needs to succeed. The bottom line truth is that innovation failure can almost always be attributed to a leadership failure somewhere along the way.

A complete treatment of the subject of leadership would consume too much space here; it's big enough for a book of its own, and there are a lot of them. I'll give a more elaborate treatment of organizational leadership and innovation in Chapter 9. One thing I like to see is corporate leaders and leaders specifically tasked with innovation inside organizations: See Chapter 9 for more leadership principles tied to innovation.

Chapter Takeaways

- Experts, pundits, and journalists have long thought about what makes innovation fail; there are lists upon lists of reasons. Many of these lists sidestep the fact that innovation failures tend to boil down to cultural barriers and a failure to focus on customers and net customer value.
- There is a tendency to look at the symptoms of failure and "blamestorm" the causes—again leading to lists, and again failing to focus on culture and customer.
- "Cultural" failures include excessive focus on process and ineffective leadership. These root causes lead to a number of other failure causes which really turn out to be symptoms: excessive risk aversion, underfunding, too much focus on products and not customers, among many. Good innovation managers address the culture and provide the kind of leadership necessary to move forward, not look backward.

CHAPTER 3

The Danger of Safety

Chapter 3 is probably the most controversial chapter in *The Innovation Playbook*.

Why? Because it's about risk management. As it turns out, risk management may be the great divide that separates styles of innovation management and, for that matter, styles of management in general. Indeed, it's often the risk management part of the corporate playbook that separates true innovation results from mere activity and, ultimately, success from failure. But agreeing on what should be in the playbook, and how it should be executed on the playing field is where managers in many corporations come to grief with their new product development functions, not to mention with each other, and it's where consultants like me are often called in to referee the play.

It's amazing to me to see just how emotionally charged the term "risk management" is.

When I speak around the country, and I proclaim the most dangerous thing that a company can do is focus on risk, the response I get is shocking. There's a warm, comfortable feel to risk management in corporations today, and that comfort is a manifestation of years of adding layers and layers of risk management—with the erroneous idea that managing risks—reduces risks!

Now before I go on to slam all things "risk," I would like to offer something of a disclaimer. Risk management does have its place in innovation management and product development. Certainly we want to validate the functionality of a device, to run it through a "fault tree" analysis to make certain it meets design requirements. We want to control the risk that a product or device could injure someone.

Indeed, we need to create a series of tests to validate that the design is safe and sufficient to deliver expected performance.

There is, of course, a wide range of risk management tools that, I hate to admit, actually help. For example, some level of early due diligence is essential when innovation initiatives are based on a new product line or manufacturing process. As noted by Robert Siminski, a patent attorney friend of mine, companies often derive more from understanding whether there are any infringement risks associated with adoption of the new product line or process, than from obtaining patents for the product or process. The problem is that risk rules the day. It is ingrained in corporate culture. Corporations manage facilities. They manage people. They manage money. They love Excel spreadsheets. They love to create controls around all aspects of their business.

But with all that said, innovation is an elusive and unruly beast that can't be controlled within the captivity of conventional risk management systems.

There's no question that product development risk management works in some fashion. It provides a way to ensure a product actually delivers its design requirements to a customer. So I can't really be critical of a basic need for product development risk management. The problem is risk management itself has become a holistic system within innovation and new product development functions of many of the largest corporations in America, and probably the world.

So how well is it working? According to the oft-quoted Deloitte & Touche study, 95 percent of new products fail. Virtually every one of those failures occurred at larger companies that had highly developed, layered risk management systems. If you take nothing else away from *The Innovation Playbook*, please consider this: The best way to manage risk is to understand—*fully* understand—what your customers' needs and values are.

What I see instead are companies becoming slaves to their own internal development requirements. What surprises me is how little focus is given to the outside world and the end user as part of a real risk management system.

Play the Game to Win

Statistics show us that organizations that have the discipline to really understand their market space and their customers have a significantly higher success rate than companies that focus on risk management. So—forgive the sports analogy—but here it is: The difference between focusing on customer net value vs. focusing on risk management is analogous to the difference between playing the game to win vs. playing the game not to lose.

Now this may sound like just a corny cliché, but it is central to the success of all great companies. How many people do you know in your life who are fear focused, or risk focused, who have ever done anything significant or meaningful with their lives? Sure, a few overcome the fear factor to do great things, but they're the exception rather than the rule. Organizations are the same. Great companies take risks that are mitigated by their keen understanding of what their customers value, not by internally focused means of risk management.

In researching *The Innovation Playbook*, I posted a question to several groups on the networking portal LinkedIn. The groups ranged from manufacturing to engineering to marketing, and others. I asked a simple question: "Is risk management killing innovation?"

And wow, I wasn't prepared for the level of emotional response—from all around the world—on that very topic. In one group I had more than 200 responses. After spending hours poring through the responses, I divided them into two categories. Category A was Playing the Game Not to Lose, and Category B was Playing the Game to Win. The group that said that risk management was the best thing that ever happened them—the Playing the Game Not to Lose group—all had an interesting agenda.

After looking at the profiles of the various people who chimed in and ended up in Category A, I found they fit almost exclusively into two groups. The first group—did you guess it?—were purveyors of risk management systems. That is, they worked for management consultants and software vendors who help companies manage risk. Needless to say, they were big believers. There was also a smaller group in Category A who defined themselves as current project managers, typically engineers, who liked the idea of not being forced to take risk and thus felt very comfortable in that category.

Category B—Playing the Game to Win—were executives of anything from major corporations to small start-ups who all said their success was based on their ability to break away from a spreadsheet or process approach, and pool customer needs and manage risk in a real world approach to understanding what their customers cared about. They then ran risk management tools through as a secondary process to make sure their ideas penciled out.

The Fear of Failure

So what happens to corporations when they develop risk management tools that become a global management focus? The important part you should understand is: *This is the natural process*. I have found that, if you look at organizational life cycles, starting from the start-up or entrepreneurial phase, to the developmental phase, to the organizational phase, to a maturity phase, you'll see that as they go up that natural curve, they add additional ways to control risk.

So how is it that organizations transmute into what I call a "hyper-risk focus." It's simple, really: *failure*.

There's an old adage that suggests the biggest cause of failure is the *fear* of failure. I don't believe there are any better examples of that adage than those found in the area of innovation and product management. What often happens is that fear begins to rule the day. Since fear doesn't sound nearly as good as risk management, we like to call it risk management because it sounds like—we're managing the risk, so everything is under control. The problem is that, in the process of fear management, we begin to look at every single product idea, every technology not as an opportunity to serve and provide net customer value, but instead as a possible negative mark on our employee file. Possibly as a demotion, or even a termination. Fear paralyzes the process.

When Fear Becomes Self-Fulfilling

In my consulting practice I help my clients license technologies. I have found that, in the medical market, often the person in charge of evaluating new technologies is not compensated for bringing in new profitable technologies, but conversely is punished if he or she brings in a new technology that fails.

So what does this gatekeeper do? You guessed it—nothing! What's even worse is that some of the country's most open innovators are actually not open at all. I have found companies that have key executives speaking at open innovation symposiums actually don't have systems in play to allow external innovations to enter the door in any real way. They also don't apply an "intrepreneural" mentality or a *portfolio approach* as Hewlett-Packard does.

After all, that's what innovation is—a portfolio. What does that mean? It means we're going to have technologies that do great, and we're going to have technologies that fail. In many cases organizations will encourage projects and project managers—as I've said before—to fail early. And as I introduced in Chapter 2, I'd like to change the vernacular to "bail early."

If you can change the focus in your organization from the top down, alleviating the focus on risk, and replace it with an opportunity to serve net customer value, you will be an innovation superstar.

Does Facebook Worry About Saving Face?

Facebook went from No. 15 on *Fast Company's* most innovative list last year to No. 1. Facebook just turned six, but has already become the platform of choice for 400 million users all over the world. Founder Mark Zuckerberg used to code the site while dashing between makeshift offices in a beat-up car that didn't need a key. Now he has 1,200 employees and a real HR person, all in a 135,000-square-foot office space. The company more than doubled its user base last year. Facebook users were updating their statuses with the word "Haiti" some 1,500 times a minute after the devastating earthquake last year.

When everyone else was pulling back the throttle during the economic downturn, Zuckerberg was doing what other emerging success stories were also doing—sinking money and time into continually perfecting his product. He grew Facebook's engineering ranks by 50 percent.

Another thing that's a little different about Zuckerberg himself is his refusal to let risk management govern his company's potential. He's a majority stakeholder, so he can't be shoved aside or fired. He hopes that this frees the company to gamble a bit. In a recent *Fast Company* article, Zuckerberg pointed out that many companies are set up so that people judge one another on failures. He can't be fired if he has a bad year, or a few bad years. And he hopes this attitude will outlast him and even liberate those who are less insulated. He sees many businesses so worried about looking successful, even when they're making mistakes, that they're afraid to take any risks and miss out on amazing opportunities.

The article can be found at www.fastcompany.com/mic/2010/profile/facebook.

The Outlier's Dilemma

There is a phenomenon I call the Outlier's Dilemma. It's a big problem: Really good ideas and really bad ideas look *extremely similar*. When we're looking at ideas, whether they're internal or external, we always try to put them in the medial safety zone. Anything outside of this central safety zone doesn't get looked at, because at the end of the day it could be looked at as crazy.

One great example is the Apple iPad. Do you really need a flat digital device that allows you to read newspapers and just about everything else? Do you really need such a high-tech contraption to do the things that you can do anyway? My answer: Hell yes! The problem is, when we look at ideas, we want to drop them back into the medial safety zone—but that is the death zone. It is the zone of incremental innovation; it is the zone of painting it blue and calling it new.

Risk management is not open to external safety zone innovations. You need to be able to develop openness, to realize the outlier is often the best choice.

Seeing the . . . *Benefits* of Failure?

Most of us were programmed from a very early age not to fail. Failure is the opposite of success, and failing means you tried and couldn't do it—or perhaps you didn't try at all.

And no doubt—as you can tell—I'm a big fan of success in the innovation space. But failure can be a good thing, too. Why? Because it's healthy, just like a tree losing its dead or dying lower branches is healthy for the tree. You learn from failure. You know what not to do, which will ultimately make you better at knowing what *to* do, and better at actually doing it. In fact, I was surprised to find out how many proverbs and sayings there are about this subject.

Fellow innovation consultants Idea Champions captured dozens in a blog post; here are a few of my favorites: (see http://www.ideachampions.com/weblogs/archives/2010/04/post_17.shtml)

> Failure is only the opportunity to begin again more intelligently.
> —Henry Ford

> Never confuse a single defeat with a final defeat.
> —F. Scott Fitzgerald

> I am not discouraged, because every wrong attempt discarded is another step forward.
> —Thomas A. Edison

It must be human nature for people to wax philosophic as they learn and move on. Regardless, as a true innovator, remember that failure is a healthy part of the game.

Keepers of the Magic Lexicon

Elbert Hubbard is famous for saying: "To avoid criticism, do nothing, say nothing, and be nothing." And that's what we've created within our new product development and innovation environments. We have created corporate sycophants who have learned the lexicon of innovation. This isn't a small problem. In researching *The Innovation Playbook*, I was surprised to find out how many expert *talkers* there were. They knew the latest terms. They quoted the latest books on innovation. They used worn clichés like "ahead of the curve" and "paradigm shift." But at the end of the day, they never actually invented anything!

What I found is that they don't understand the process. In fact, their only value proposition to the organization is as keepers of the magic lexicon. Really?

When you engage with great organizations, it's about reality. It's about a focus on serving customer value. We have to go back to our organizations and find out: Have we created nothing more than "innovation-speak?"

What's In a Tag Line?

Recently, at a major conference, I was walking on the exhibitor floor. It was hilarious! Every single company used the words "invent" or "innovation" in their tag lines. But a closer discussion and analysis revealed that these companies were anything but, and even the organizations that do understand good innovation systems—don't apply them.

Einstein told us that "insight is not a cure." Knowing what needs to be done doesn't fix the problem, and believe it or not—this may sound shocking coming from a management consultant—more than likely, the last thing you need is another bloody system,—and especially, a risk management system.

IBWA—Innovation By Walking Around

I was surprised to find out there are more than 170 different risk management or new product development processes being propagated around the country. Now, these systems are designed to "McDonald-ize" and to create systems around something that really has to be done through a system I call "innovation by walking about," or IBWA. You have to do the heavy lifting of connecting to your customer—customer connectivity is risk management control process Number One.

But there's a caveat. I don't necessarily equate this to so-called "customer relationship management," or CRM, because CRM is really nothing more than an attempt to mechanize the process of connecting to people at a visceral, emotional level—and that's where success lives. Imagine, if you will, walking in your home's door at the end of the day and reporting to your spouse that you've decided to implement broad-based "marital relationship management" methodologies as a means to provide "improved connectivity" and "mitigate the risk of conflict" in your home. I don't know about you, but I'd probably soon see the business end of a cast iron skillet.

Perhaps that metaphor is somewhat over-extended, nonetheless it's really important to take the right approach to gaining customer insight. I'll be back in Chapter 4 to talk about the myths and realities of collecting customer insight. I will also give you a more complete playbook in Chapters 6 and 7.

The System and the Solution

So when I use the term "risk management system," what am I really talking about? Are these systems simply checklists to make sure all the bases are covered in designing and introducing a new product? Or do they reach back into the idea generation and prototyping phases to manage, control, stage, check, and evaluate new ideas and the development of those ideas?

As it turns out, many of today's systems do both. They not only help guarantee that the bases are covered, that a product does what it is supposed to do, safely and securely, but they also help a (usually) dispersed management and engineering team manage and control its own activities. I'm a believer in the checklist part, agreeing wholeheartedly with Atul Gawande's excellent book *The Checklist Manifesto*. In today's complex and fast-paced world, as Gawande points out, it has become more important to "check the boxes," as the world's aviators have known for years, lest some really simple but critical item is missed.

We don't want to introduce a car with brakes that don't work when it hits a bump, and we don't want to introduce food with any potentially harmful materials, and the checklists should guide us away from such failures. But what happens when the risk management process travels all the way back into the "ideation" process in such a way that anything really new or different never makes it past the first checklist? It happens, and it's happening more and more, as people become more comfortable managing risk and less comfortable with change.

Perhaps it is the very speed and volatility of the current business environment that causes risk management to become the ruling force. Perhaps because it *is* more systematic and cut and dried, people find it easier to say "no" than "let's do this." Perhaps it's today's corporate reward systems, which tend to punish failure individually while rewarding success to groups and/or top managers within an organization, that are the culprits.

What I see today is that companies need to not just eliminate risk management entirely, but take risk management and its systems in perspective. If they help innovation along, and they help guarantee the success of good ideas, they are good. If they hinder innovation, and especially if they hinder the generation of customer-centered business ideas, look out below.

What to Expect from Risk Management

Risk management systems do have their advantages. They provide structure, a common language, and tools for managing complex projects and large numbers of projects simultaneously. They help with communication and many of the standard elements of project management. And these things are good, particularly when the system is managed well and has the right tactical tools—networked meetings and so forth—sitting behind them. But I want to make two things clear. First, risk management systems don't substitute for thinking. Second, risk management systems don't substitute for good marketing homework, that is, for proper assessment of customer needs. Organizations that expect their new product development systems to do their thinking for them, to figure out where value can be created for customers are headed for trouble.

Keepers of the Gates

Ask almost anyone in a new product development function and they'll tell you they've had experience with what I call a "staged approval system" model. For those who haven't dealt with staged approval systems, they are, as the name implies, models that break up the new product development process into stages with approval "gates" allowing progress onto the next stage. Different users and different companies have different stages, but they usually look something like ideation, develop analysis, develop business case, develop prototype, test, and launch. Each stage has a "gate"—a thorough management or steering committee review to decide whether the project should go further.

Frequently, the stages mentioned above are divided into several smaller sub-stages, which may include detailed risk analysis, resource analysis, or customer testing; in some cases I've seen companies try to manage products through 10 to 15 stages.

As I mentioned earlier, staged approval systems do help complex organizations manage complex projects. But all too often the process, not the customer, becomes the master. Everyone works to satisfy the needs of the gatekeepers, and the gatekeepers tend to feel like they're doing their job if they say no. In many examples I've witnessed, they have too much power, and they are too disconnected from customers to make the best gate-keeping decisions. In addition, it's not hard to see how the extra bureaucracy and layers of approval bog down the process in addition to stifling creativity.

For the users, and especially the gatekeepers of staged approval systems, the old saying "If you have a hammer, everything looks like a nail" may apply. While the gates help to allocate resources and to weed out obviously bad projects, they are often held up to the task of measuring the immeasurable—the customer value, the customer passion, the innovator's passion—that make breakthrough innovation work. It's too hard to get a "good" project through all the approvals.

Still, I do see the need for some process control, to make some order out of chaos and to allocate resources efficiently. But somehow the organization needs to also be able to embrace breakthrough projects, to take chances, to open gates that might not be opened with a hard, numbers-oriented risk analysis—for projects that have breakthrough potential and obvious customer value. On top of that, the gatekeepers need to be at the forefront of customer connectivity, not the isolated, internally focused individuals we usually see in those positions.

When staged approval processes run the show, incrementalism is the likely result. Incremental improvements are relatively easy to measure, and since they build on existing products, the gates are usually already partly opened. In fact, staged approval approaches are often applauded for managing incremental innovation; it's what they're best at. But in many instances, they break down altogether and nothing happens at all. Risk-adverse managers rule the day, and innovations are shot down at the business-case stage or earlier. Some may get patents, but it ends there; innovators and R&D departments are happy because they got a patent, but nothing gets to market. If your organization grinds through a lot of resources but has little to show at the end of the day, save for a few incremental improvements ("Paint it blue, call it new"), it's time to question your staged approval process, if you use one.

Asked and Answered

One test I use is to ask clients: "Would the Apple iPod have ever gotten through your new product development process?" If the answer is no, the process is probably too risk adverse and cumbersome; it should be scrapped and reinvented, zero-based style. If the answer is yes, then your process has the flexibility, the market focus, and the recognition of breakthroughs necessary to be an innovation superstar. The most likely answer, however, is "I don't know," and that's where you as a manager or as part of an innovation team need to evaluate your processes and systems critically and decide if what you have really works or is just an impediment to successful new product development.

Two questions I also ask when in front of clients: "Does your organization have the kind of leaders and the kind of leadership that can get a breakthrough project or idea through the gates?" and, "Do you have a Steve Jobs or someone with his vision and passion who can evangelize a product or idea past the gatekeepers, and who can get the gatekeepers on board with the idea of net customer value in the first place?" Often it isn't the process—it's the people who execute the process—who are the problem. Staged approval systems run by truly passionate, innovative people *can* really work—it's all about climate.

I'm often asked: "What should organizations expect their innovation processes and systems to do?" My answer: They should help manage and share good ideas, and they should promote—not inhibit—a culture of innovation. And these processes should align to overall business visions and strategies, not to the internally focused gods of risk and cost control. I also warn clients that these systems are not designed to guarantee success or avoid failure completely, and that the best processes and tools actually help an organization learn from those failures.

When the system becomes part of the solution to developing world-class innovations and bringing them to market, and not just an end in and of itself, you've found success.

The Attack of the Organizational Antibodies

I'm sure you've had this experience yourself. Come up with a good idea, and run it by your peers and superiors in a meeting. Before you've finished your last sentence, someone in the back of the room pipes up, announcing that he or she "is playing devil's advocate"—and proceeds to find every negative he or she can think of about your idea and lay it out on the table for all to see.

Yeah, you've been there. So have I.

It's a funny thing that happens in the corporate world. People have a much easier time finding out what's wrong with the work of others than doing something new, innovative, and exciting themselves. One colleague tells me a story of an impromptu last minute presentation on a new service program made to a top marketing executive and her staff. He thought he nailed it. He actually did. A day later, he got the feedback: "He used the wrong colors on his presentation slides."

People like to play find the fault. It's easy. They can take a paycheck home every day with impunity. But have they created any value for their customers? Have they really created any value for their organization? True, if an idea really is bad, people should speak up. But to nit-pick things to death, bringing up this fault and that risk over and over—I say, that's crap.

Beyond simply being easy, the reality is that some people—and some organizations—simply are uncomfortable with change. When a new idea comes along, half (or more) of the people in the room simply think it's their job to chime in to point out what's wrong with it. I call these people "organizational antibodies." Like real antibodies, they're tough, and they come back again and again to do their job—against any foreign substance they might find.

The reason this is important is that systems rarely work without people; in fact, it's the people using them that make them go or not go. So when people fall back on their roles as organizational antibodies, they're causing the innovation management system to fail. That's bad, and it's worse when, as is very often the case, they're getting support as antibodies from their management teams. It's still worse when top management folks are the antibodies themselves—now you've got a real problem.

These antibodies may just be lazy, or they may be especially risk-adverse individuals. They don't really understand the business or the customer, or they aren't passionate about what they do. As a manager (or as a consultant, as I often see it) there are at least three things you can do.

1. *Stop rewarding the behavior.* Don't give any "attaboys" for people who simply find fault, and absolutely don't promote them, give stock options, and so on, for this kind of work. (This happens all the time.)
2. *Accentuate the positive.* Don't let someone drag the ideas of others through the mud unless they have a positive suggestion to make at the same time.
3. *Connect them to the soul.* People who make a living being critical of the ideas and suggestions of others simply aren't thinking about their customers, or really, the long term health of their business. These people need a lesson on both the soul of the business and the soul of the customer. Reset their expectations by getting them out on the front lines. Teach them to put the customers first.

The One-in-Ten Syndrome

In some organizations, the antibodies are everywhere. There are nine out of 10 people in every conference room, in every finance department, in every site procurement or site facilities organization sitting there paid, waiting, and ready to knock your innovation off the rails. Know that "no innovation" means success to these people, because they all "found the fault" as they were supposed to. If your organization has nine "no" people for every one who's trying to move it forward, guess what? You're business won't get anywhere. On top of that, you might be in the wrong job.

Diffusing the Bomb

When I look at innovation management systems—and I've had the opportunity to go in and fix very sick companies—I realize they've developed or implemented risk management systems as a way to control product failures – product failures that would vex the organization, or product failures that would vex the careers of certain individuals within the organization.

But not surprisingly, virtually nothing came out the other end. What did come out was so incredibly slow that it had little to no market relevance by the time it saw the light of day. What we, as a consulting organization, have had to do in most of these companies is to rewire them to get rid of the layers and layers of unnecessary bureaucracy that make some product manager—or consulting firm—look like they earned their keep. The net effect was that all these layers and processes served to filter out innovations that should have been theirs—when they should have been wired to their customers in the first place.

This is no small deal. In some cases, we're talking about millions, or even billions, of dollars of opportunities because our throughput through our NPD function was absolutely killed. Diffusing the bomb is absolutely necessary.

From there, I like to start with a zero based approach. For an exercise, I tell clients to pretend that there's no system in place at all right now. The next step is to create a system that is fluid and fresh and customer connected, and that rewards employees. What if we created a system that was fun again? What if we had a chance to spend the *carpet time*—that is, time to closely observe customer behavior and needs further described in Chapter 7—with the customer and do really cool stuff?

Anger Management

Isn't that a better way to control risk? When I decided to write *The Innovation Playbook*, I had to ask myself one very basic question: "Do I want to write a book that will increase my popularity and to sell a system by using the book as a brochure?—or—am I willing to irritate some people and say the things that everybody else in this space really wants to say?"

Colin Powell once said, "Pissing people off is both inevitable and necessary. This doesn't mean that the goal is to piss people off;

and pissing people off doesn't necessarily mean that you're doing the right thing. But doing the right thing will almost invariably piss people off."

So here it is. Chances are that your innovation system is not open because it's afraid. It's driven by fear. Chances are that your new product development function is extremely slow, because of all the unnecessary analysis that shouldn't be done, but it *is* done because the new product development function doesn't really understand the market or the customer.

Chances are the people who have the highest level of customer contact in your organization never have a voice to say where there are opportunities to add additional customer value. Chances are the people who make most of the decisions in your company are completely insulated from the customer, and often from the very market. Chances are people are punished for taking smart risk and for pursuing innovations that serve both the company and the customer. Chances are nobody's ever rewarded for doing cool stuff and taking smart risk. Chances are risk rules the day.

I hope I didn't piss anybody off, and yes, it may apply to you, but from my research, I can assure you that it applies to 80 percent of companies.

It's Fixable, or at the Genesis

There is good news, and that good news is that it's fixable. The better news: It's *easily* fixable. Not only is it easily fixable, it will also provide a completely different experience. Now this is something that may make some companies uneasy, but what about fun? Have we lost that? I mean—really? Let's have fun again. Let's have some fun doing stuff that is so cool that it blows away everyone who sees it.

As a successful inventor myself, it's been interesting. When I drive to drop my kids off at school every morning, people hide from me. Why? Because I'm going to walk them back to my car. I'm going to open the trunk, and I'm going to show them the latest cool product that I'm involved in. Being involved in the genesis of something new; to bring something to the universe that wasn't there before and to successfully commercialize it so that it adds value to other people's lives is why I got into this in the first place, isn't it?

We have the coolest job. We're in the creation business, and what I hope is that we can take the fear out of the equation.

I know we have to be smart, and as a Certified Management Consultant, I "get" organizations, and I get the need to have controls and reports. So you're forgiven. But let's do it in a way that connects us back to the people we love: our customers. Let's have fun again.

Fire in the Belly

In *The Innovation Playbook*, I will offer some alternatives to the more rigid, more linear approaches to risk management that are fluid, that are customer connected, and that are *fun* again. I'm not suggesting you throw the baby out with the bathwater—and if you like your current risk management system, it's okay. Because at the end of the day most of those systems are actually good; it's not the system itself (you system purveyors will be glad to hear this)—it's the *use* of the system I'm critical of.

Again, one of my favorite analogies compares risk management to fire. Fire, used properly, will warm you; used improperly, it will burn you. Unfortunately, the use of fire requires adult supervision. Often organizations are so enamored with an idea—and it's a false idea—that managing innovation by spreadsheet can help them create normal controls just like they would in their financial functions.

The reality is creativity, customer connection, and innovation comes from the belly. It's visceral, and it can't be done through McDonald-ized approaches.

When I look at the greatest companies, like Sierra Nevada Brewery, like toymakers Spin Master and Air Hog Toys, I see companies that are so unbelievably connected to their customers, and they're so passionate and proud of what they do that the focus is on creating cool stuff for customers, instead of developing systems that will "protect our jobs."

"Nothing" Rules the Day

That leads me to another point. Beyond some of the hurdles created by risk management systems, and some of the behaviors exhibited by the organizational antibodies, quite often risk management is adopted by departments—I'm not bashful about saying this—as an excuse for doing nothing. If we have a risk adverse environment, the best thing an employee can do is absolutely nothing, right?

It's interesting *how big* a problem this is. Organizations are told not to make mistakes; they're ridiculed for failure, they are upheld as organizational idiots when something goes wrong—and, not surprisingly, nobody in the organization wants to expose the system itself to ridicule. Even some of the best organizations that—theoretically—encourage smart risk taking still basically prevent new idea promotion and sometimes create toxic consequences for people who have chosen to take smart risks.

A Short Primer on Smart Risk

If we know that taking smart risks is necessary, here's the big question: What exactly is a smart risk? One way to describe a smart risk is, of course, any risk that results in success, right? That doesn't help much, I know. More insightfully, taking smart risks actually means taking risks that are based on a high level understanding of what the market and the customers want.

I know that sounds obvious—but what's amazing is that it's *not* obvious to most companies. They're more interested in a one-dimensional look at it. They do a "feature benefit and a review analysis" of revenue potential, return on investment, and so forth. Instead, the analysis should start by being highly connected—not by CRM or traditional "Voice of the Customer" methods (see Chapter 4) through IBWA—Innovation By Walking About. That said, I know that CRM and VOC can provide valuable data and some degree of insight, but that data and those insights are much more valuable if you already have a gut understanding of the customer in the first place.

Anyway, this is how you take smart risks. A risk clearly in the direction of customer needs, preferences, and value is far less risky than a risk taken without such clarity. Such a risk becomes "can you deliver" versus the question "Is this the right thing in the first place?" The former risk is much easier to manage. Another way to put it: Innovation risk taken with customer certainty is a lot smarter than innovation risk taken with customer *un*certainty.

What Makes Apple Shine?

Some of you may be asking yourself: "What about Apple?" Guy Kawasaki postulates that "nobody can accuse Apple of being market driven." It's true. I happen to be a big Apple devotee and I love and consume their products wildly. But what they are—and they're *very* good at this—is customer connected. Does that mean that they go out and "co-create" with their customers—for many the penultimate sign of customer connectivity? Well, sometimes, sometimes not. But they understand their customers, and they use their internal expertise not to invent what customer want, but to create, as it turns out, what their customers *must* own!

Apple does some things that are just amazing, and, as with In-N-Out Burger and Sierra Nevada Brewery (see Chapter 1),—what they understand is the *total customer experience*—the entire cycle of customer experiences, what I like to refer to as the *customer service cycle*. By that I mean this: When you buy a product from Apple, it comes in an absolutely beautiful box. The box looks like it is holding the Fabergé egg, and it has been designed, crafted, and engineered with the same precision and the same "wow" as the product inside.

When you open the box, it's not what's included that's amazing; it's what's *not* there. There's *no manual*! Are they trying to save printing costs? Probably, but the truth is that the product is so easy to use (as well as beautifully elegant) that it does exactly what you expect it to do.

So back to the central question—how do they control risk? It's simple. They know their customer—they really know their customer—and they execute accordingly and execute perfectly. When you can do that, and make that *part of a philosophy*, rather than a mathematical system, you will become an innovation superstar.

No Creeps Allowed

If you're already an innovation superstar, make sure you don't allow what I call *risk creep*. Risk creep is inevitable. It happens to every organization—"the bigger we get, the more we've got to protect"—becomes the mantra.

When I was in college, everything I owned was in a shoebox. But when I started earning money, and started buying homes and cars and all kinds of gizmos and personal property, I became afraid that I could lose it all. I think that philosophy is alive and well in corporate America.

Moreover, it becomes an easier job to protect something that it is to go out and increase, improve, or build something new. Just follow the rules, the policies, and the procedures. Just keep the thing in sight. Play not to lose. It's an easier job, and it's an easier job to justify for empire-building types in organizations who like to build empires. That leads straight to the One-in-Ten syndrome, and when you're there, you know you're at the end of your "creep." Losing business to competitors and then losing your business altogether, is what happens next. Just ask anyone at GM or Eastman Kodak or any other once-innovative company gone awry.

Further, employees who could be fired for taking risks—they have no choice but to do nothing.

Carmaker at a Crossroads

Until early 2010, carmaker Toyota Motor Corporation enjoyed no rival as an innovative company constantly seeking to push the innovation envelope, both in product and in process design, to deliver the industry's leading net customer value proposition. Everyone loved their cars, everyone loved their technologies and the way they integrated them into the cars, and everyone loved the price of Toyotas—an obvious sign of process efficiencies and innovations behind the scenes in their factories and engineering departments.

Then along came the sticky accelerators on eight different models, brake system failures on the renowned Prius, and a great deal of internal and external upheaval over these matters. Not that they are unimportant, but one wondered as the story unfolded about the short-term and especially the long-term effects on the company's innovation culture. Could that company, from CEO down to design engineer to factory worker, possibly regain its focus on what got them so far in the first place? Innovation? Or would they be subconsciously or even consciously sucked into a new order of risk aversion preventing even *smart* risks to prevent such a thing from happening again, effectively slowing or even snuffing out new innovation?

Only time will tell. Failures, if managed well, are short-term speed bumps. Managed poorly, they'll take a company down the wrong road for good.

Chapter Takeaways

- Play the game to win, not to "not lose." Winning companies focus on delivering net customer value; very little of their organizational bandwidth is consumed by risk management. They are wired to their customers.
- Manage failure—don't manage risk. Make sure the product fits the requirements that you've discovered through a high level of customer connectivity. That's where innovation really lives.

- Use risk management to verify that the product does that but do it quickly—the market won't wait.
- Create an organizational philosophy—an organizational culture—of pride. As I walked through the beautiful brewery at Sierra Nevada, all I could think was "Wow—here's somebody who's extremely proud of their business." Not a speck of dirt—it was hospital clean—but it had a very different feel to it than a hospital. It was warm and inviting. It was a great place to work for people who love what they're doing.
- Create an environment that fosters customer connection and pride. Get rid of the organizational antibodies. We've all heard the nomenclature around innovation; the lexicon keepers must go. Or, at the very least, they must change their language. Let's talk about customers. Let's be real. Let's forget the processes and systems that are just there to protect somebody's job.
- Check your focus. What does your organizational focus look like? Change your focus to playing the game to win, not just playing not to lose.
- Remember that some failure is healthy for your organization. You learn from your mistakes, and you get some organizational pride for the attempt. Better to have loved and lost than to never have loved at all, right?

C H A P T E R

4

What's Mything in Innovation Today

By now, if you've followed me through the early part of this book, and especially Chapters 2 and 3, you have a pretty good flavor for the major ills afflicting today's corporations when it comes to innovation. They all boil down into common themes in various combinations of causes and effects—risk aversion, bureaucracy, lack of customer focus, poor performance measurement, wrong culture, and a failure to appreciate the importance of innovation in today's economy.

I've also shared with you that a lot has been written about innovation—what's wrong with it, how to fix it, how to jumpstart it, how to manage it. An Amazon keyword search on "innovation" brings back some 39,042 results—*Innovation to the Core, The Innovator's Dilemma, The Art of Innovation,* just to skim the top of the list. I realize there aren't 39,000 separate book titles on the subject of innovation—but you get the idea. Similarly, if you pick up almost any business magazine—*BusinessWeek, Harvard Business Review,* and others—you'll find something on the latest innovation secret of the day.

Not that these treatments are all bad, but you could make a career out of simply reading them all. Many are academic in nature. Many suggest "process" solutions that actually take away from innovation. Many try to turn innovation into an exact science—which it clearly isn't. If there's one thing I want you to take away from *The Innovation Playbook*, it's that innovation isn't an exact science—any more than achieving success in football or any other sport is an exact science.

If you've read along, I've been clear that innovation is about customers, not about processes. I've also conveyed my disdain for "panacea du jour" solutions to the ills of corporate innovation. More "stage gate" systems don't work; more spreadsheets don't work; and more programs to motivate inventors to create patents don't work, either (unless you want patents instead of marketable innovations).

Beyond that, I see four common myths perpetrated upon the innovating public and its management teams over and over. Often these myths come from books, from self-styled corporate leaders who, frankly, think they know more than they do, or from the innovation consultants (shame on us) who should be pushing beyond these myths to begin with.

The myths are:

- The Better Mousetrap myth.
- The I'm Really Connected to My Customers myth.
- The Open Innovation Will Solve Everything myth.
- The Product Is the Technology myth.

The rest of this chapter deals with the nature and pitfalls of these four myths, and how to avoid their adverse impacts on your innovation culture.

Myth #1: "If You Build a Better Mousetrap, Will They Beat a Path to Your Door?"

Dr. John Lienhard is a professor emeritus of Mechanical Engineering and History at the University of Houston. Now, right away, you might ask: "Why do we need to know this? What's so special about John Lienhard?"

John Lienhard is one of the leading authorities on the history of technology and innovation. Those who have heard of him probably heard his National Public Radio program called *The Engines of Our Ingenuity*, a short, regularly broadcast series of radio programs telling the story of inventions and "how the inventive minds work" behind them. Incredibly, the show has recorded 2,579 episodes since it was started in 1988.

One of his episodes, Episode 1,163 recorded back in the mid 1990s, hit the bull's-eye with me. It's called "A Better Mousetrap."

Lienhard starts with the ancient adage "Build a better mouse-trap, and the world will beat a path to your door," which is widely attributed to Ralph Waldo Emerson, although it seems to have been extrapolated by none other than Elbert Hubbard from a far more quaint writing: "If a man has good corn, or wood, or boards, or pigs to sell, or can make better chairs or knives, crucibles or church organs than anybody else, you will find a broad hard-beaten road to his house, though it be in the woods."

Regardless of who said it, the mousetrap quote has always intrigued me. Because it's *wrong*.

Work Smart, Not Just Hard

What Emerson—or Hubbard or whoever—meant, of course was that quality and ingenuity prevail in the marketplace, and he or she who has the latest and greatest will prosper. So people went to work inventing better mousetraps—better spring mechanisms, better trigger mechanisms, and so forth. Innovators built so many new mousetraps that, according to Lienhard the U.S. Patent Office has issued over 4,400 mousetrap patents. And some 400 people still apply for mousetrap patents each year!

Yet, here's the crucial truth, as he goes on to point out: "Only 20 or so of products covered by those patents have ever made any money."

This article does a beautiful job of articulating my point that just because you invent something doesn't mean that there is a market for it, even if the thing you invent actually works better. Why?

The mousetrap phrase has been the motivational mantra for hundreds of thousands of would-be successful inventors and innovators. But the trap here—and in this case it isn't a mousetrap—is that these innovators focus on the function and not the benefit or, as we'll learn to call it out of habit, meaningful net customer value.

In order for an innovation to work in the marketplace people must need the product, and they must recognize they need the product. It must be affordable and better than competitive solutions. Sure, a small improvement in spring or trigger technology might benefit the customer, and it may also enable you to deliver the product less expensively. But will you win in business just doing these things? No, not in the long term anyway.

In the long term, someone else will come up with a breakthrough, and you'll find yourself in the hole. In this case, customers are actually fairly happy with the current mousetrap solutions, so far as they go. They work, and because the traps are inexpensive, they can be thrown away with the dead mouse to avoid the discomfort of mouse disposal.

Segments and Sub-Segments

Now this isn't to say that better mousetraps are not possible. They are. Here's the crux of the matter: To innovate, you must find a breakthrough. That breakthrough may address the needs of the whole market, but more likely—and more *attainable*—it may address the needs of a segment or sub-segment of that market. That is, there may be an underserved segment of the market that has its own appetite for delivered net customer value.

Here's what I mean. A lot of people are squeamish. They don't want to see a mouse virtually broken in half on a traditional spring trap. So one possible innovation is a sort of "garage" trap where the mouse gets stuck inside, so the user doesn't have to see the dead mouse. There may be other trap designs that are more humane or keep the bait away from insects or provide other benefits to carefully targeted groups of trap buyers.

The bottom line is, if you don't provide improved net customer value you don't have an innovation. And one of the quickest ways to find new net value to deliver is to serve segments and sub-segments of your market, and serve them well. But you can't do that by making minor tweaks to your product or service.

So don't focus on building a better mousetrap just for the sake of the incremental improvement—or worse, for the patent (there's a long line at the mousetrap patent Examiner's office!). Find targets—sub-segments—and deliver value like crazy.

The Good Ship Enterprise

One of my favorite examples of a segment-based innovation has nothing to do with technology per se, but it's a great example of clear focus on an un-served or underserved segment in the market. It worked far better than the incremental tweak deployed in the face of head-to-head competition in the highly competitive market of rental cars.

Enterprise Rent-A-Car has four main competitors for its market share—Hertz, Avis, Budget, and National. The company began innovating its business model and customer experience by focusing on a different user need: a car to drive when a customer's car is in the neighborhood repair shop. Enterprise built up an extensive network of local and neighborhood offices and developed a different business model where insurance companies pay for most of the rentals. These innovations led to the company delivering rental cars to people for many purposes, resulting in a different—and vastly differentiated—customer experience. The company went from a $1 billion profit in 1996 to $7 billion in 2007, leaving the former market share leader, Hertz, far behind.

One question I always ask when I see this kind of business insight and adjustment: "Could it happen in one of today's gigantic corporations bound to tradition, size, and short term Wall Street interests?" Interestingly—and somewhat coincidentally—Enterprise was founded by a man named Jack Taylor who served honorably on the USS Enterprise aircraft carrier in World War II. Whether or not Taylor turned around a real-life aircraft carrier, I don't know, but he sure turned his car rental business on a dime. Perhaps, as a privately held family business, it was easy. But that doesn't mean a large publicly held corporate ship can't be turned—think, once again, Apple.

Niche and Get Rich

In many cases, good innovations really address what I call niche markets—small, underserved segments of the market that either didn't know they needed something, or never had it delivered to them the way they wanted it. Gourmet coffee drinkers. A niche? Twenty years ago, certainly yes. Then, along came Starbucks, who found this underserved niche to be far bigger than anyone thought possible. They innovated the corner coffee bar, and did it in such a way as to not only replace the corner tavern as a hangout, but appeal to several new customer segments—college students, self-employed professionals looking for a respectable "third place" to work, mothers of young children looking for a good morning hangout.

The Starbucks niche went wild, and driven so far by a hugely successful net value proposition, it became a whole market, with Starbucks itself, of course, leading the way and reaping the advantage. The point is, don't forget about niche markets.

I'll also take this opportunity to recommend a great book on niches and niche marketing written by Peter and Jennifer Basye Sander and called *Niche and Grow Rich*, published by Entrepreneur Press in 2003.

Myth #2: "But I AM Connected to My Customers"

I hear this one all the time in my consulting and speaking engagements. The conversation goes something like this: "I am connected to my customers. We spend millions on market research, customer surveys, and we just implemented a new Customer Research Management (CRM) system. So of course I'm connected to my customers."

I shoot right back, "But how much do you know about what they really want? How much do you know about their true experience with your products? Their true feelings? What kinds of products that you *don't* produce today do they want?"

"Uh, well," the conversation continues, "I think we know a lot. We know what they buy. We know about their demographics. We know how often we touch them at our various touch points. We think we have a pretty good idea what they own and whether they are profitable to us."

What's wrong with this picture? Well simply—you can't innovate with this kind of information. Sure, you know a little about what your current customers own. But what do you know about their experience with your products? What do you know about what they *want*? What do you know about needs they have that your products *don't* fulfill?

Sure, today's market research Voice of the Customer (VOC) and CRM systems are helpful in establishing at least some basic customer knowledge. They allow you to better understand market segments, customer value, and who buys what, and sometimes, why. Most CRM systems go a step further to manage customer contacts towards generating new sales—of existing products. They do little to help define new products (except insofar as they collect customer feedback in some meaningful way). None of these systems get to experience and the more visceral threads of true customer needs.

The idea for an Apple iPod would have never come from a CRM system, and probably not from a VOC framework.

Listening to the Voice of the Customer

Voice of the customer is what might be referred to today as traditional market research. Typically combining qualitative research (like focus groups and individual interviews) and quantitative research, such as outbound surveys, in-store surveys and the like, they collect lots of customer data on purchase behavior, satisfaction, and relative importance of certain features, and sometimes, stated needs or preferences. For the most part, it gives a report card on previous purchases, on products already owned.

These VOC methods are typically used to collect this rear-view data and to build customer profiles and satisfaction profiles with existing products. Of course, we all know the dangers of driving by looking in the rearview mirror; these methods don't tell us much about what customers want to buy next except by extrapolation, and that extrapolation may be dangerous. Just as important and as mentioned above, they don't tell us about customer needs or preferences about products that they *don't* have.

Sometimes VOC methods are used in new product development to evaluate a product concept or prototype or to capture observations about alternative or competitive products. Sometimes they can take the form of structured individual in-depth interviews, which can provide a lot of information about customer judgment and feeling. But they stop short of actually observing customer behavior and experience with a product, and again, they don't provide much information about products that a customer doesn't have.

As a new product development device, VOC depends heavily on the quality of the research—the discussion guides, the questions asked, and the sample selection. They can provide invaluable input about desired design features and specifications. The more closely product development teams are involved in research design, and research deployment where appropriate, the better.

Most VOC methods are traditional, as are most interpretations of the results. The results of VOC methods lend themselves more to incremental improvements than breakthroughs. They have trouble assessing more abstract or organic concepts like experience, future customer needs, or needs that customers don't even realize they have, like the iPod. It's difficult to get interview subjects and survey responders to think outside the box towards new products, and thus it's difficult for innovators to get meaningful signals about the next new thing.

Still, VOC methods help and are better than nothing, but I find that many companies rely too much on them. Stronger focus on experience, net customer value, and carpet time will be better. All of these efforts are depicted in more detail in Chapters 6 and 7.

The "Customer" in Customer Relationship Management

About 10 years ago, CRM systems came into vogue as the latest and greatest end-all mechanisms to connect to customers. Collect data from all customers at all "touch points" to the organization—sales, service, after-market sales, mouse clicks on company sites; overlay it with some additional data collected either directly from the customer or from external customers, and you'd know anything you needed to know about your customers. All millions of them.

Of course, advances in IT made it all possible. CRM systems were used to identify prospects, "cross-sell and up-sell" customers when they came into points of contact, and fuel tons of quantitative analysis behind the scenes. It would also reduce costs, because sales and support functions would know about the customer they were talking to and be able to prioritize or de-prioritize them on the fly, or target products or services to their needs.

But the end result was that we got a lot of shallow, rear-view pictures about a lot of customers. We got no qualitative or visceral perspective of what those customers felt or needed. Furthermore, with the exception of a handful of very active customers, we didn't get very much or very reliable information.

Part of the problem, as well, is that the CRM approach assumed that customers *wanted* a relationship. Clearly, that wasn't always the case, so as innovators or as anyone else reading the information, there were a lot of potential and actual customers out there we didn't know much about.

But the deepest failing of CRM, of course, is that no matter how much "touch point" data we collect, we still don't get that intimate knowledge of customer needs, preferences, or desired value propositions from the company. Further, in most organizations, people in innovation functions weren't very closely connected with the data; it was mainly owned by sales and support personnel. When used correctly, however, CRM and related knowledge data could be used to identify "most valuable customers" to target for further research, although most applications based this on who had *already* bought your products, not who was likely to—if you offered the right innovations.

As Tim Beadle, Director of the Atrium Group, put it in a December 2009 article in *Marketing Week*, "What's Wrong with CRM?":

"Too many people forget that CRM is about customers, NOT non-customers who MIGHT become customers." He goes on to say: "CRM systems envisage a serene path from suspect to prospect, to customer, to repeat customer, to evangelist. Their entire existence is predicated upon this, their internal business rules demand it. But people don't behave in a linear fashion, so all too often the CRM system gets in the way, requiring a salesperson to jump through all kinds of hoops to get a new customer into the system simply because they failed to follow the prescribed path. Furthermore, they envisage that all data is perfect and all system users know exactly what to do. It isn't and they don't."

These comments reflect the challenges of using the CRM approach as a sales tool, and even more strongly reflect the challenges of using CRM as an innovation tool. That said, the advent of CRM and especially its godchild "Customer Knowledge Management," or CKM, within an organization is a step in the right direction; at least we're paying close attention to *some* of our customers. Keep in mind, though: We do learn something about those customers, but we must go further to identify the bastions of true customer value.

Conduits of Connectivity

So then, how *do* you develop relationships with your customers—or what I call "conduits of connectivity?" There's an old management theory that was propagated back in the 1970s called Management by Walking About, or MBWA. The idea there was that, as you walked around the floors of your company, you could see opportunities to improve efficiencies, get more connected to your employees, reduce costs, improve sales, and so on. It was a really intelligent approach to getting *inside* your company.

The best thing you can do in the area of developing conduits of connectivity in the area of innovation is to spend time with your customers. I know that sounds really simple, but most companies don't do it. In fact, we talk about what we call the *inverted pyramid*. With the inverted pyramid—I call it the "inverted pyramid syndrome"—most companies have their executives at the highest levels—the top of the pyramid—making most decisions about new product and service offerings, yet they have the least amount of contact with actual customers.

Conversely, front-end people—the customer service representatives, service technicians that have high levels of customer connectivity—usually have virtually no voice in the products and services offerings available to your valued customers. So the first thing that has to happen is that people really involved in decision making need to get out to see where the opportunities are.

Recently we had the opportunity to work with a surgical company. We were surprised to find out that there was no one from inside their surgical product development team who had actually been in surgery within the last 24 months—*2 years*. Here they were developing technologies for a market that they didn't even see. We changed that, and the results were amazing.

That's what it means to get connected. Another great example—and again, it's one of my favorites—is the Sierra Nevada Brewery. When they're getting ready to launch a new product, when they feel that they've really gotten it right; they go into their tap room, which is a beautiful restaurant and bar, and they sit there with the patrons who have been coming there for years. They typically do it on Thursday nights, which are "locals" nights usually filled with serious beer drinkers who are very passionate about their product. They allow them—*encourage* them—to truthfully answer questions like, "Is this product right?" They don't just listen to the experts (the high level beer drinkers), they listen to the occasional beer drinkers as well to find out whether a product really hits its mark.

But they go beyond that. Ken Grossman, their CEO, is an amazing guy. His openness is incredible. He'll talk to his competitors and ask them their opinion. He'll talk to people who would be seen as the enemy by corporations today, and the beauty of that collaboration is amazing. As a result, he consistently makes the best product in the world. This is what it means to develop conduits of connectivity.

Remember: *Manage by Walking About. Innovate While Walking About.*

And What about Benchmarking?

Benchmarking was all the rage 10 to 20 years ago—find out what your competition is doing, measure yourself against it, and everything will come out okay. You'll know how you're doing against the competition.

Okay, that's nice. But can you use benchmarking as an agent of innovation? Not so, as so clearly spoken by management consultant and guru Tom Peters: "I hate benchmarking. Benchmarking is stupid. Why is it stupid? Because we pick the current industry leader. Then we launch a five year program, the goal of which is to be as good as whoever was best five years ago five years from now—which to me is not exactly an Olympian aspiration." He then goes on to share a quote from two professors in the *Financial Times*: "To grow, companies need to break out of a vicious cycle of competitive benchmarking and imitation."

I don't believe benchmarking is all bad, and it can tell us where we've fallen behind our competition. But as a tool to find breakthroughs and to get ahead? Think again. The real innovation imperative is to get connected to your customers. Rely on traditional market research, and you'll get lost in the weeds.

Myth #3: "Open Is the Answer"

The term "open innovation" was originally promoted by a University of California at Berkeley professor, Henry Chesbrough, in his book, *Open Innovation: The New Imperative for Creating and Profiting from Technology* (Harvard Business Press, 2005).

The basic principle of open innovation rests on the changing natures of the workplace and the scientific community. The traditional "closed innovation" vertical shops like those found at IBM or Xerox or Bell Labs or Procter & Gamble became somewhat obsolete with the advent of tech startups, larger and more highly funded research at universities, and with the mobility of research workers, and soon, if not now, the internationalization of research. These trends were especially true in research of basic technologies; companies can no longer afford the scale, breadth, and depth of this basic research within their own walls, and if they could, it wouldn't happen fast enough anyway.

Open innovation was seen by Chesbrough and others as a way to share and speed up research and development, especially basic technology research. Modern tech companies like Cisco, Adobe, and others import and export their research to and from several sources and, in general, make themselves more permeable to the flow of knowledge and ideas. They hire interns, consultants, and academic research partners. They partner with other established companies or startups. They conduct joint research and license technologies from each other. There are some intermediaries or knowledge brokerages like InnovationXchange and InnoCentive in the marketplace to help facilitate these exchanges.

You can probably already anticipate my bottom line on open innovation. Open innovation is more geared to the exchange of basic technology than to the finer points of discovering and capturing what customers need, want, and love. Open innovation gets us there and hastens the process of delivering net customer value, but it doesn't show us what net customer value is in the first place.

That said, open innovation shouldn't be disregarded; it *does* work and is an important ingredient in the innovation formula in today's fast moving business and technology world. One of my favorite motivational speakers, Les Brown, is fond of saying: "It works when you work it." The problem is most people don't truly have the culture and the life-support systems for open innovation.

Why Do So Many People Make Such a Big Deal about Open Innovation?

I find that there are two main reasons that explain the popularity of open innovation. It's become such a big deal at many companies that some now even have a Vice President of Open Innovation. There are dozens of open innovation symposiums around the world each year.

The popularity of open innovation comes from the fact that most corporations practice closed innovation. People on the research and development and innovation management side of the company see that innovation is extremely closed. They're very closed, very private, about their own innovation, and are not open to external innovations or ideas. Because of this, the concept of open innovation became explosive. It just made sense. Open innovation is a fantastic tool that allows companies to do a much better job of quickly accessing innovations that serve their customers and ultimately build success for their company.

So the first reason open innovation quickly became so popular is because the problem was so big. But worse—and probably more to the point—the second reason is that open innovation is the latest Grapefruit Diet, the latest panacea or singular effort to solve the world's problems to hit the streets. I don't mean that it doesn't work, it's just another well-known and popular tool, and organizations are known to adopt well-known tools as quickly as possible to make sure they're doing what they know their peers are doing to grow their businesses. It's keeping up with the Joneses, business style; more cynically, it's management by cliché—keeping up with the latest buzzwords and trends—for companies that are clueless about what's really happening in their business.

So the bottom line is that open innovation is deservedly popular, but typically, in my experience anyway, it is not being deployed in the way in which it was designed, especially beyond the realm of basic technology research.

Why Do Companies Think They're Open When They're Not?

Openness in innovation is a multidisciplinary challenge. We need to make it system-wide; we need to make it a systemic part of the organization—but rarely does that actually happen. Usually people adopt what they think are open innovation methods only to bring in a fraction of what true open innovation methods could bring them. My advice is: If you're going to commit to this, and in many cases, you should, make sure you look at open innovation in a way it was designed. Make it part of your holistic system. Open innovation, kept separate from closed innovation processes because of security—or more to the point, insecurity—won't work.

The "Not Invented Anywhere" Syndrome

One of the biggest obstacles to overcome in innovation—or any corner of the business world, for that matter—is the so-called "not invented here," or NIH syndrome. The root causes are numerous, but in NIH-land managers don't trust or value what they don't create themselves. They either don't' understand it, feel threatened by it, or worse, simply view it as part of a knowledge turf war in which someone else's success detracts from theirs.

NIH happens within corporate walls; one manager applies NIH to build walls around his department to resist the ideas of others. It's a big innovation killer *inside* organizations, so can you imagine how this kind of thinking also gets in the way of inter-company open innovation? (Actually, I've seen cases where internal NIH is stronger than external NIH—it depends on the size of the egos among the managers within an organization).

Regardless, strong NIH tendencies lead to another principle I call the "not invented anywhere" syndrome. Companies and organizations within companies tie themselves up with NIH syndrome. They don't take advantage of what's available outside, so they must reinvent the wheel on their own. Guess what—they don't have the time, resources, bandwidth, initiative, or ideas to really do it. Throw in a layer of risk aversion and guess what—nothing happens!

Throwing a Line in the Water

As I've pointed out, companies have a tendency to "hunker down" in recessions or soft economies. They become more "closed" to their own ideas, let alone others. This mentality flies in the face of what logic might dictate: maintain innovation for the future and use "open" forums to get it done faster—and cheaper. To help, consider what I call "inside-out" innovation, which is, putting some of your own research and innovation out there for public consumption—to stimulate a similar flow in return.

What Can Companies Do To Be Truly Open?

Later, in Chapter 8, I'll provide an assortment of tools to show you how to apply what I call "real world openness" in accessing information. I'll also show you some real world tools that aren't very well known, but are extremely valuable. In advance of learning those specific techniques, the best advice I can give is to be open minded to external resources and look at open innovation as a win-win solution to help you get to market faster with the latest and greatest technologies. In addition, don't forget about using open innovation to get closer to the core net customer value proposition—not just to build better mousetraps.

The Tide Turns at Procter & Gamble

A few years back, the traditional closed innovator Procter & Gamble Co. made a big change in its in-house R&D process. They adopted an open-source innovation strategy called "Connect and Develop" with the goal of tapping into resources available outside P&G labs, including networks of inventors, scientists, and suppliers for new products that could then be developed in-house. It was a big deal and difficult to execute in such a traditional environment. They reworked much of the research organization and created a new job classification called "technology entrepreneur," or TE, and placed about 70 of them worldwide—in technology hot spots, such as places with university labs.

Anyone who had seen the highly closed, secretive, and secure nature of P&G in the past would find this shift—perhaps like their TV-commercial before-and-after cleaning tests—to be rather amazing, almost unbelievable.

Myth #4: "The Product Is the Technology"

You can probably see what's coming here—perhaps I'm becoming too predictable.

I'm going to tell you there's much more to a product than just its fundamental technology, features, speeds and feeds, no matter how cool it might be. A product innovation can be about service. It can be about channels. It can be about the box it comes in, or the instructions on how to use it. It can be about personnel or the facilities in which they work.

Now that might seem obvious—especially for you seasoned marketers out there. You know about the "Four P's"—Product, Price, Promotion, Place. Of course you do, and how you position the product with respect to each "P" versus your competition ultimately determines market success.

But what I see all the time is this: Marketers think about the Four Ps, but does the organization devote its energy to innovation in all four of these areas? Most likely, if they do, it's in the Price category—innovations to reduce process costs in order to come to market with a lower price.

But what about innovations in promotion? In Place, which can include not only physical movement, but channels, and probably the packaging the product comes in?

And what about all of those intangible factors beyond the Four P's? Innovations in service and support? Innovations in documentation, training, instructions for using the products? Innovations in employee morale and satisfaction that create the passion and promise that motivate employees to innovate in the first place?

All of these areas, not just the product itself, are ripe for innovation and should get—will get—innovation focus from truly innovation-centric organizations.

A New Product—or a New Problem?

One must think, as well-informed marketers and business leaders do, about the *whole* product. Too many companies grind and burn on new technologies. But no matter how innovative the technology, if a customer can't figure out how to use it, or can't get one, or can't get any information about it in the store, or has to deal with a surly or uninformed employee at the end of a support line, you probably haven't invented a new product, you probably have a new *problem*

(unless you get lucky and everything goes right during and after product launch.)

Secret to Whole-Product Innovation

Not surprisingly, the bottom-line secret to whole-product innovation is to think beyond the product itself. Just remember, the coolest products can still fail in the marketplace if customers don't understand them, can't use them, or can't get the help they need—or can't get them at a reasonable price.

When one thinks about the whole product—or *layerization*, as I like to call it—one thinks about the Apple iPod. The technology was pretty cool, but pretty basic. The simpler "Shuffle" models are technically little more than a flash drive with some software. The mid-range models are a disc drive with software. The more advanced models add a fantastic "touch" customer interface. They are great innovations. But now, layer in the excellent iTunes service, some cool colors, very cool retail outlets, even a cool box—you know the rest of the story, especially if you're one of the millions who own an iPod.

But successful whole-product innovation simply requires two thought paradigms, both of which need to be part of your organizational innovation culture.

1. Focus on customer experience.
2. Think (literally) outside the box.

The Experience of LUV in the Air

An all-out focus on the whole—and true—customer experience around a product will bring out many areas for innovation and allow you to create important *value propositions* for your customers. One of my favorite examples is Southwest Airlines. Their stock trades on the New York Stock Exchange under the ticker symbol LUV, an original reference to their home airport, Love Field near Dallas. But as many Southwest customers know, LUV took on a more significant meaning in recent years relating to their love of their customers, which they openly tout in their advertising and, beyond that, practice in their business.

But what Southwest really did so well—and so much better than its competitors—is to really understand the customer experience of flying, including all the things that happen before and after the flight. When customers fly, they want to get where they are going safely, with some degree of comfort, and as cheaply as possible. So Southwest offered a four-point value proposition.

1. We are going to fly one type of aircraft (Boeing 737s), saving money on fuel and maintenance costs.
2. We are going to offer you only a small snack—peanuts—on your flights, no meals. (*Now copied by many other carriers, who are delivering even less.*)
3. We are not going to ticket through travel agents, and we're not going to "interline" baggage with other carriers.
4. If you accept the first three, we're going to give you the lowest possible fares in all markets at all times.

And how customers accepted this proposition! For this and other reasons, Southwest continues to beat the industry year in and year out, to the point where its market capitalization recently exceeded that of all other U.S.-based carriers combined.

What was the magic here? Good execution, for sure, and good management was a big part of it too. They hedged successfully against the recent fuel price increases, something other airlines were unable to do. Sure, it's reported they had the money to do it, but I also regard it as another innovation not directly tied to the product—a financial innovation.

But the real secret was a close look at the flying experience and what customers were getting versus what they wanted. They figured customers would accept more spartan accommodations in exchange for a lower price. Since that innovation, Southwest went on to implement the easiest-to-use web site in the industry, the easiest, simplest, and most straightforward frequent flier program, and more recently (perhaps not an innovation) they bagged the baggage fees charged by everyone else out of a simple notion that such fees would irritate customers beyond what little incremental revenue it would generate. Right on.

Was Southwest Airlines thinking outside the box when they ditched meals in the late 1980s? You bet. A meal was an assumed part of the flying experience. But they got away with it. Not only did they get away with it, customers understood and appreciated the change. No more flights filled with the aroma and mess of dirty dishes. Flights were short enough and timely enough that you could grab a bite in the airport if you thought you'd be hungry.

And getting rid of first class seats? Brilliant. They took a lot of room, cost a lot of money to service, and made "the rest of us" all feel second tier. Give me good service (and leather seats for everyone now) and I'm a happy camper. I don't care about first class or first class upgrades, and can't afford either anyway. And do I always have to fly to Boston's Logan Airport, or New York's LaGuardia or JFK, or Chicago's O'Hare? No—nearby Manchester, New Hampshire, Islip on Long Island, or Chicago Midway will often, if not always, make sense in the interest of greater convenience and lower prices.

The point is—these are outside-the-box matters with respect to the basic service, flying and transportation—but Southwest stayed focused on the whole product and all the experiences and amenities that came with it and won over a lot of customers. They changed the industry. But I've always been surprised that they haven't changed the industry even more than they have.

"Are other carriers resistant to open innovation?" one might logically ask. Perhaps true. Or perhaps those carriers just don't understand their customers, preferring to remain in the realm of serving perk-conscious business travelers whose tickets are paid for by someone else. We all know what's happened with that—those payers are getting wise, and more business travelers are flying Southwest now. Other carriers don't get it, fly with their "rearview mirrors" only, or can't execute it (as United's "Ted and Delta's Song" imitations proved).

At the end of the day, Southwest Airlines is right on track with its understanding of its customers. It is right on track with its notion of the "whole product," its possible value propositions, and it's outside-the box (in both senses) thinking. And Southwest isn't alone—recall the customer experiences I shared in Chapter 1 with In-N-Out Burger and Sierra Nevada Brewery. They get these kinds of details and value propositions right, too. It serves them well, and it serves all of us well too.

Freudian Slips: Psychoanalyzing Your Company's Innovation

Perhaps I should have been a psychoanalyst, or was one in another life. Why? Because I enjoy psychoanalyzing the innovation mindset and behaviors at companies or with audiences at speaking engagements. It's kind of fun, actually, assigning an innovation personality type to the groups and organizations I see. Mind you, I'm not recommending that every innovation consultant or expert acquire a couch in their office.

You might rightly ask how this discussion fits into a discussion of "what's mything in innovation today." It isn't an exact fit, I'll admit. But many companies live in a mythical world of thinking their innovations and innovation processes serve their customers and their true strategic objectives, assertions that fall flat once you take a look at the true masters their innovation serves. Many companies simply aren't focused on what they *think* they're focused on. When innovation serves the wrong masters, it will almost never produce the desired business results.

Without further ado, here are four innovation personalities I commonly see.

Invention-Centric

Recall the explanation of the difference between invention and innovation from Chapter 1. An invention is a new and perhaps intriguing product or service that does something new or better; it is a new technology or an application of technology—a handheld GPS for instance. It doesn't have to solve a customer problem, and it doesn't have to do it economically. In other words, an invention in and of itself may have no intrinsic net customer value. But make it into a whole product that really does deliver value, and it becomes an innovation.

Invention-centric companies are focused on creating patents and inventing for invention's sake, for meeting internal new product generation objectives. For each invention, the focus is on what a product does—its functionality—not who it serves. Most inventions arising from such a culture never make it to market; they have fuzzy value relevance to customers—that is, customers just don't get it—if there's any relevance at all.

Techno-Centric

Closely related to invention-centric organizations are those I refer to as techno-centric. Techno-centric organizations often don't even get as far as inventions—their focus is on the basic technologies themselves. Again stopping short of marketable products, these organizations may be just as content to produce something for a technical journal as to create products with meaningful customer value and return. They are looking for unique technologies more than applications of existing technologies. Occasionally breakthroughs—like inkjet printing—result, but most of the results never leave the company's shipping dock. Except for the few really cool breakthroughs like inkjet, customers rarely see a value proposition at all, let alone a clear one they can get behind. In today's competitive environment, the techno-centric organization is on the decline.

Feature-Centric

More common today is the feature-centric innovation culture, where the focus is on new or enhanced product features—bells, whistles, and the like. The good thing about feature-centric innovators is that, at least, they are looking for ways to deliver something to the customer. The bad news—the culture usually produces incremental, not breakthrough, value. We often see faster "speeds and feeds"—faster processors, more memory, more pages per minute. The focus is on what it does more than how it really benefits. Do I really need the latest XX gigahertz processor? Probably not—and so what? The company can clearly describe the innovation, but how it actually benefits the customer is less clear. Customers get it, but they don't get why they *need* it.

Such innovations tend to keep a company ahead of its competitors for fleeting moments, if at all. Worse, when a feature-centric organization is compelled to do something "breakthrough" or to create a new technology or to reinvent some aspect of their business, they have a hard time pulling it off.

Guru-Centric

Following the style of the techno-centric organization, guru-centric organizations tend to center their innovations around individuals within their organizations. They put their innovators—or their product development organizations—on pedestals, and assume anything that comes down from the ivory tower is gold. A guru-centered company thinks it knows more about its technologies than any competitor, not to mention its customers. It often comes to market from a position of arrogance; what they know is more important than what they create.

Time for Transition

Up to this point, my main objective has been to illuminate and describe some of the common problems and misconceptions with innovation in large and small organizations today. As you've seen, the disconnects between innovation process and customer focus are numerous and are key parts to the story. I firmly believe organizations devoted to creating true customer value take a lot of risk out of the equation.

Fancy risk management systems and bureaucratic environments not only don't mitigate the risk of missing customer needs, they make it more likely, as they stifle true customer-focused breakthroughs and get everyone involved to think too much about risk.

Along the way, I've dropped a few hints and tidbits about how to align your organization correctly, focus on customer value, and deliver great innovations. From here forward, in Part II, we'll go much deeper.

I'll start it out by defining and giving examples of what I call "Innovation Superstars"—those companies that get it right—mind you, not perfect—but get enough things right and are holistic enough in their approach to deliver true value, and convert that delivered value into financial success. That template will serve well as we take apart some of the key components of superstardom.

Next, I'll explain how to really get in touch—how to establish conduits of connectivity—with your customers. I'll describe net customer value in some detail—what it is, how you determine it, how you describe it, how you bring it back to your key innovators. I'll talk about "carpet time"—processes to really get close to customers, their experiences, and what they need.

From there, I'll expand into processes of management that make innovation work, including my flagship RealOpen system. Then I'll expand—further—into how to integrate excellent innovation into your corporate culture, whether your organization is large or small.

Chapter Takeaways

- It's easy to get caught up in innovation myths, losing sight of what innovation should do and how it should work in your organization. Much has been written about innovation, and much of it turns into panacea *du jour* solutions that cause more trouble than they fix. Be customer centric, minimize process friction and execute, and you'll win at the end of the day.

- "Better mousetraps" are normally a poor path to success. Focus instead on underserved customer segments and design breakthrough products or services *for them*.
- It's easy to think you're customer-connected when you aren't. Typical market research and analytic tools like VOC and CRM, while serving many good uses, do a poor job of assessing what customers *want*—especially if you aren't already providing it. They should be supplemented with more direct conduits of connectivity, putting more decision makers on the front line, and those on the front lines already should be empowered to bring information back into the innovation process.
- Open innovation is powerful—if approached and used correctly with the right expectations.

PART II

INNOVATING YOUR WAY TO BUSINESS EXCELLENCE

CHAPTER 5

Anatomy of an Innovation Superstar

As a management consultant, it wouldn't surprise most of you that, like Tom Peters before me, I'm constantly and continuously engaged in the search for excellence. I look for excellence in business like so many others. But I go a step further, and I think it's a really important step.

To learn any lessons of business excellence, I think you need to look deeper than just to the business itself. Most consultants, analysts, journalists, and writers, myself included, search the corporate world for signs of excellence in business strategy and in business performance. But I go a step further to look for a different set of qualities in a business: The qualities or "glue" that binds it all together—excellence in innovation.

My focus is innovation because innovation is how we get from "strategy" to "performance," in most organizations. Unless the strategy is to declare bankruptcy and liquidate in the near future, we need innovation. We need innovation to bring new products to market. We need it to produce existing products more efficiently. And we need it to deliver the components of customer value that lie beyond the shiny bright object itself.

We all can think of superstars in business—companies that rise above the rest in strategy and especially in business performance. Wall Street is all over the companies that deliver great earnings and near-term shareholder value. If you want to find a superstar company that does everything right in its marketing, in its operations, and especially in its financials, you can start with the "buy" and "strong buy" rating lists offered by Wall Street analysts. They, of course, focus on performance, and if you read the reports of a good analyst, you'll get an idea of their take on a company's strategy.

But in my mind, that's more or less where it stops. Unless an analyst specifically calls out a company's "new product pipeline," or some such, you don't get much of a feel for how a new company thinks about—or executes—innovation. You don't get much of a feel for their customer focus, nor what they think a customer values from their products. You don't get a feel for how efficiently or effectively a company brings new products to market. And you don't get much of a feel about whether the processes or the overall culture of the organization fosters innovation, or gets in the way.

So I'm taking it upon myself to become an innovation analyst. I'm going to identify what it takes to be an Innovation Superstar. But I'm going to go a lot further than that. An analyst may (or may not) tell you what you need to know to decide whether to invest in a company. Fine, so far as it goes.

But my goal, in *The Innovation Playbook*, goes far beyond telling you whether a company is good, bad, ugly, or just plain indifferent as an investment, or even as an innovator. I want you to become an Innovation Superstar yourself, and I want your company to likewise earn that stature. I want to show you how to become a winner in your marketplace, not just in the stock market. Part II of this book is about defining what an Innovation Superstar *is*, then offering the secret sauce you'll need to become one.

What Does It Mean To Be an Innovation Superstar?

I'll admit that sports analogies are sometimes overused and don't always explain things very well. But here, the term "superstar" really works. Superstar, marquis player, you name it. A superstar stands out among the rest. But what is it about these players that make them superstars? Here are a few thoughts:

- Superstars are consistently better than the rest.
- You can count on superstars to deliver
- Superstars are role models; you want to be like them.
- Superstars are good in all aspects of the game, not just one part of it.
- Superstars (usually) have a balanced and accessible personality to go with their talent.

- Superstars are team players, and they make everyone else better.
- If superstars were a culture, you'd feel comfortable being part of that culture.

My goal in this chapter is to lay out what I think it takes to be an innovation superstar. I will use examples to explain, and then share a more complete case at the end.

Bones of an Innovation Superstar: Customer, Process, Culture

This chapter is called Anatomy of an Innovation Superstar. I chose that title for a simple reason. Just as with the anatomy and physiology of a human being, no two versions are alike. Humans of all sizes, shapes, builds, bone structures, musculature, sensory perception, and intellect have achieved excellence. There is no single DNA pattern, nor even a few DNA patterns, that are destined to produce excellence in human function.

And so it is with companies. No two companies are alike. No two companies embody the same structure, culture, focus, or personnel. No two companies produce exactly the same product (though many are close), nor do they deliver it to their customers the same way.

So just as with human superstardom, I look at corporate innovation superstardom as a unique blend of factors leading to success. No two companies, no two *superstar* companies, are alike. But what I've observed over my 20 years of working in this space is that they all have certain "bones"—certain traits or combinations of traits, that *in balance* make them successful innovators.

Balance Is Important

Want to find the best place to live in the United States? It's not hard; we hear about them all the time. Palo Alto, California. Jupiter, Florida. Lake Forest, Illinois. Beverly Hills. Palm Beach. Grapevine. Sure, they're great places with great houses, park-like settings, nice downtown areas, great shopping, great climates (mostly). But can you afford them? Sure they're great—if money is no object.

Are these places superstars? Only if you have enough money. They do a few things very well,—and other things—like affordability—not well at all. Some friends of mine, Bert Sperling and Peter Sander, wrote a book called *Cities Ranked & Rated—More Than 400 Metropolitan*

Areas Evaluated in the U.S. and Canada (Wiley/Frommer's, 2nd ed., 2007). In their book, places like Des Moines, Iowa, and Roanoke, Virginia, do well. Are they superstars in any category? Hardly. But they bring a favorable combination of attributes that makes them at the end of the day very livable. It's not so much about the good stuff but rather the lack of *bad* stuff.

I look at the same thing with companies. In the game of innovation, a company that does a few things well but a few other things very poorly will not be successful. A company that has great processes and great culture, but does not focus on customers, will not succeed. A company that is very customer focused and has the right culture and employee mix—but is tied down by process—won't succeed. A company that focuses on its customers and has relatively streamlined processes—but its employees are overworked and live in fear of failure—won't succeed. You get the idea.

Dissecting the Anatomy

From the previous discussion (and the title of this section) you're already starting to gather what I look for in the corporate anatomy in my search for innovation success: Customer, Process, and Culture. The "CPC" model, if you will. It might be loosely analogous to Head, Body, and Legs. Perhaps that's carrying the anatomy analogy a bit too far, but maybe not? I'm having fun with this—you should too.

The Customer

First and foremost,—a good innovator must focus on the customer, and specifically, on delivering value ("net customer value") to that customer. What the customer wants—like the head on the shoulders—drives all other activities. The rest of the corporate anatomy must respond to the customer's interests, else the activities in the organization can't really be considered innovation.

I look for the following in a company's Customer anatomy:

- External auto-focus
- "Love thy customer"
- Go-to-market mentality

I'll cover each of these as we move through the chapter.

The Process

Process is necessary to make anything work in an organization, especially a large organization. But when process becomes an end in itself, not a means, it needs some rework. The Process "body" should support the Customer "head" and nothing else. With most innovation superstars, the less we can say about process, the better, although some like Hewlett-Packard have come up with unique processes worth discussing and emulating. I look for:

- Process serves innovation (not the other way around).
- A framework for success—right tactics, right tools, right systems, right measures.
- Open for business.

The Culture

Culture, these days, is an overused term. It's hard to define, and many experts and consultants consider customer focus as part of the culture. I think it's so important that I call it out separately. I make the Customer the head, or brains that decide what should be done, while Culture is a set of legs that move it forward. It's how the organization thinks, feels, and works together to achieve excellence. It is about pride, passion, and environment. The general question is, "Does the company provide the right environment for employees to succeed, and thus, for innovation to succeed?

A company with the right Culture does things right in the following areas:

- Collective passion
- Craftsmanship
- Fear No More
- Right Team

Does "Fixing the Culture" Make You a Superstar?

Before cutting into the details of the anatomy of an Innovation Superstar, I'd like to step aside for a moment to flesh out some of my comments about Customer and Culture, and why I view them as distinct and separate components of the Innovation Superstar anatomy. It seems like "culture" is the new buzzword of today's corporate sleuths—the armies of consultants and ombudsmen and commentators and journalists and writers. Most talk about culture now. But culture issues may really be issues of *focus*.

The topic of organizational culture is extremely popular now, and for good reasons. Most organizations nowadays have a really bad culture, and it is particularly poor in its ability to foster an innovative environment. But is culture the problem? In my mind, it's a scapegoat for something else: focus. The right culture combined with the wrong focus still won't bring success. Bad culture may be a symptom of the wrong focus, a prevailing and unwavering *internal* focus.

Internally focused organizations keep their eyes on their own profitability, maximizing brand value, increasing efficiencies, reducing cost of goods sold, and so forth. As organizations become larger and more bureaucratic, it seems like everything they do is centered on how they can help themselves, and that's the beginning of the end. Still, we need to have controls, and of course, we need to make certain that we've addressed our own needs.

I was a lifeguard for years. And in college when I was a lifeguard, the one thing I'll always remember is that when worse comes to worst, the lifesaver comes first. That may sound counterintuitive, but the reality is that you have to protect yourself if you're going to go out and rescue somebody. The same is true if you want to serve your customer. You have to make sure that you're a healthy company that has the infrastructure to deliver value. But when internal focus becomes *hyper*-internal focus, all hope is lost.

Internal focus spends a lot of time on blame, or "blamestorming," as I have previously mentioned. Meetings are about assessing blame for any given problem within the organization. Externally focused organizations, on the other hand, put the focus on accountability. Accountability to customers, to shareholders, to employees, to the greater good of society. It's not about punishment; it's about accepting responsibility for situations so the organization can learn and grow, while helping the organization meet its objectives. Accountability doesn't have to be negative, but blame is always negative. Internally focused organizations do a lot of blaming, whereas externally focused organizations count on accountability.

Internally focused organizations are very process driven; they love to construct methods, systems, policies, and procedures around everything in the building. In many cases, that's good. The problem is that process sometimes becomes more important than people, and then you create organizations that are truly, truly sick.

Anatomy of an Innovation Superstar   101

I had a hard time deciding whether "external focus" fell under "Culture" or "Customer" in my anatomical scheme. I chose Customer. Why? Because it goes hand-in-hand with being sensitive to customer needs. And like all other components of the Customer anatomy, if it isn't right from the beginning, no amount of Culture excellence will help you.

The Customer Anatomy

The Customer anatomy is all about how the organization thinks about and relates to its customers. Being centered on the customer, what the customer needs, and how to deliver value to meet those needs, is Job No. 1—not Job No. 55 out of 56 as implied on the "Idea Creations" list in Chapter 2. It's not a job of delivering the minimum amount of value to get by and just match the competition. It's how an organization views the customer, connects to the customer, and decides how to deliver value to the customer. It really is—or should be—the brains of the innovating organism.

External Auto-Focus

As a management consultant, I can almost walk into a building and look at the physicality of the people that work there—the expressions on their faces—and I can tell you almost instantly what kind of organization they belong to. In fact, study after study shows that organizations that have a high employee satisfaction index—that is, organizations that aren't about blaming, and aren't about processes—provide tremendously higher value, quality, and customer satisfaction. Thus, it starts with external focus.

External companies, rather than looking at risk, look at opportunity. They see the opportunity in virtually everything. Not just any opportunity, but an opportunity to become more efficient, to provide better products at a lower price, to serve everybody in their ecosystem—and that's what's magical about great companies. These companies know how to be innovation superstars.

Externally focused organizations avoid "techno-focus." Techno-focused, or techno-centric, organizations tend to look at their technology or product as an independent thing, a bright shiny object. It becomes that without regard to how it lives in the external world.

But we're not in the business of creating bright shiny objects, are we? We're in the business of creating wonderful multisensory experiences for our customers. To the extent we can do that, we rule. And that's what innovation superstars do so well. So don't focus on the bright shiny object, focus on the experience. Think of it this way: The bright shiny object is no more than a delivery system for a human experience. It's incredible to me how companies have lost this fundamental principle that has been proven over and over again.

Another characteristic of bad culture or of an internal or self-centered culture is a reactive approach towards the market and a reactive approach towards customer value. Externally focused companies know that they need to be in front of a customer's needs, so they are proactive. They find ways to deliver new value before the competition. They surprise their customers with new value that they didn't even expect in the first place. Internally focused organizations, on the other hand, become reactive. They respond to customer complaints and dissatisfaction. Again, externally focused organizations prevent that from happening by being so well connected, by living in the outside world, by getting off their asses and going out and *living* with their customers.

The External Auto-Focus Checklist

- Does the company—and its management—really place customers first?
- Does the company create mission statements and strategies that really address customer needs and benefits?
- Does the company view financial performance as a result of excellent performance in the marketplace? Or are systems, cost cutting, and so forth ends in and of themselves?
- Does the company think more about long-term customer value or short-term financial performance?
- Is the company proactive or reactive?
- Does the company focus on problems? Or opportunities?

Love Thy Customer

"Love thy customer" is a core idea of innovation superstardom. As the name implies, it's about forming a caring observance and relationship with customers, individually and as a whole that is special enough to get true insight into what they need and want. Of course, such "conduits of connectivity" are the first big step toward delivering net customer value.

As an example, I had the privilege of working with a large ophthalmology practice, MECA, located in Memphis, Tennessee. They had a policy they called "High Tech, High Touch." At the time it was considered to be absolutely ridiculous, the idea that an ophthalmologic surgery center would have something as arcane as the word "touch" in their mission statement.

The bottom line is: They knew something amazing. The owner of the practice, Jerre Minor Freeman, MD, is one of the smartest people I've ever met. He realized he wasn't in the treatment of ophthalmologic disease business; he was in the *experience* business. Wow—what a breakthrough for an ophthalmologist to step away from what could have been an egocentric mentality based on his efficacy as a surgeon.—But he realized that his business was about taking care of people, and that the only purpose of technology was as another tool he could use to deliver wonderful value.

So what's the flip side of love thy customer? Well, you guessed it; it's "hate thy customer," and unfortunately, that's where many companies wind up. I was recently at a resort in Lake Tahoe, California. I was surprised, after listening to some of the people working in the place, to learn that they referred to "tourists" as "terrorists." They hated their own customers, and it showed. The end result for that resort, by the way, was financial collapse. This story, of course, recalls the Circuit City example I shared in Chapter 1.

Hating your customer is a very bad business policy. But it's easy to do. The first time a customer comes into your supermarket, slips on a grape, and sues you, all of a sudden your focus changes to grape risk management, and everyone who walks in the door is no longer a customer, but rather a perpetrator. Or possibly a terrorist.

It is important to realize, perhaps as a part of the cost of doing business, that some customers *are* bad. The problem is that many companies will reference the bad customer with every interaction, experience, and decision. They become centered on loss prevention rather than customer acquisition or retention. The reality is that hating your customer will have a long-term and inevitable effect on the financial viability of your business. Such "failure referencing" is a bad habit, and a hard one to get out of—I'll address it more in Chapter 9.

It's interesting to note that doctors who treat their patients extremely well, regardless of their medical efficacy, have a significantly lower incidence of malpractice lawsuits and a lower incidence of problem patients. It's also interesting to note that people who have a hard time communicating and connecting with and serving their customers have more problems. The more you hate your customer—believe me—the more you're going to hate your customer!

As a reader of hundreds of books on innovation and creativity, it is interesting to me how conspicuously absent the discussion of the customer really is from these books. There are systems, there are methods, there are spreadsheets, there are formulas, there are processes, policies, and checklists, you name it, but again, where's the customer? On the checklist I shared in Chapter 2, customer priority was second from last as a cause of innovation failure.

Hating thy customer is a problem similar to risk management. You can suffer from customer hate creep! Eventually, day by day, one bad customer at a time, you can change your whole business: your products, your services, your packaging, your delivery strategy, your support strategy—everything—to try to target that minority, that rare instance, of a bad customer. You live in fear.

Have you ever noticed that you can easily have two very accurate vantage points? You can assume that most people are good and generally do the right thing. You can also accurately do the same thing about, generally, people being bad. And of course, you'd be right in both instances. However, there's a phenomenon that is difficult to put my finger on, but when we focus on the idea that customers are generally good, it's incredible how customers tend to be—generally good. Whereas when we think of customers being bad, well, you get the idea, customers are generally bad.

I know this sounds like kinder-science, but it gets to the core of innovation. The ability to connect and to assume your customers are good and worthy of your quality and innovation and ultimately, your experience—that's what makes this all worthwhile. Even more important, it's the key to driving the organization's culture.

Innovation superstars go the distance to *love* their customers. Southwest Airlines, especially compared with the competition, loves their customers. They fly clean airplanes on time. Their web sites and frequent flyer programs are easy to use. They have fun with their customers on board the flights, telling jokes, even making the usual seat belt and oxygen mask lectures fun and interesting. Flying Southwest not only gets you there, it is an enjoyable experience from the time the reservation is made until the time the bag is picked up on Carousel Two.

The "Love Thy Customer" Checklist

- Does the company go the distance to really understand the customer?
- Do they focus on the total customer experience, or do they just collect and measure data on customers—customer satisfaction, and so on?
- Do they place the right people—decision makers—in front of the customers?
- Do they have good processes to collect information from customer-facing personnel?
- Do they do "carpet time?" (covered in Chapter 7)
- Do they try to understand what noncustomers (future customers) want?
- Do they understand what motivates their customers to buy their products?

Market-Focused Innovation

This one's pretty simple. What good does it do to invent something if you can't bring it to market? Yet so many companies do just that. Some of the more techno-centric organizations, in fact, simply judge their innovations by the number of patents they receive. Patents are nice, and I suppose if you're part of some kind of academic or nonprofit organization, the knowledge itself and the recognition serve as a useful end.

But I come from a different world—the business world. Successful innovation is judged by the revenues and profits and return on investment gained by the company.

So I like to see innovations actually result in marketable products with strong customer acceptance. I like to see R&D folks, and even management, actually spend time pounding the pavement to see how their products are doing in the marketplace. They're talking to customers, talking to retailers, talking to service technicians, absorbing how well their product is doing in the marketplace. Of course, they're also looking for new ideas.

One thing I also look for is strong feedback loops between the people in the front lines who man the call centers, help desks, service departments, installers, and so forth. Too often the R&D folks sit behind big high walls (literally and figuratively) within their organizations, all but impervious to valuable information gathered on the front lines. I like to see strong conduits between these front line folks and the innovators, through formal and informal channels. A suggestion box with participation really encouraged for ideas, not gripes, is a start. Getting front-line participation in idea generation meetings and so forth is a great idea.

The Market-Focused Innovation Checklist

- Is the goal to bring products to market or just to innovate for innovation's sake?
- Does the company *succeed* in bringing a high percentage of its innovations to market?
- Do people inside the company (and R&D) get excited when a product comes to market?
- Are innovators and decision-makers closely linked to customers and customer needs?

The Process Anatomy

Process is the major component of the superstar anatomy. By now you've read my concerns about process, and how it has a tendency to take over organizations and get in the way of innovation, rather than helping it along.

I don't advocate getting rid of process completely. People need some structure and framework in which to operate. Project reviews must continue and products must be tested before being brought to market. From my experience, the application of process varies all over the place, but it is important to have process especially in large, geographically diverse companies with complex products.

We've already examined the downside of process: excessive bureaucracy, slow time to market, people living in fear of getting through the next process stage, and thus watering down their projects or abandoning them completely. We've already observed that, in some companies, the easier job in the organization is to shoot ideas down or find fault, actions which effectively destroy value rather than create it. We've already observed how process can become the focus, in lieu of the customer, and this misguided focus leads to misguided innovation, or kills innovation altogether.

We've also seen examples where innovation progresses at a reasonable pace, but could be faster and better if augmented with ideas and technologies from outside the organization. The "not invented here" syndrome dilutes or waters down what's possible.

While less is often more, I look not for an absence of process, but for process that truly fosters the innovation process, and that the innovators in the organization are comfortable with.

Process Serves Innovation (Not the Other Way Around)

It's hard to put this idea into a short phrase, but when I engage with a company, it doesn't take long to assess whether the process is a help or a hindrance. When the first thing you get from the people you're meeting with is a 68-slide presentation on their innovation processes—with little to no information on their customers, customer needs, customer involvement, innovation successes, and so forth, alarm bells start to go off.

I try to imagine myself working in the organization. Would I get so frustrated with the layers of process—the forms to fill out, the reports to write, the checkpoint meetings—that sooner or later I'd forget about what I was working on? Would I feel like my project was "guilty until proven innocent" instead of the other way around? Would I feel like I had to win the approval of nine or ten "find the fault" people to move forward with the simplest steps? If it seems that way, I'm probably not dealing with an innovation superstar.

On the other hand, if the process seems to add good ideas, connect me with customers (either directly or through the front lines of my organization) and provide sufficient resources to execute a breakthrough innovation, that process is serving innovation, and the company passes muster as an Innovation Superstar candidate.

The Process-Serves-Innovation Checklist

- Is the innovation management process an asset or liability?
- Do innovators spend more time serving the process or innovating and serving the customer?
- Does the customer play a significant role in the innovation process?
- Can the process act and react quickly? Can it decide quickly? Can it add speed to critical projects?
- Is the process streamlined or bureaucratic?

A Framework for Success: Right Tactics, Tools, Systems, Measures

This element is a more detailed take on the "Process Serves Innovation" construct. Here I often ask more specific questions of the organization about specific "piece parts" of its processes. To a degree, the answers give me a stronger impression one way or another about whether process serves innovation. Occasionally I spot a really innovative tool or approach, like Hewlett-Packard's Garage internal innovation communication portal, or their Idea Campaigns—short two-week forums to solicit feedback on a concept or idea across the organization.

The Framework for Success Checklist

- Do the systems and tools help the process?
- Are there internal communication forums to elevate the importance of innovation?
- How would you rate the internal communication devices around innovation? Video conference and other tools? Portals, newswires?
- Does the company actively solicit employee ideas, and is there a good process to do so?
- Does the company run idea campaigns or something similar in order to first, collect ideas, and second, collaboratively develop them more quickly?
- Does the company have good systems or tools to collect customer feedback?
- Does anyone look at this customer feedback and report on it on a regular basis?
- Does the company have mechanisms or the ability to fast-track a new product or service based on customer feedback?
- Does the company have feedback loops to test the assumptions of a new product before release and after release?
- Does the company measure the success of its overall innovation efforts?

Open for Business

This item may be more focused on culture than process. But given today's speed of business and technology change, I simply don't think it's viable to innovate in a vacuum. Building on the ideas and research of others, including academic and other forms of public research, customers, other companies in the value chain, and even domestic and even foreign competitors, is becoming increasingly important in today's economy. A company that turns a blind eye to these external resources is probably spending more than it needs to and taking longer to get products to market than necessary. Even worse, a company wrapped up with "not invented here" syndrome, where ego becomes more important than getting the job done, is sowing the seeds of failure.

When I talk to companies, I look for examples of where they've gone outside to leverage technologies or even the processes of others. I look for innovators and innovation managers who are at least aware of what others are doing in the space.

Open for Business Checklist

- Is the company generally aware of innovation activities outside its four walls—what competitors are doing and how they do it?
- Do any of a company's success stories obviously incorporate learnings from the external world?
- Does management actively seek outside knowledge or resources to augment customer, product, or technology knowledge?
- Has the company learned to co-create with other companies in the space? With customers?
- Are innovators and managers proud or complimentary of the successes of others? Or just their own successes?

Will Japan Out-Innovate the United States?

With all I've laid out about innovation superstardom, and its component parts—customer, process, culture—one begins to wonder whether the United States is in position to maintain its historic edge in innovation. Will some emerging nation take the reins and lead the world in go-to-market innovation? I often ponder that question.

In particular, one can justifiably wonder about Japan. The Japanese understand their customers. They are experts at process. They have the teamwork, passion, and craftsmanship to pull almost anything off, from leading-edge consumer electronics to top-drawer hotel service. But with a few exceptions like the Sony Walkman, the Japanese aren't really thought of as innovators despite the fact they file many more patents year in and year out than their United States counterparts.

(continued)

Is it because they have traditionally focused too much on process? Perhaps the cultural need to save face gets in the way of risk taking? Perhaps they have historically been socialized not to take risks or think outside the box, so they don't exercise as much creativity as they are capable of. It isn't clear, but especially given their customer focus and their penchant for design and quality, it seems that their perceived weaknesses are fixable and that the United States has a lot to worry about if the goal is to remain No. 1. In contrast, the United States must redirect its focus towards customer and culture to keep its top billing.

The Culture Anatomy

Although I suggested earlier that today's emphasis on culture as both the creator and the solution to most business problems had become a little *too* pervasive, I still maintain that culture is an indispensible enabler of innovation. It's simple—if you get the customer right and the process right, does that guarantee innovation success? Only if you're lucky. If your organization lacks the passion, the skill sets, the talent, the personal ownership, the freedom to act where acting is needed, you're still likely to fail. So while the customer focus "head" tells you what to do and the process "body" accomplishes tasks, the culture "legs" support it all and allow it to move forward.

I've identified four specific culture elements: Collective Passion, Craftsmanship, No Fear Factor, and Right Team. I'll discuss each below. The bottom line I try to assess with each organization is: Does the culture reward and foster innovation? Is innovation an important component of the organization's overall business strategy? Is the organization invested (both literally and figuratively) in innovation?

If not, look out below.

Collective Passion

Passion is the stuff of entrepreneurs: a clear crisp focus driven by a spiritual energy to do something special for your customer. That something special can be an amazing new product, technology, or service. Collective passion, in my mind, is something more special and unique: It is the ability to scale passion up into the size of a larger group or organization. This is key. Very few companies have the unique and special skill and ultimate commitment to institutionalize the passion for their business. All innovation superstars achieve sustainable success by keeping their eye on the customer with a powerful fueling force of collective passion. How do they do it?

I've had the privilege of working with an amazing company based in Seattle, Washington, called *Sur la Table*. Sur la Table is a national gourmet retailer, and their whole world is about kitchen tools and kitchen gadgets. I remember going to their corporate headquarters and spending some time with their buyers and some of their media people. In fact, the day I was there the CEO was on her way home to try out a new pizza oven they were considering adding to their catalog. They are people who absolutely love gourmet food. Discussing the latest quality gourmet food and tools and the latest innovation to make your life and your culinary experience terrific was almost like talking religion—that's how passionate they felt about their business.

I'll never forget the energy and the feeling of passion at Sur la Table. If you ever have a chance to go to one of their retail stores or to look at them online or to get one of their catalogs, you can see the results of people who absolutely love what they're doing. It's not just what they do for a living—it's truly part of their DNA.

Innovation Superstars live with passion. Personally I believe that, with the exception of some mutated accident, it's impossible to invent—and to deliver high levels of net customer value unless you do it "from the belly." It's a visceral thing. It isn't inherently intellectual, and you can throw as many processes and policies and procedures and consultants as you want at it, but at the end of the day, if you don't have fire in the belly, you aren't going to be an innovation superstar.

The dividends from being an innovation superstar are colossal. Conversely, ignoring these components can lead to titanic failure.

Innovation superstars love what they do. They wake up every day with exuberance. And it's not just the customer; it's the "stuff." They love the technology, they love the business, they love the space.

Is that feeling, that ethos, alive and well in your organization? Do you love what you do? Do you love the people who create the bright shiny objects you bring to market with layers of new and exciting value? It's an important question. In my view, all innovation superstars have a *collective* passion.

The Collective Passion Checklist

- Does the company *understand* the importance of successful innovation as part of its long-term success? Are they driven by the long or the short term?

- Does the company appear to have passion for its customers?
- Does the company appear to have passion for its products?
- Does the company feature breakthrough innovations in its portfolio? Are breakthroughs more important than tweaks?
- Are the people within the company passionate about what they do?
- Does the company—and do people within it—love what they do and it shows? Do they have the "mojo"?
- Are vision statements and corporate brand promises passionate? Or dry and dull?

Craftsmanship

At the risk of sounding old-fashioned—and unfortunately, it probably does—I believe that one amazing component that is alive and well with all innovation superstars is craftsmanship. Often when we think of the term "craftsmanship" we think of hand-crafted wood items or hand-sewn quilts or hand-painted this-or-that. But I believe craftsmanship is alive and well in all things. It is about quality *that is connected to what a customer feels*.

Craftsmanship is about creating value for customers that elicits a visceral response above and beyond the mere function of a product or service. It requires a real connection to what customers value and the skill to craft it for them. Unfortunately, the trend today is that most organizations focus on minimizing components, on increasing manufacturing efficiencies with a core objective of reducing cost of goods sold. Craftsmanship, in my mind, is creating multiple "fibers" of experience for your customer. It's about the way it looks, the way it feels, the way it smells, its reputation, the way it makes you feel *about yourself*. It's the convenience, the timeliness, the ease of learning, the ease of use—the more such "fibers" you connect in this multisensory being we know as humans, the more that craftsmanship is alive and well.

But craftsmanship isn't always about something old or traditional. There are new forms of craftsmanship and new ways to deliver craftsmanship. Take Facebook as an example. In my family, as well as family members and individuals and companies around the world, Facebook has provided an amazing way to stay connected. It's almost like my neighbors—who I've been out of touch with for years—are now like neighbors. I get a chance to know what's going on in the lives of people I care about every single day. That's a form of craftsmanship, because it touches us on so many levels; it's multidimensional.

That sort of craftsmanship is so valuable to so many that it has become an explosive phenomenon—simply because the market responds to what they feel. They respond to what they experience, and that's what craftsmanship is all about. I find that a sense of craftsmanship is alive and well in all of my innovation superstars.

The Craftsmanship Checklist

- Do a company's products reflect a pride of craftsmanship? A superior quality, fit, form, and package?
- Do a company's products or services consistently *exceed* customer expectations?
- Do a company's services (sometimes around a product) reflect a pride of craftsmanship? Ownership?
- Do a company's communications—web sites, ad collateral, etc.—reflect a pride of craftsmanship?
- Do people act like owners of the company?
- Do a company's facilities reflect the same level of craftsmanship, care, and pride of ownership as its products?

Fear No More

As the widely quoted axiom holds: "The biggest cause of failure is the *fear* of failure." It's an unbelievable cosmic truth that so many forget. Fear is the most insidious of all human emotions. Yet, organizations often try to use fear as a tool of manipulation—even more oddly, as a motivation tool! Believe me, innovation and creativity do not prosper in an environment that is driven by fear. But, since fear sounds so cryptic and so primal, organizations have decided to call it other things. Of course, the most common term, or euphemism, for "fear" is "risk." "We have to be careful about X"—that's fear. "We have to control Y"—fear. "We have to make sure that Z doesn't happen." Fear.

The systems that have been created around risk management are really all about *fear* management. And I can tell you that, in my 20 years of experience as a management consultant, I don't think there is any dynamic that has killed more wonderful companies than this encroachment of risk-creep and fear.

It turns out that, ironically, fear *is* your enemy. It's your enemy for a lot of reasons. First of all, it s-l-o-w-s y-o-u d-o-w-n. And at today's rapidly increasing speed of business and speed of technology, that's death. It is imperative to employ broad-based fast tracking methods in all aspects of your business. But if you're required to do too many checklists and too many what-ifs and too many financial projections while your competitors are delivering insanely cool stuff to your customers, you lose. We've seen this in the car industry. We've seen it in other old-line businesses. We've also seen it even in more modern tech companies. It's important not just to manage the business, but also to manage fear.

When my youngest daughter was in kindergarten, she was asked to get up in front of her classmates and explain what her father did. Having heard me say what I do many times, she got up in front of her class and proudly proclaimed "He's in the failure business!" Of course, she was right.

To invent means to fail, to innovate means to fail. And that's why there have been so many methods, so many systems put together to try to control the unruly, cosmic beast that is risk. But the idea that you can eliminate risk completely is nuts. In fact, as the saying goes, where there is risk, there is likely to be reward—and where there is no risk, there is likely to be no reward. No risk can only happen on something that has been done and proven already, and while proven products are certainly good to have in a portfolio as a cash cow, they don't last forever. They *can't* last forever—as Kodak so painfully learned and as Microsoft worries about every day. The innovation pipeline must have something in it, and so risks must be taken.

You get reward by exposing yourself to risk. This is a cosmic law. I've never been able to break it, and if anybody does, please call me because I've been trying to figure out how to short-circuit the process by pulling failure out of innovation. But the reality shows it can't be done; less than 1 percent of all the patents applied for with the U.S. government make it to the marketplace.

When you look at the statistics, at the number of products that are successful compared to the hundreds and thousands of products that are launched, the numbers are unbelievably bad. But if we know we can look at innovation as a portfolio rather than an individual act, we can be comforted with the fact that at the end of the day, we can still be successful at innovation. But instead, companies have tried to do everything they can to pull risk out of an inherently risky proposition. The more they talk about risk, the more they think about fear and the more they try to manage fear, the less that happens.

In fact, most large corporations today have all but stopped inventing. Sadly, most of the resources go towards things like strategic acquisitions, often of start-up technologies that have already earned market validation. Maybe that's the right strategy—a strategy where we smaller entrepreneurs create while large companies acquire. In a sense, that outsources innovation, and that might be a good strategy for some companies.

But it seems to me that this is where a lot of companies lose their soul, their connections with their customers. They lose the ability to drive the relationships with their customers to new products and to fast-track their products to market. What if there is no suitable technology start-up to acquire? What if the market is looking for something besides bright shiny things—what if it's service or delivery that differentiates the product? Soon, a bad acquisition is made—or no acquisition at all—and the company starts down the path to a broad decline. Companies like Sun Microsystems, Microsoft, Hewlett-Packard, and Exxon have all made bad acquisitions in an effort to acquire technologies that probably should have been grown internally.

But if you are a company and you do want to create, managing fear is absolutely fundamental. All innovation superstars look at risk reasonably. They deal with—or extinguish—fear, and focus on the opportunity to serve their customer.

The Fear No More Checklist

- How does the company's reward system treat failure? Can an individual innovator—or innovating organization—fail without harsh repercussions?
- Does the company applaud failure as a necessary evil in the innovative process, or as even a good? Does the company ever *celebrate* failure?
- Is the company quick to bail on a downside project, with sufficient rational observation but before it turns into a more expensive failure?
- Does the company "failure reference"—that is, dwell on past failures—or do they "success reference"? (More in Chapter 9.)

The Right Team

Lastly, along with "love thy customer" and the rest of the "customer touch" components, we arrive at one of the more human elements of the innovation process: teamwork and the team itself. Basically what I look for is a team that really walks the walk, rather than just hanging those ubiquitous Successories posters all over the walls.

All innovation superstars have teams that work, and they work for a variety of reasons. But before I get into that, it's worth spending a minute to talk about what's *wrong* with most teams. If you were to talk to most management consultants, they'd probably tell you that each one of the various multifunctional team members has a different personality type, and that there's a "collision in the psycho-dynamics" of the marketing person, the operations person, finance, and so on.

But the truth of the matter is—they're wrong. Teams need to be made up of good people. Healthy people, people who are happy. People who love the bright shiny objects and everything that makes them into a whole product. People who love customers. People who love other team members.

I know this sounds like La-La land, but at the end of the day you cannot fix bad people. And the biggest problem in most team architectures is that you have one or more bad people. I know this sounds almost too simple to be as profound as it actually is, but if you want to get good results you have to have good people. Why? Because good people understand the needs and sensitivities of others. In fact, when we looked at most teams, we found that the biggest problem with most team members was that they were very selfish! They were self-serving and egocentric. Everything was about them, them, and them. Effective innovation culture cannot survive in this environment.

Going back to my comments earlier about internal and external focus, we want to hire people who are externalists in terms of their ability to look at others, the needs of others, the opportunities offered by others. So that's the challenge to becoming a superstar—hire good people, because great companies and great innovators are made up of good people. Remember that great people aren't necessarily creative geniuses—they're *value experts*. They have a sense for what others need and care about and how they can deliver it efficiently.

Not only do great companies hire great people, but the other part of the equation—is that they treat them well. Such well treated, great people are far more likely to do a good job serving their valued customers, especially with effective leadership. I'll cover these topics, especially leadership, further in Chapter 9.

The Right Team Checklist

- Are employees treated well? Does the company do things to make them feel better about themselves, their work, their jobs, their health, their career?
- Does the team have a positive attitude? Body language?
- Does the team think of customers as part of the team? Does it empathize with customers?
- Does the team think about the entire customer experience versus just the product or bright shiny object?
- Do team members really work as part of the team? Is the language centered on pronouns like "we and us," or is it instead "I, me, they, and them"?

Chapter Takeaways

- Innovation superstardom is based on a healthy and balanced combination of customer focus, process, and culture.
- Customer focus is analogous to the head of the anatomy; it drives and decides everything else. Component checklists include External Auto-Focus, Love Thy Customer, and Market-Focused Innovation.
- Process focus is analogous to the body; it supports bodily function without getting in the way. Components include Process-Serves-Innovation, Framework for Success, and Open for Business.
- Culture is the legs that give further support and keep everything moving forward in the right direction. Component checklists include Collective Passion, Craftsmanship, Fear No More, and The Right Team.
- These elements and ideas are all defined in further detail in Chapters 6 through 9, with Innovation Superstar examples given in Chapter 10.

CHAPTER 6

Creating Net Customer Value

Creativity is a joke.

Huh?! Is this right? Or did it mistakenly get through some kind of edit at the publisher?

No—it's what I meant to say.

I recently had the opportunity to sit in a creativity session. It was entertaining and fun and there were poster boards flying and confetti and it was interesting and engaging. But at the end of the day, it wasn't really necessary. We actually don't lack creativity at all. Just go to your local kindergarten if you want to see creativity.

I would say we do lose some creative edge year after year beyond preschool. That said, I still don't think we need to be more creative, and creativity initiatives get you nowhere. Now, where exactly am I going with this?

One More Time: Invention and Innovation

Here's another shocking proclamation: Not only is creativity a joke, so is innovation! That's right; I'm proclaiming in *The Innovation Playbook* that innovation is a joke. Why am I saying that? Because for some reason individuals, especially inventors, are under the erroneous assumption that inventing stuff is the key, and that's where value is created. Well, if that's the case, why do less than 1 percent of the products covered by the nearly 2,000 patents filed with the U.S. Patent and Trademark Office every week actually succeed in the market?

The answer is simple. People misunderstand where value is actually created. If you don't understand this principle, you cannot succeed at innovation. Yet, surprisingly, many companies are in the "creativity and innovation" initiative business. I strongly believe this thought process is misguided, and if you look at the great organizations around the world, their focus is not on creativity; these companies look at innovation as just an instrument. Their focus is not on innovation. Their focus, rather, is on creating customer value through innovation.

Where There's Risk...

How do you create customer value? Here's the bad news: You've got to be willing to fail. You can't get around it. Even as a successful inventor, I've spent half my life trying to get around the cosmic law of risk and reward. I've often wondered why inventors and innovators believe they can somehow circumvent this law. What is that law, you ask? The answer is: An innovation is only as valuable as the meaningful net value it delivers, no matter the risk.

Almost always, risk equates to success. There is no such thing as a breakthrough technology that wasn't risky. In the book *Polarity Management: Identifying and Managing Unsolvable Problems*, by Barry Johnson (HRD Press, 1992), the author talks about the difference between managing your risk and delivering value to your customer by taking risks. Of course, it's a great point. We need to find the equilibrium risk and value in our organizations.

But It's Not Just about Risk...

I may have confused you just a bit. First, I told you that creativity alone doesn't do it. That should be pretty clear since undirected or misdirected creativity can make for some nice, colorful storyboards or products that, unfortunately, don't interest anyone and don't sell. Then I said innovation is a joke and, moreover, that successful innovation entails taking risk. But there's still more to the story.

Here's the reality and the real message. Innovation is not a joke *if* certain conditions are met. And here's the main condition: It must deliver real customer value. An idea that is simply creative, but goes no further or takes risk but goes no further, isn't going to cut it. It must be ready to go to market, and to go to market, it must be something that a customer is willing to buy, that is, something worth more to the customer than the money he or she would part with to buy it, and is worth more than a competing product. But to register a lasting impression with the customer, it must deliver more value than the customer *expected*. To be an innovator you need to create something that is exceptional (see Net Customer Value Strata following).

The Bottom Line

I'll be back to elaborate on these ideas a bit more, but first I want to revisit the distinction between *invention* and *innovation*, because the idea is so important. You must be redirecting your thought processes, and your organization's thought processes, to be truly innovative:

- An invention is an idea transformed into physical or intellectual reality.
- An innovation is an idea designed to meet—or preferably, exceed—a customer need.
- An invention becomes an innovation when—and because—it delivers net customer value.

At this point—finally—it's time to take apart net customer value.

What Is Net Customer Value?

So what is customer value? More importantly, what is customer value today? The answer to that question is simple: It is something remarkable. In the old days, you could bring your product to market and "ad spend" your product to prosperity, at least to some extent. However, today, in a world of digital media, that opportunity has vanished.

So what is "remarkable"? Remarkable is a product that provides noticeable, conspicuous value at a parity, or lower price, than competitive alternatives. Another great book is *Free, Perfect, and Now: Connecting to the Three Insatiable Customer Demands, A CEO's True Story*, by Robert Rodin and Curtis Hartman (Free Press, 2000). I like the title because it's what customer value is all about.

We live in an unbelievably competitive marketplace; no longer can we create the mediocre. We need to understand what our customers value in order to make certain we create innovations and solutions that don't just perform but far exceed expectations.

The next step is to drill down and gain a further understanding of what customer value—or define what "net customer value" actually means. Net customer value refers to the value of the experience derived from a product or service, not just compared to what the customer paid for it (that's part of it), but compared to what they *expected* from it. So when we deliver more than the baseline level of pervasive or ordinary expectations, that's when we become exceptional, and we become exceptional in different tiers, or what I call "strata."

Innovation Superstars have found ways of maintaining exceptional net customer value using innovation as a delivery mode. So if innovation is the delivery modality, what is the delivery target? The target is simply the customer's experience. The experience is the difference between what they thought they were going to receive—their baseline expectation—versus what they actually received.

Customer Value in Tiers

That's tiers, not "tears," by the way. To enhance the illustration of net customer value, and when it's being delivered and when it isn't, I've organized and classified "value" in tiers, or "strata," according to their success and prowess in delivering net customer value (see Figure 6.1). When you look at my customer value stratification, you can see the differences among different levels of achievers—and more importantly, where most organizations fit along the implied continuum.

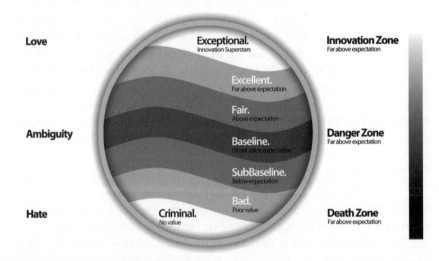

Figure 6.1   Net Customer Value Strata

Criminals Among Us

If you look at the strata, at the very bottom is something I call "criminal." I call it criminal because criminals take away from us and give nothing in return. Worse, sometimes they take from us and return pain.

Recently, I sat down at a restaurant with my family. The experience was bad, the service was bad, and the food was simply toxic. I paid $150 for indigestion. Frankly, I would rather a burglar had kicked in the front door and taken my wallet, because I could have at least forgone the indigestion.

Many companies—without knowing it—operate at the "criminal" level. The "criminal" and the "bad" levels are the two that operate in the "death" zone. It's not "will their business fail?" but a matter of "*when* will their business fail?" This is the most dangerous area in which to live.

What's sad is a lot of companies started out with the goal of delivering great customer value, but have fallen into this area because they changed their focus, their gaze, from external to internal priorities, from the external delivery of meaningful net value to customers to the internal focus of protecting themselves. They developed bureaucracy—systems, policies and procedures—that drove their business, instead of utilizing customers and customer needs.

The restaurant that made me sick found ways of improving productivity and reducing food costs. I suppose that's good for them, but it's bad for their customers. They hired low quality employees who were poorly trained—good for them, bad for the customer. They provided a speedy process that got people in and out. Table turns increase profit—good for them, bad for the customer.

I talk about these focal issues with great frequency throughout *The Innovation Playbook* with good reason—as we begin to focus internally, we begin to lose sight of what we do for a living, which should be delivering exceptional levels of customer value.

From Criminal to Just Plain Bad

Above the criminal level is what I call the bad level. "Bad" means the business hasn't yet sunk into the abyss of criminal, but it has lost its way and is delivering significantly less than what the customer expected. They have few to no initiatives to create new customer value; as a result, they're in the "death" or "dying" zone. One more slip, one more competitor, one more step in technology evolution, one more style change or change in consumer tastes, or one more notch downward in that company's deliverables and they're done. They're vulnerable. "Bad" could be called "vulnerable," while "criminal" is beyond vulnerable. The strata are not static; they're dynamic. Typically, when someone drops into the bad zone, they're on their way to criminal, and ultimately going out of business.

Below the Baseline

Above the bad level, or stratum, of customer value is what I call "below baseline." Now I want to address the below-baseline expectation because, in my estimation, 60 to 70 percent of businesses reside in the below-baseline level of expectation, or at the baseline level in what I call the *pervasive* baseline expectation.

All customers have a different idea of what they are going to expect when they engage your product or service. But generally there is a pervasive expectation that is universally accepted. The problem with the below baseline area is most companies don't know they're there, because they're probably capturing enough revenue, and maybe even enough growth to sustain that stratum, so the concept of being at the low end, the marginally acceptable end of the customer expectation, is hard to fathom.

A recent study showed that, for every customer who complained about a product or service, there were some 2,000 who didn't complain but were also dissatisfied. Most companies, when they see that one complaint in 2,000, are left with the impression they only have a small problem, an outlier, if one at all. What is missed is that this number may statistically represent a much larger problem.

Sub-baseliners are *usually* sinking. For the most part, sub-baseliners are organizations that have turned into an organizational, or internal, focus rather than an external or customer focus. More than likely, sub-baseliners are descending into the abyss of the bad or critical zones with the next bit of competition, technology change, or bad news. Now that's not to say sub-baseliners aren't fixable, but rarely do they realize their sinking situation in time to save the day.

Delivering the Baseline

Now let's talk the "basal" or baseline level of customer expectation. If I go into an economy hotel, I expect to pay a low price for a clean room, and I would prefer not to hear a lot of gunshots during the night. That's it—if it is reasonably clean and comfortable at a rock-bottom price, and in a reasonably good part of town, I'm happy.

But if I check into the Four Seasons and I get just a clean room in a nice area, I'm going to be highly disappointed. So you can see that what you pay for something and what, more importantly, you *expect* to receive, in contrast to what you do receive, is the secret of developing and inventing customer net value.

If you apply this concept of baseline expectation to any innovation or technology, you can easily see that breakthrough technologies like the iPhone provide a completely game-changing technology that delivers amazing levels of customer value for about the cost of a standard cell phone. The iPhone did this, and its success was explosive.

The other problem with living at the baseline level of expectation is that it never stays the same. Consumer needs shift, consumer tastes shift, expectations of technology and technology performance shift. Customers want more, faster, and cheaper. As an obvious result of that, companies that are not highly connected to their customers will not know where their expectations are, and risk delivering products, technologies, and solutions that are subpar.

Knowing—and keeping track of—the baseline level of expectation is something that must be hard-wired into your organization. I'll talk about that more in Chapter 7.

In reality, the baseline level of customer expectation is really a danger zone. Not certain death, but a danger zone. Why? Because somebody else is working on a product, technology or solution to earn a place in the market by making your answer to the customer's expectation obsolete.

North of the Baseline

Now, finally—north of the baseline level of pervasive customer expectation is what most customers *really* expect. It is what I call "above baseline." But above-baseliners are also in a very dangerous zone. It's dangerous because companies operating here may be operating under the erroneous assumption that they are successful because they're above the level of minimum expectation. For some industries and some technologies they may be right—until, of course, that baseline moves further north.

The problem with being above-baseline is that you're typically in a situation where you assume you're doing better than you really are in terms of delivering customer value because you're doing it better than most people expect. Remember that ultimate innovation success is about being exceptional, and being exceptional means understanding what people expect and literally taking it to the margins.

The Superstar Tier

Once we're able to leave the above-baseline area, where we're hovering over the sea level, we begin to enter what I call the innovation zone. That is where we really learn to use and blend creativity, technology, and product to deliver meaningful net customer value—things people really get, things they really want to own—truly great products. This is the zone you want to be in, because a large majority of your competitors, probably 90 percent, aren't here. You get an amazing competitive advantage and it allows you to build brand equity and a reputation for delivering value.

Today, especially in the digital world, that is extremely important. Your ultimate goal is to rise from the "good" level into the exceptional band. The exceptional level is the habitat of the innovation superstar. They know what their customers expect, and they set their sights on meeting or exceeding those expectations. Superstar Tier businesses hard-wire themselves to those customers to keep their fingers on the expectation, and on changes to that expectation.

This may seem simple, but the shift from external to internal focus, excessive risk management, and a more general inability to see the world through the eyes of their customers has caused many a company to lose its way. Without a clear focus on preserving innovation superstardom, the natural order of things seems to be to descend from that perch towards the baseline. Once that descent has started the financial and risk management people take over things, and then what happens? The descent accelerates. It becomes a race to the bottom. Of course, that's a vicious cycle to avoid at all costs

Superstars may or may not be recognizable at first glance. Apple certainly has achieved superstardom; few would disagree, and few see them falling back towards the baseline anytime soon. But other companies, like John Deere (more in Chapter 7) hang out very quietly in the superstar zone, and have for years. It's possible to do—with the right customer connectivity, the right processes, and the right culture.

The Innovation Cycle and the Customer Experience

Many business experts, consultants, and authors have explored the importance of the "total customer experience" focus—the idea being that a product needs to be thought of as a "whole" product, from initial customer contact through purchase through delivery through use through service and support through the eventual disposal of the product. I too am part of this school of marketing and product management.

Most companies—and many experts—focus on how you can go wrong by *not* considering the total customer experience. I agree; you can go dead wrong. Sure, the product works, but the customer can't figure out how to use it, can't get decent support (I'll be back with a great example of *that* in the next chapter), and overall has a miserable time with it. Are you going to achieve a level of brand excellence with this approach to the marketplace? Most likely not—unless your product is so far and away the cost or the technology leader—that people don't care. Even that situation doesn't last long, for competition usually closes the gap.

Experience Is Opportunity

From an innovation standpoint—as well as an overall business excellence point of view—I prefer to view the customer experience as a huge opportunity. An opportunity to innovate, top to bottom, side to side, through the entire experience. An opportunity to rise far beyond the product to deliver net customer value. The ability to do this well separates the superstars from the rest, and few get it right. Why? There are lots of reasons—or excuses—but here are three I often run into or observe as I view the real world.

The experience isn't sexy enough. R&D designers and product development folks like to think about technology and all the exciting stuff technology can bring. They tend to be product-centric and techno-centric, and they can't get their arms around mundane things like packaging, instruction sheets, and call center manners. So they often simply avoid these matters, and leave them to someone else in the organization. That may be okay, because perhaps a highly paid PhD engineer shouldn't be working on call center scripts. The problem is that it often falls through the cracks—nobody else picks it up—or if they do, they haven't studied innovation and they can't really do it. So the matter stays buried within the cracks, and the customer experience continues to, well, suck.

It's all small stuff. The same R&D or product development folks—and the rest of management—may simply not be aware of, or even care about, failures in customer experience. To them, it's all small stuff. They assume the customer is such a big fan of their product that the big thing is the product, and nothing else is terribly important. Again, the example I'll share in Chapter 7, in which my Internet service provider essentially told me to go to the Internet to solve my problem myself when the service was down, is a great case in point. If anyone had thought about this detail—or the myriad other details that come up in a customer experience—chances are they would have done something about it.

Outside our area of expertise. Product development and R&D people may bail on customer experience innovation because it takes them into areas they know little about in marketing, operations, channel management, and so forth. But too many organizations drop the ball right there, not placing enough impetus on these other organizations to innovate. I believe every group or function in an organization should have its own laboratory and be chartered or sponsored to come up with its own innovations, and be rewarded and able to showcase those innovations just like the product development function. The entire organization—not just the product development lab—must participate in innovation.

The Innovation Cycle

Bringing this all back together, I see too many organizations fail to maximize opportunities to innovate through all parts of the customer experience. I like to use a concept and diagram I call The Innovation Cycle to try to get organizations to think holistically about the customer experience and the innovation opportunities that lie in that path.

The Innovation Cycle is the entire experience a customer receives beginning with what I call *brand noise* and ending with the *last touch* on your product or service. Brand noise comes from a customer's notion of your product, your service, and/or your company received directly or subconsciously; this cycle evolves into preconceived ideas about what they might expect when dealing with your company. Brand noise is how you serve customers even before they become customers, and in essence, combines your brand reputation with what I call presales value. For example, I provide a variety of free resources to visitors to my business web site, whether or not they ultimately become a customer. This is extremely important because most customers want something free in advance; they want to sample the recipe. Is this giving away something free? Absolutely! All Innovation Superstars do it—in the right time and place, with pride and frequency.

The first touch happens when customers first engage with your company, physically or virtually, and can be something such as ease of parking at a fast food restaurant, maybe how clean the grounds are surrounding the parking lot. Do people see discarded cigarette butts as they approach the door, are the windows clean, are the customers greeted with a friendly smile, does it smell good, was the product priced fairly, is it easy to buy, does the package communicate extreme value?

After the commitment to the company and the product, usually a purchase transaction, they now enter what I call the *experience cloud*. The experience cloud is made up of all the things the customer values, depending on the product or service—functionality, ease of use, sensory inputs like sight, sound, and smell, whether it is clean, whether the people working for the company seem to be on your side. And don't forget superlatives, especially here but throughout the cycle (see Figure 6.2): Was there more in the box than I expected?

The "relationship cloud" describes all the things that happen, the interactions between consumer, product, and company, during ownership. It's a cloud in my concept because you don't always see what goes on inside, and the interactions can be numerous and varied. It's typical to assume all customers use and respond to your product in a similar fashion, but that's clearly not the case. "Carpet Time," my subject for Chapter 7, is my way of establishing enhanced conduits of connectivity with customers to see what's really going on inside the cloud.

Eventually the customer disengages with the product, whether immediately leaving the parking lot of In-N-Out Burger, or more gradually, as with a physical product they own, that they no longer use as much and are considering replacing. Finally, the product is left or disposed of, and the cycle is over—but the value to you as a company may not be gone because the customer may come back or refer the service to others.

Again, the important thing is to think of the cycle as what it is—a cycle—and to look for exciting opportunities to innovate throughout. Every stage of the cycle is a golden opportunity to

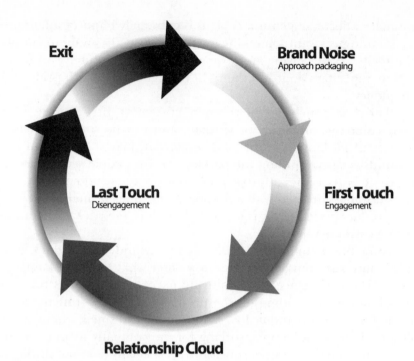

Figure 6.2   The Innovation Cycle

add net customer value, and to differentiate yourself from the competition.

In all parts of the innovation cycle, and especially in the relationship cloud (see Figure 6.3), keep in mind that what you *invent* as an organization is net customer value; the *innovation* process is a way to deliver it.

Sweating the Small Stuff Can Get You to Big Stuff

Think holistically about the experience. As you've probably picked up I'm not a fan of incrementalism—the "paint it blue, call it new" style of innovation that seems more directed to satisfying the need of new product development departments who want to proclaim success at something, rather than to delivering new customer value. A small tweak in the customer experience can bring big rewards.

The cloud. Invent customer net value. Use innovation as the delivery system.

Figure 6.3   The Relationship Cloud

I don't know how many extra airline tickets Southwest Airlines has sold because they thought outside the box to make the mundane "seat belt speech" interesting and fun. But is that an innovation? I'll let you ponder. Someone thought outside the box. You have to say the FDA required safety speech, but why not add a little humor to get people to listen, and even get a few laughs to relieve the boredom and, for some, apprehension of the impending flight. I would imagine that at least a few additional tickets were sold as a direct result of this departure from the typical aplomb.

But here's what I *would* surmise. Taken together with other in-flight humor, and a truly warm and friendly touch applied by the gate agents, and the low fares, and the easy-to-use web sites, and the absence of baggage fees—you have all the spokes of a wheel of great experience, from the first thought of buying a ticket to the pickup of that valise at the baggage claim. Southwest Airlines is your friend, your helper, and your companion throughout the experience. The company *gets* the experience.

So I say the small stuff can be critically important. Enough small stuff, or small stuff applied in the right place, becomes big stuff. Are the seat belt jokes "painting it blue and calling it new?" Hardly, in my book.

Finding the Soul of the Customer: Using Experiential Sliders

With the principles of baseline expectations, the innovation cycle, and the relationship cloud in mind, I want to introduce another important thought process geared toward really getting at what delivers tangible net customer value. The thought process is based on the idea that net customer value is not one-dimensional, it's not just based on price or pleasure or even the shopping experience; it is not monolithic in nature. Rather, several dimensions are interconnected into a broad and holistic "take" on value. It gets to what I call the soul of the customer.

By way of example, think of a restaurant experience. "Value" in this case isn't delivered just by the food, just by the price of the food, just by service, nor just by the ambiance and cleanliness of the facilities. It is all of those things together. And any one of those dimensions can be delivered well—or poorly—according to the value strata I've just outlined. If you do everything at the superstar level, you will win. That said, you probably have some leverage to deliver only baseline in one area, while delivering at the superstar level in another, but that's a judgment call.

Anyway, I offer a tool I call Experiential Sliders as a thought template for constructing your customer net value proposition (see Figure 6.4).

Following is a brief explanation of each of the sliding scales.

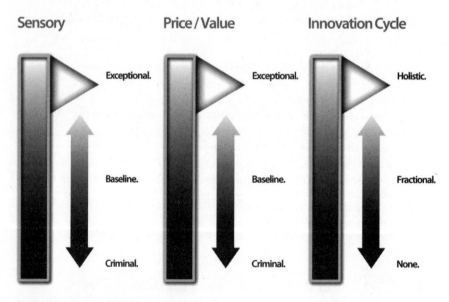

Figure 6.4   Experiential Sliders

The Sensory Scale

Never forget that your customers have a multilayered sensory system, and that each one of those systems needs to be covered as part of the overall experience. Smell, taste, feel, sight, sound, ego, and emotional connection are all part of the sensory experience. The emphasis placed on each of these drivers is obviously based on the type of business product or service you're engaged in. Clearly if you are in the restaurant business, smell and taste are far more important than if you're selling USB drives.

The Price/Value Scale

What we expected to pay versus what we received is an experience driver that comes into play in virtually all business products and services. I recently ordered a computer accessory online. The video, the testimonial, the shopping list of amazing features persuaded me to buy the product. When I received the product it was anything but amazing. So what did I do? I sent it back. Remember, even if your customer is totally happy with the sensory slider or the "Innovation Cycle" slider (see next), if the price was far greater than what they expected to pay, then the net experience still registers as bad.

The Innovation Cycle Scale

Relatively more complex and just as important is what I call the Innovation Cycle, which is really the complete set of other experiences *through time* with the product and company. Here is where you need to be extremely careful and holistic in your approach, for one bad or criminal element within this cycle takes you to "none" and can negate a whole lot of good in the rest of the cycle, not to mention what you've achieved on the Sensory and Price/Value slider.

As an example, I recently purchased a luxury car for my wife. The buying experience was phenomenal. We were welcomed by a highly trained and very personable sales associate. They provided us extra little goodies and even stuffed animals for the kids. But shortly after the purchase a service problem turned into a nightmare. Not only will I never buy that type of vehicle again—I will do everything I can to share my poor experience with all my friends to save them from the same suffering. The bottom line: This criminal act destroyed all the other superstar value. Even if they had delivered baseline, or what

I call fractional value with their service, they would have preserved my relationship and loyalty as a customer.

The other bottom line: Superstars provide a holistic value throughout the entire innovation cycle.

The Webb Triangle

The subject of this chapter is net customer value, and the goal of the chapter is to provide understanding of what it really entails, and to show all the possible ways it can be delivered. Inventing net customer value ideas is not the end of the process; you must proceed to innovate them, that is, bring them to market in a way that not only serves the customer but also the organization—can it be produced and delivered to market? At an acceptable cost?

I like to use a model that I developed called the Webb Triangle for a basic back-of-the-napkin analysis of a product's likelihood for success. The Webb Triangle is an opportunity approach towards a balanced analysis of the viability of a new product or service offering. It is not risk-centered and it is nonlinear.

At the top of the triangle (see Figure 6.5) we see the need assessment: Does anybody need or want this product, does it take advantage of an opportunity, does it solve a meaningful and widely recognized

Figure 6.5   The Webb Triangle

problem? On the left-hand side we ask if it can be manufactured and/or delivered in a way that exceeds customer expectations at a competitive price that still delivers acceptable profit? On the right side is the "sell" angle: Is there a market large enough to provide the revenue that offers a return on the developmental investment? Does it survive in the competitive ecosystem? Is it a superior species?

The point isn't to approach net customer value in a vacuum, but to begin to think about balance between customer and corporate interests at an early stage. This model isn't designed to limit the ideation around net customer value, but to put an extra level of thinking into it.

Revisiting the Four P's

Almost anyone who has taken a business marketing course has learned about the so-called Four P's of marketing—product, price, promotion, and place. It's worth another look at the P's because they can also be used to build your understanding of net customer value and, ultimately, your net customer value proposition or position.

Those in the services business, or who added a significant service component to a product, revisited the Four P's and turned them into Seven P's, which includes the traditional Four P's plus Process, People, and Physical evidence, the last being the sensory environment of a facility or even a communication being delivered. The last three P's represent the systemic vision from the marketing point of view,

Now, services marketing academics and experts from the sector have recently added an eighth P. From Christopher Lovelock and Jochen Wirtz's *Services Marketing: People, Technology, Strategy* (6th edition, Pearson International, 2007) we now have Eight P's of services marketing, defined as follows:

1. **Product elements**—The core and periphery service elements at the center of the company's marketing strategy.
2. **Place and time**—Delivering product elements to customers can be done physically and/or electronically, depending upon the service. Speed and convenience are essential to the customer and are important value-adds.
3. **Price and other user outlays**—Money is only a portion of what customers may part with when purchasing a service; one must also consider time and convenience.

(continued)

4. **Promotion and education**—Speaks for itself, but the marketer must make sure communications not only provide information, but also persuade the customer of the service's relevance to the customer's particular problem.
5. **Process**—The means by which the firm delivers product elements.
6. **Physical environment**—The appearance of the place where the services are delivered may have a significant impact upon whether the service was satisfactory.
7. **People**—Front-line staff will have a direct impact on perceptions.
8. **Productivity and quality**—Improving productivity is a requisite in cost management; but quality, as defined by the customer, is an essential service that differentiates itself from other providers.

Mind your Eight P's, and you'll be on the right track to net customer value success.

A Darwinistic Approach to Net Customer Value

At this point, I must tip my cap to my fellow marketing and innovation consultant and expert, Dr. Geoffrey Moore, who was well known for his 1992 epic *Crossing the Chasm—Marketing Disruptive Products to Mainstream Customers.* A more recent book of his, published in 2005, is called *Dealing with Darwin: How Great Companies Innovate at Every Phase of Their Evolution.* It gives us an interesting categorization of different types of innovation—which really turn out to be different ways to deliver net customer value.

Moore cleverly relates the different types of innovation a company might need—or choose to undertake—to the stage in a company's life cycle.

Much has been studied and written about corporate life cycles, and they all boil down to identifying three basic phases of corporate existence—sometimes drawn out further into sub-phases, pre-phases, post-phases and so forth, but we won't go there. The three simple phases are the growth phase, the maturity phase, and the decline phase.

The Innovation Zone(s)

Moore applies four *Innovation Zones* to these phases. These four zones as defined reflect the needs of the organization more than the needs of the customer, but drilling down a step further, they translate into customer needs as well. The four zones—matched to the phase of organizational evolution are:

1. The Product Leadership Zone → Growth Phase
2. The Customer Intimacy Zone → Maturity Phase
3. The Operational Excellence Zone → Maturity Phase
4. The Category Renewal Zone → Decline Phase

Moore makes his point this way: "Whenever we hear the word *innovation,* we tend to call to mind its most dramatic form—*disruptive innovation*—the sort of thing brought to life by brilliant inventors, rebellious artists, and daredevil entrepreneurs. That is indeed an important type, and it has pride of position (as part of the Product Leadership Zone). But ... it has a great many brothers and sisters with whom to share ..."

Fact is—with one caveat—I completely agree with Dr. Moore. We should not always look for the so-called disruptive innovation. In fact, too much of an organization's resource can be spent looking for the disruptive innovation at the expense of other kinds of innovations that deliver real net customer value, the appropriate net customer value, given the business you're in and how it integrates with the customer experience. An airline should focus on innovating to improve airline service, not on developing an outer space flight product. (Okay, that example is a bit over the top, but you get what I mean.)

Oh, and I mentioned a caveat? I'll get back to that in a second. But I first want to share how such life cycle thinking can shape the net customer value equation and thus the kinds of innovation you might strive for.

Life Cycle Innovation

As described above, companies go through three essential stages in their life cycle: the growth phase, the maturity phase, and the declining phase. Moore applies four innovation types to the three phases as outlined above. The innovation types, or styles, best fit the phase of the company's business—and the expectations of customers of a business in that phase. For instance, customers expect different kinds of innovation in the media business from Google in the growth phase than Time-Warner or Viacom in the mature phase or McClatchy or Gannett in the declining phase.

I'll review the best-fit innovation types because I do think they provide a road map showing how you should orient your organization to deliver value, depending on where your organization is in its evolution. While they provide a good road map, I'll urge you, don't get too caught up in staying within one silo or another—the lines can be blurry. I'll explain that in a moment.

The Product Leadership Zone

In the growth phase companies are looking to define their products and define their markets. Moore calls this the Product Leadership phase, defined as: A company putting new products—and a new brand—into the marketplace. So naturally, this is the place where most breakthrough, or disruptive, innovation occurs. Note while the *center* of this innovation is usually in the physical product, many companies find disruptive breakthroughs in the service, delivery, packaging, or some other "whole customer experience" of the product. Did FedEx invent air freight? No, they just made some stellar innovations both in the operational side of it and in the customer interface and positioning ("absolutely, positively overnight"). Did 1-800-Flowers.com invent flowers? No, but Internet, customer interface—you get the idea.

Anyway, here are the four types of innovation, according to Moore, that flourish in the Product Leadership Zone. Note once again the point here is not to emulate the innovation style *per se* (although that can happen too), it is to seek and define net customer value in a manner consistent with these styles. I'll use Moore's core terminology, but substitute *Value* for *Innovation*, since that's what we're really focused on here.

1. *Disruptive Value.* Here, as the name implies, the goal is to bring breakthroughs to market. There can be a product, or like the iPod example, an entirely new product—or service—category. It isn't hard to think of examples. The point is, if you're in this growth or startup phase in particular, you want to think of ways to create substantial new value for customers. In many cases, it will be value they didn't even know they wanted. When they say: "That's a great idea, I want one of

those," or "That's a great idea, why didn't I think of that?" you'll know you're on the right track.

2. *Application Value.* Moore suggests application innovation as being not so much finding breakthrough new products, but finding breakthrough applications of existing products or technologies. Many of the innovations on the Internet are really new applications of existing technology. The idea here is to create net customer value by taking an existing technology and repurposing it so a customer can get new value from it. Handheld consumer GPS systems leverage existing military technology, obviously in a new and highly value creating package.

3. *Product Value.* This is the conventional innovation space, innovation for an existing market with existing products but differentiated through "new features and functions current offers do not have." Net customer value is brought here by substantial forward movement (not "paint it blue"); Moore gives the examples of adding wireless capability to laptops or cameras to cell phones. Net customer value is provided by adding something new—a current technology or an altogether new one—to a product to make it better.

4. *Platform Value.* Platform innovation is about taking relatively complex and sometimes unrelated technologies and bundling them together into a platform to make them—essentially—usable, thereby delivering net customer value. The myriad electronic parts and software components necessary to build a PC already existed in the late 1970s and early 1980s, but the innovation was really packaging it all together into a platform a customer could use, and thus get value out of it, which is what IBM, Intel, and Microsoft worked together to do. Here, the individual parts provided no value whatsoever; it was the platform that created net customer value.

The Customer Intimacy Zone

Here we move on to innovation styles more likely to be experienced by a mature organization. The emphasis in this zone is to make a product more attractive to the customer; to build loyalty; to make yourself as a brand indispensable to the customer, not just the product itself. Tractors are tractors, for the most part—what John

Deere gets is the loyalty, breadth, and depth of its customers' needs, and it knows how to meet those needs by adjusting the products and bringing more value to the customer beyond the product. The four ways to deliver net customer value, again from Moore, in this zone are:

1. *Line-extension Value.* Here we may bring value by extending a product line into greater options at the low end or high end. Netbooks might be a low-end line extension innovation, bringing net customer value by offering a new slimmed down package at a reduced price. Automakers have thrived on line extensions for years, however, one might argue whether or not they really brought new net customer value—did they provide more compared to price? Compared to *expectations*? If not, they don't qualify as innovations. The trick, of course, is to extend the line in such a way as to create new *value*, not just confusion. The latter happens a lot.

2. *Enhancement Value.* Here, according to Moore, we take existing products and add "finer levels of detail." It is like the "Product Innovation" in the Product Leadership Zone, except the additions are finer—new flavors for food or drinks or new audio systems in cars might qualify. Again, they must add net customer value, not just "paint it blue."

3. *Marketing Value.* Here, we aren't creating a new product at all, but rather a new way to market, explain or deliver it to the public. Redbox is a new and highly innovative way to distribute DVDs; "clicks and bricks" Internet and store pickup shopping options, as used at Sears and others, is another example. Again, is there new net customer value in these ideas? You bet.

4. *Experiential Value.* This is like Marketing Innovation, but more directed to the total customer experience. The product doesn't change much; it's the experience that is enhanced by some idea or innovation, large or small. Chocolates on the pillow, a restaurant or hotel system that remembers your preferences, new airline check-in procedures all qualify. Here you can deliver a lot of differentiating net customer value without inventing a new product at all.

The Operational Excellence Zone

In the Customer Intimacy Zone within the mature phase, the focus was on amendments to either the product or the experience or both. Now the focus shifts more towards improving internal processes in order to reduce cost, improve quality or some combination of the two. While many of these innovations seem internally focused by nature, they do in most cases have the potential to deliver net customer value if executed properly and benefits pass through.

- *Value-Engineering Value.* Here, the idea is to reduce total ownership cost by finding the right combinations of components, materials, and labor for a product. It doesn't make sense to put a disc drive in a PC that lasts 20 years; the goal is to achieve balance, through innovation, to optimize the performance at a price, thus delivering new net value. Note that net customer value can be achieved by means other than reducing product cost or price: For instance, by reducing the cost of one component, the savings might be applied to beefing another up, delivering better performance or longevity.
- *Integration Value.* Here, customer net value is delivered by combining features or technologies to make something simpler or to give it a simpler customer interface. Moore gives the examples of mutual funds or all-in-one printer/fax/scanner/ copiers. At this level, the value and the innovation are not really about the product, it's the packaging. Kraft "Lunchables" pre-packaged, do-it-yourself lunches also come to mind.
- *Process Value.* Now we get to the conventional cost-cutting value achieved through process innovation, with abundant examples. As Moore points out, sometimes process improvements can deliver net customer value *other than* by reducing cost, as Dell's direct model did for a number of years. Oftentimes such a customer benefit is secondary to a primary cost saving objective; one could think of bank ATM machines in this way. The question to ask, of course, is whether you can deliver net customer value—by cutting cost or providing other benefits—through a process innovation.
- *Value-Migration Value.* This one doesn't roll off the tongue so well, but has to do with moving the company to somewhere

else in the food chain to deliver greater value (and often more profit, as well.) The movement is usually away from commodity products, and a classic example is the IBM and HP example of companies moving from computer hardware products to integrated solutions to full-blown consulting. The value is delivered through a more holistic product the customer wants or needs; the innovation is re-crafting and repositioning the business to deliver it that way.

The Category Renewal Zone

This zone is reserved for companies in a declining phase—a besieged group that has grown a lot recently. These companies are looking to salvage something through innovation, which usually means finding some new way to deliver value from an old technology or brand or relationship base. It works more often than you might think. There are two types of net customer value creation found in this zone.

1. *Organic Value.* Here the company is simply trying to get something new out of something old. Eastman Kodak has a brilliant brand image in the imaging field and a lot of technology around it. So why not use that to deliver new forms of value through in-store printing kiosks, photo sharing sites, digital cameras, and other ways to process and display digital photo media? This example, of course, pertains to declining companies, but it also applies—probably more often—to declining brands and sub-businesses within a business. Sure, Kraft is a healthy, mature food products brand, but it still tries to find organic value by introducing new packages and flavors and textures of Ritz crackers and Oreo cookies. There can be a lot of net customer value "spark" in such corporate ashes.

2. *Acquisition Value.* Now a company finds ways to deliver new net customer value by merging, selling, or acquiring another brand to go with it. There may be brand or distribution or technological synergy or simply a more complete product offering involved. Providing this kind of value can work well—banks and financial institutions have been doing it for years (although some of the recent bank mega-mergers were not

about customer value at all). But such attempts at acquisition synergy can prove disastrous if customer net value and the value proposition aren't thought through; I'm still trying to figure out why Daimler-Benz ever acquired Chrysler. There, in my mind, customer net value was destroyed (for Mercedes owners, anyway), not created.

Soft Lines, Not Barriers

Now here's the caution I referenced a few pages ago. These "lines" between the different stages in evolution, and the different innovation "zones" should not be taken as too definitive. As we've seen, the value-delivering strategies appropriate for companies in the declining phase can be used for products or even entire businesses that might be declining in an otherwise healthy organization.

But here's the real issue to watch out for. Just because your organization is mature doesn't mean it should completely eschew the kinds of innovations prevalent in the growth phase. What if Apple had given an internal "no" to the iPod and its brethren because it thought itself in the mature phase in the Mac business? Imagine that lost opportunity.

In the same vein, the caveat I have with Moore's approach is that he seems to reserve disruptive innovation for companies in the start-up or growth phase. While I certainly see such creations of net customer value driving such innovations in that space, I actually think disruptive innovations—and the creation of disruptive net customer value—are a good thing anywhere on the life cycle map. New, disruptive ways of defining and capturing markets not only help the financial bottom line, but they also do a lot for a company's image and even its sales of other—non-disruptive—products. Profits and PR—not a bad thing. Again, I cite Apple as a prime and fundamental example.

So while my main message is "think like who you are, and learn to deliver value accordingly," I also believe you should strive—perhaps as a stretch goal—to find those new products, those new markets, those new ways of packaging or delivering a product—that bring huge, disruptive new levels of net customer value to the marketplace. Just don't let that pursuit consume all of the value-delivering and innovating resources within your organization.

Chapter Takeaways

- It's all about creating net customer value. Net customer value refers to benefit provided to a customer at a given cost and compared to the benefit of existing products.
- The difference between invention and innovation: Invention is the transformation of an idea into a product or service; an innovation is an invention that creates net customer value.
- Value can be defined into strata—from "criminal" and "bad" to "baseline" to excellent to exceptional. These strata define how a company's offerings stack up against the competition in relation to net customer value—and also predict where a company is going financially.
- The quest for net customer value should be directed towards all parts of the customer experience and the Customer Innovation Cycle, not just the product or service itself.
- The thing to really focus on, or "invent," is net customer value. Innovation can be looked at as just a way to deliver net customer value—the "how" in response to the net customer value "what and why?"
- The dimensions or components of customer net value are not monolithic; they work in combination to comprise a holistic value delivered to the customer. Any one component delivered in the "bad" or "criminal" strata can ruin even superstar value delivered elsewhere. Think in terms of Experiential Sliders when you develop your net customer value framework.
- The type of net customer value you deliver depends in part on where your business is in its lifecycle. That said, the lines are blurry, and there's always room for an exciting, new, disruptive innovation in every business.

Carpet Time

More than 20 years ago, my wife, Michelle, and I decided to start a family. Once I made that commitment, I personally pledged to always be certain that I made time available to spend with my kids. The only way I knew to do that was to glue myself to the ground long enough to really hang out with them.

So I created a policy called "Carpet Time." At the end of every day—and I still do this—I walk in the door of my home, set down my briefcase, and sit and visit with my kids. Now this may sound corny—or even hard to believe—but I can tell you it has been an amazing experience for me and my kids.

During the 1980s, "quality time" was an oft-used pop-psychology phrase. "Quality time" in those days was propagated by busy parents who didn't make time available for their children on a regular basis. They used "quality time" as a way to make up for the lack of "quantity time." And of course, it didn't work. Children assume that *all* time is "quality"—but what they're really looking for is "quantity."

And so it is with customers.

In order to understand what customers really care about—or in many cases more importantly, what could be going wrong in the course of delivering meaningful value—you have to spend carpet time with your customers, to see them, feel them, and experience them. I know—it would be great to be able to computerize this process so you could get back to the business of managing operations, financials, and so on. But really, this is the heavy lifting required for sustainable health in your business.

A few days ago, my DSL service went down. I called my DSL service provider, and while on the phone, the message proclaimed, in a phrase that sounded all too familiar: "Please hold. A service representative will be with you shortly." Then—unbelievably—it went on to say, "If you're unable to connect to the Internet, please go online and look at our services at . . ."

Are you kidding me? The message said that if I couldn't go online, I should go online to solve my own problem. A kindergartener could understand that such an instruction was a horrible disconnect. Yet, at the end of the service call, they still gave me a 15-page "service survey" to fill out. Undoubtedly it was put together by a consulting firm propagating "Customer Relationship Management."

Wow. We have to use common sense. We have to *really* get to know our customers. And the only way to do that is to spend time with them.

For example, if you're driving down an Iowa back road and you see two older gentlemen in front of a run-down country store, don't be surprised if one of the fellows playing checkers is a new product development person with John Deere & Company. John Deere spends an amazing amount of time in the field *living* with its customers. The company knows it doesn't just sell farm equipment—it sells *livelihoods*. By understanding the challenges of fuel costs and efficiencies, John Deere has been able to create some of the absolute best technologies in the world.

In fact, John Deere products are more than just a means to an end for its customers; doing business with the company is more like being part of a religious order. Truly, when you have a company with a huge revenue licensing stream for its logo simply because people want to wear its shirts, hats, and jackets, that's a pretty good sign that the company has done an amazing job of systematically identifying what its customers want—and delivering it with mathematical certainty.

How Do You Tell if You're *Really* Customer Connected?

Before going into the mechanics of carpet time, I have a question—a question you may have as well. How can you, as a manager, marketer or innovator, tell if you're really customer connected?

Sure, it's easy to *feel* customer connected—you've done your market research, sat in on the focus groups, and tried the product out yourself as though you were a customer. You brought a sample home for your best friend and your mother-in-law, too. But do these things really mean you're connected to your customers? Do they really help you get the real and honest feedback, the picture of how your customers use, perceive, like and dislike your products that you really need to define customer net value and move forward with innovation? Hard to tell at this point.

While it's hard to know exactly when you're connected and when you're not, I suggest the following "test of threes" to help out. Try it for yourself.

- Can you *quickly* describe three things your customers like about your products?
- Can you *quickly* describe at least three things that frustrate the heck out of customers about your products?
- Can you describe three experiences with your products your customers have had and told you about recently?
- Are you getting at least three useful inputs or comments per week about your products?
- Have you been "in the field" at least three times in the past calendar quarter?

If you, and the people in your organization, can answer "yes" to all of the above, you might not be completely connected, but you're well on your way.

How to Do Carpet Time

Carpet time can be a simple and truly literal experience. For years toymakers have sat with children on carpeted living room floors in real homes and watched them play with toys. They watched their initial out-of-box experience, or OOBE. Toymakers watched kids learn how to assemble or set up the toy. They watched them learn how to use the toy and play with it. Toymakers watched the kids to see if they would do inventive things with the toy, things the designers had never thought of. They listened, not only for sounds of joy or frustration, but also for new ideas. "Gee, I wish this robot had realistic sound effects." "I wonder what would happen if I . . ." And so on.

The end result of such carpet time was a better understanding of what these juvenile customers *did* with the company's products, how much they *liked* or *disliked* the company's products, and what new ideas or concepts with or around the products might make them more interesting. Really, there's no better way to understand how a customer finds value in your product than to watch him or her *use* it.

That said, watching enough customers—at least adult customers—use enough products in a controllable, unbiased setting to get the information you need is, to say the least, challenging. With kids, they don't really know why they're being watched, and so their behaviors can be taken as generally real. Tell an adult that you're watching them use one of *their* toys, and you may not get a natural read on what they perceive about your product.

Carpet Time for Adults

Just because it's a challenge to get your customers into a room and onto the carpet with your product doesn't mean you should eschew carpet time. You just have to be a little cleverer in how you go about it.

Basically, at day's end, carpet time is all about powers of observation, and just being observant in general. There are formal and not-so-formal ways and settings to make these observations, each having some advantages and disadvantages. The truly customer-connected individuals and organizations use a mix of the two, and most importantly, are constantly watching.

Here are some formal and not-so-formal ways to do carpet time.

Focus Groups

If used properly, traditional focus groups can work well as carpet time. Focus groups are obviously contrived—not natural—settings for customers and potential customers to discuss the features and value of your product, and if done well, can provide a lot of information. That information can be absorbed by a lot of people in your organization, since you can bring lots of guests to the viewing room, make videos, and so forth. But people in focus groups always know they're being watched, and some may go out of their way to please you (or displease you if they have a grudge against your products). And focus groups can be expensive. But a well-moderated focus group, with clear objectives and a good moderator, can produce a lot of good information.

Innovation Safaris

While focus groups are valuable for most companies and products, too many researchers stop there. Even worse, they stop before that point, relying on simple VOC and CRM surveys. You can't know what customers really think, really do, or really need simply watching them from behind glass walls. It's important to get people out into the field, whether it be a farm field for Deere or an electronics retailer for a TV manufacturer or a kitchen for a prepared food products company. This can be done one-on-one as in "wandering around," which I discuss next, or in an *innovation safari*, where a group from your organization hits the field. I'll elaborate on innovation safaris shortly.

Wandering Around

This past year, a colleague of mine went to a Staples office products store in a small town in the California mountains. His intent was to find a quick, cost-effective way to make copies of a picture of his kids for a Christmas letter. He had one copy of the picture. He approached the self-service machine and started making individual copies to cut and paste in a nine-per-page layout to make the final run. A Xerox service rep just happened to be at the store at the same time. He saw what my colleague was doing, took the picture, pushed a few buttons in a little-known "multiple image" section of the keypad, and presto! Multiple copies, quick, easy, cheap.

> "How did you do that?"
> "Simple. Just push this button, enter the number of images, choose a layout, and go."
> "I never knew these machines had a feature like that!"
> "Hmmm. That's interesting. I never thought about that . . ."

Now, did this service rep learn something? Perhaps he learned that an otherwise competent copier user could not, would not, have ever found that useful feature on his own. Maybe could there be something to help customers learn what features are available and how to use them? This little bit of carpet time, if used properly, could help Xerox connect an innovation already in place to its customers. Or it could have just as easily been used to develop another one. Or, with a lot of companies, it might have simply gone to waste.

The innovation safari is a "many-on-one" or "many-on-many" approach usually requiring some organization and expenditure. These safaris are great, and focus groups are great, too. But I believe all employees in an organization—top to bottom—should wander around. Wander around to see their products being presented, sold, and used in the marketplace. Wander around to find very real, very personal, one-on-one observations on how customers use, don't use, or perceive your products and your product *experience*.

You should wander around on your own. Employees should be encouraged to do this on their own, during business trips, even during family shopping trips when it makes sense. Visit some retailers or strike up a conversation with someone on an airplane to ask them what they think of your product. Or a competitor's product.

It doesn't just stop with the carpet time itself. You, and all employees, should have an intra-corporate venue to download all of your experiences and observations, good or bad, for others to see. Intra-corporate web portals like HP's "Garage" or the use of Brightidea's' "WebStorm" idea collection portal, as Adobe and many others do, will help with this. Trip reports also work. But employees should always be encouraged to share their observations, whether formally or informally, within their organizations. Sooner or later, it gets into the mindset. Who can see the most interesting things about their customers? When these are the stories that are told at the water cooler, you know that *carpet time* has become part of your culture.

Electronic Carpet Time

One of the first-order applications of what I call digital innovation is the use of the Internet to tap into what customers think, feel, and say about your products.

Indeed, the Internet has, in the past 15 years, made it possible to connect more—with more of your customers—than ever before. It has changed the entire landscape for researching and marketing a product. In the context of carpet time, what's really important about the Internet is that it allows customers to give real time feedback to you about their product experiences, and to share those experiences with each other. You, of course, can listen in.

While electronic feedback and reconnaissance can be a bit impersonal, it does have reach—you can literally touch hundreds of customers every day. And, as we'll see in the case of Adobe, if you take the time to respond to customer feedback, you'll set up a dialog and get a lot more value out of it.

There are two approaches I'd like to highlight for doing electronic carpet time. The first is what I call "listening posts," and the second is the idea portal similar to that of Brightidea's WebStorm or some other web portal that collects and organizes customer feedback.

Making the Most of Carpet Time

It's not enough just to provide for carpet time—you must work at it to make it effective. Simply spending time with customers alone won't do the trick.

Regardless of what kind of carpet time you choose to engage in, there are some guiding principles I suggest you keep in mind. You may recognize these principles as similar to those found in almost any general treatment of interpersonal relationships. That's not a coincidence, because learning what customers think, feel, and do with your products is a matter of getting close to their thoughts and feelings. Here's a short list:

- *Have an open mind.* Most people have a natural bias towards thinking they're right, and thinking their *products* are right for their customers. That bias and the cognitive dissonance that can surround it can cause you to miss important signals from the customer. If you find yourself feeling angry that a customer spoke poorly of your product, or simply doesn't get it, you should get over it. You must be open to any and all of their feelings and their responses.
- *Stop, look, and listen.* It seems pretty basic, but I find that people don't really listen when they are face to face with a customer, or they listen for what they want to see or hear, not what's actually happening or being said. Also, practice *active listening*—that is, ask good, supportive questions to try to get the customer to disclose more in a nonthreatening way.
- *Be perceptive.* Don't just listen, but also watch for nuances, body language, signs of comfort or discomfort. Try to discern whether the customer is or isn't having a positive experience. It's usually not hard to tell.
- *Be empathetic.* This follows the "open mind" point closely. Learn to see, feel, touch, and hear the customer experiences from

their side of the fence, from their end of the phone. Obviously, someone missed out on this notion—if they did carpet time at all—when setting up the Internet service provider experience I told you about.

Aside from these behavioral tenets with carpet time, it is also essential that you focus on the whole product experience. Observe as much as you can about the complete experience, from initial brand noise and first touch all the way through to the disposal of the product, walking out the door, hanging up the phone, and so forth. Think about important elements peripheral to the product itself—instructions, documentation, packaging, service, cleanliness, appearance, and ambience.

Also, employ your carpet time to find not only baseline expectations, but also what creates emotions like delight or surprise in your customers. Find the unexpected benefits and the little snags. Sweat the small stuff—don't just focus on the dominant elements of the product or service but also the little things like unpacking time for a product or wait time for a service call or even the manners and positive attitudes of the people involved. Finally, measure what you can, but realize that most of what you observe probably isn't measurable. Don't ignore something just because you can't measure it—and remember that measurement isn't everything.

Now, I'll move on to explain a few carpet time tools in greater detail and then share the Adobe superstar case example, a paradigm of excellence in the area of carpet time.

Carpet Time Tools: Innovation Safaris

One of the tools we use in our practice that is extremely effective is the *Innovation Safari*. An innovation safari is most often a facilitated process in which we take clients out—typically an entire R&D or new product development team—into the field with a program that allows them to really observe, and to talk to, and to listen to their customers. Not for 15 minutes or half an hour—but for *several days* at a time. Several days of intense hands-on observation, in multiple locations if it makes sense.

Immediately after the innovation safari, we come back together at the office for an "ideation" session. During that session we transmute our observations from the field to meaningful products and services.

We recently had the opportunity to do this with a client in California. With just one innovation safari, the client generated millions of dollars of new technologies. Once an organization has completed one or two innovation safaris, they typically make such safaris part of their innovation system.

What they have learned is their surveys and other methods don't really connect them to the soul of their customer. Remember this: The voice of the customer can miss a lot. The customers may answer a few important questions, but are they honest answers? Moreover, are they answering questions you don't ask as well? The reality is—it's the soul, the spirit, the experience, the true belief of the customer we go after these days, and you can't do that with automated or computerized means.

Carpet Time Tools: Listening Posts

One of the first elements of so-called digital innovation is an element that belongs here in the carpet time section, while most of the rest of the digital information is about creating the innovation itself. I call this element *Listening Posts*.

Just 10 years ago, it would have been hard to quickly, and in real time, identify what people think about product concepts, service concepts, brands, and so on. But today, you can host questions on a variety of very vertical social networking sites and get extremely good and valuable information.

In researching *The Innovation Playbook*, for example, I routinely posted questions on highly vertical sites to get expert opinion on the current lay of the land. It was amazing to see the quality and speed with which I received extremely powerful and valuable information that just 10 years ago would have cost thousands, maybe tens of thousands, of dollars to acquire.

The other great thing about listening posts is they allow you to scan the Web automatically through tools like "Google alerts," where you enter in key words and Google will search the Internet for you and automatically send you an email whenever those words are published online. This keeps you in tune with the kind of noise that's on the Internet about a specific item, product, or product category. I use this tool every day—at any given time I have 15 to 20 or maybe more Google alerts coming my way to help me stay on top of any colossal changes in the area of innovation. Such listening posts are an amazingly powerful tool; they usually cost nothing, they're fast, and they will reduce failure prior to a product launch by helping you take the temperature of your target in real time.

Carpet Time Tools: A Few More Bright Ideas

There's a small company based in San Francisco that I think all innovators and innovation managers should know about. This company makes some clever and effective software products that collect and aggregate ideas from employees, partners, and customers and turn them into reality. Especially for large organizations or very dynamic industries, their solutions do an amazing job of helping collect, in real time, this true voice of the customer.

The company is Brightidea, Inc. and its business is *Innovation & Idea Management Software*.

More than 300 businesses around the world use its Software-as-a-Service suite to collect ideas from employees, partners, and customers and turn them into a reality. These companies utilizing the software include accomplished innovators like Adobe, Bosch, Cisco, Sony, Harley-Davidson, Experian, Emerson, British Telecom, Bristol-Myers Squibb, and Honeywell.

One of the key products in the Brightidea portfolio is WebStorm 5.0, a product that creates what Brightidea logically calls an *Innovation Social Network*. Companies, including many of those named here, use WebStorm software to create idea and communication portals for their customers. Because of their interactive nature, both the companies and their customers benefit from these idea platforms.

WebStorm is a true electronic carpet time tool. By giving customers the opportunity to not only share their ideas in a WebStorm portal, but also to voice their opinion on others' ideas through votes and comments, companies gain valuable customer insights. WebStorm allows organizations, in an easy-to-use format, to collect information on how customers use their product, talk about their products, and engage with their product. Customers, likewise, have the ability to share ideas and suggestions with companies in a low-barrier, two-way environment, and the ability to collaborate with other customers. It also allows companies to create contests and other promotions to stimulate input.

WebStorm can gather and manage ideas from an unlimited number of employees or customers. It also ranks, categorizes, and archives all input, creating a permanent record of feedback and institutional knowledge for the organization. The product helps companies identify highly engaged customers, get the customer voice into product development, test new ideas with customers, and build a community of loyal customers and evangelists for the company.

I've been impressed with the ability of Brightidea products to really facilitate the electronic carpet time process. See http://www .brightidea.com/webstorm.bix for more information.

Carpet Time Tools: Poster Board Sessions

Another great way to stay highly connected to your customers and to understand what's going on at street level is to do what we call *Poster Board Sessions*. A few years ago, one of our clients, California Guest Services, a concessionaire for national and state parks, had a very thin profit margin and a seasonal business, and it was extremely important that they find new profit centers in order to continue to stay profitable.

We asked a few basic questions. One was, "How could California Guest Services generate new revenue while delivering a unique and special value to its customers?" The second question we asked was, "What methods can we deploy to save money without adversely impacting the employee or the visitor, that is, the customer?"

What happened was a one-day poster board session where each and every employee brought their own poster board. They had one employee representing each of their parks. As a result, they found over $2 million in new profit and saved over $1 million in costs while actually improving the experience of both the employee and their customers.

This was attained simply by asking frontline people to participate by answering two simple questions through the poster board method. When presenting it in front of their peers, they wanted to do something that was both smart and entertaining. It was a fun day and extremely profitable.

Poster board sessions should be at least a quarterly activity in most companies.

Adobe Sets an Example

I defined the Innovation Superstar and its key anatomical components and traits in Chapter 5. I could, and perhaps should, have given a complete case example of all the traits and how they worked together right then and there. But I chose not to. Not only was that chapter pretty long already, but my ace example, while it is a true superstar in all aspects and elements of the business, simply stands out—in the "Customer" portion of the superstar anatomy.

My example is software toolmaker Adobe Systems, Inc. of San Jose, California. Adobe makes a number of software tools, the most well known of which are Acrobat, the universal document processing (.pdf) software and related "reader," and its Photoshop and derivative products for processing and enhancing images of all sorts.

My goal here is not to talk about Adobe products—or profits, however, but about Adobe innovation, which is one of the most successful innovation programs on the planet. I've been familiar with the Adobe way for years, but in researching this book, I got a very helpful low-altitude flyover from Lisa Underkoffler, a product manager in the company's "acrobat.com" division and champion of a new collaborative product called "Buzzword."

I asked Lisa to give me an overview of the important aspects of Customer, Product, and Culture, the three anatomical components of superstardom.

Customer Touch: SynchDev

SynchDev is a cross functional idea development team with members from different parts of the Adobe organization, certain customers. And *potential* customers. The idea is to generate some ideas, get some validation, and paint some reality on the ideas and product concepts already in process. This team reviews a lot of existing products, looking for holes and gaps in this product. Members of the team include product managers, developers, product marketers, and quality assurance team members, with a sampling of customers added to the mix.

The obvious goal is to answer the question: "What do we need to do next?" But there are more subtle questions the team tries to answer about the customer situation and especially change in the customer situation and requirements: What are people doing today that's different? Have customer needs changed? Has the environment changed? Has what they do—and need to do—with the product changed or evolved in any obvious or subtle ways?

Customer Touch: The Idea Portal

While the SynchDev teams are a more obvious and structured way to capture customer feedback, the acrobat.com group within Adobe also runs a live and active idea portal using Brightidea's WebStorm tools. In addition, there is a feedback link in the product itself, which sends e-mail to the entire team working on Acrobat.com. While many companies have deployed some form of electronic suggestion box, the novelty here is the way Adobe uses the approach. (See http://ideas.acrobat.com)

Customers can give feedback on products, how they're using them and what problems or issues they may be encountering. From their feedback, the Adobe team not only identifies potential improvements, but also learns a great deal about current customer vocabulary, that is, what they do and how they describe it but also correlations between use of different products, media, and hardware. The gap between how Adobe *thinks* customers use products and how they *really* use them is reduced.

What makes the site and the process work, however, is that contributors are treated like customers. It isn't a black hole; rather, all suggestions and inquiries are answered individually and personally (not with form letters) in a style that makes Adobe seem more human in its business space. The folks writing the responses are product marketing and product development people, not customer service people, who don't have the time or bandwidth for such handcrafted responses.

The result is a user community that is not so much a fan club, or worse, a group of complainers, but rather an integral part of the new product development process. These customers feel close to the new product development team, and vice versa.

Interestingly, this approach was initially adopted by the Acrobat .com group despite great concern from general management, who thought (as many do) it would be a project too cumbersome and time-consuming to answer incoming messages and keep the conversations going. But the group has shown the value of the interaction, and other groups within Adobe have started to adopt the approach.

Customer Touch: 1:1 Visits

To capture customer feedback, Adobe, like many companies, tried the survey (voice of the customer) approach, and left it behind, mostly dissatisfied. The company felt it was unable to identify true present or future needs, but still uses surveys for validation.

On the other hand, Adobe has made a substantial investment in customer visits, and has made them a part of their ongoing customer research and new product development process. These visits don't so much take on the form of a deep and long innovation safari, where marketers and developers may spend days or even weeks at a time with a customer, but are more like short Saturday afternoon visits, an hour or an hour-and-a-half long, where Adobe team members can learn more about the true customer environment and even use them to show and tell new products. One goal of these visits is to do a "contextual inquiry," that is, to sit with customers in an informal way while they actually do their work.

The team again has product marketing and new product development members, but usually has at least one senior management team member involved, sometimes even the CEO (see my later comments on the "inverted pyramid"). Every one-on-one visit is reported to the rest of the organization via a trip report. Unlike the typical safari, these visits are shorter and occur frequently—consider it more of an afternoon drive-by than a safari. But it works and works well—not only to serve Adobe's needs by keeping track of the customers' pulse, but it also helps build a better image of Adobe in customer minds.

Process and Culture Superstardom

As laid out in Chapter 5, it is often true that the less said about process, the better; less is more. Not surprisingly, Adobe considers its customer touch (carpet time) processes an integral part of its new product development process, and treats these activities accordingly.

Beyond that, Adobe also champions a fast development process, both for new products and new releases. Development project team members stay close to customers throughout the development, and are free and willing to admit they are wrong at any time during the process.

According to Underkoffler, "Risk isn't something you spend a lot of time talking about." The company feels that if they've done their customer homework through SynchDev, the portal, and customer visits among other tactics, that takes a lot of the risk out of the equation. Most teams within the organization are "creative and energized," they understand their market well, and they know well with a new product idea "where they can be elastic and where there is risk." Again, the bottom line is: Knowing the customer reduces the inherent risk of most projects.

Adobe has additionally gone the extra mile to involve not only customers but also employees in defining and improving its products. A slogan, created by one of its founders, appears often on intranet sites and other places: "Good ideas come from all places in the company." To that end, the company has set up an actively used Brightidea's WebStorms intranet for employees to submit ideas and innovations. The company also uses "wiki" pages set up by development groups; all wikis for projects across the company are available to all employees.

The company has had special, if not unique, challenges in implementing this culture across all of its businesses, since it has made numerous acquisitions over the years. Management has turned this challenge into opportunity by absorbing the best customer connectivity tactics from these acquisitions, and by implementing pillars of its own culture in the new subsidiaries while leaving them somewhat independent to operate.

Adobe has exhibited a balanced deployment of all the characteristics of an innovation superstar, and gets particularly high marks for its use of the carpet time concept. The result has been a customer driven, results oriented corporation that has survived the test of time and growth, and continues to be, despite that growth and the pressures of Wall Street, an innovation superstar to this day.

The Inverted Pyramid Syndrome

Most organizations suffer from what I call the *inverted pyramid* syndrome. By that I mean the people at the top of the organization, who make most of the decisions that affect most of the customers, have the *least* amount of customer contact. Conversely, the people that have the *most* customer contact—the customer service people, the service technicians, the field representatives, the sales reps—the entire frontline of most organizations have absolutely no input or impact whatsoever as to what kinds of products and services and improvements and enhancements will be ultimately added to a product line or service offering.

That's obviously a mistake, and to become truly successful at innovation, an organization should be turned upside down. By doing that—by providing ways for your frontline people to communicate

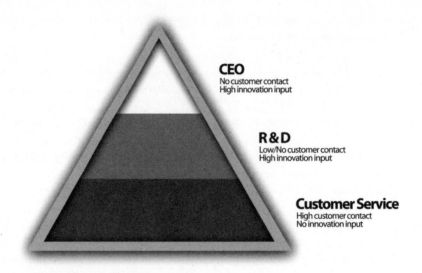

Figure 7.1   The Typical Pyramid

problems, ideas, and observations in real time, you'll build a bulletproof organization, at least insofar as customer satisfaction and innovation go.

The typical pyramid, shown in Figure 7.1, features the CEO at the top and more importantly, farthest away from the customers, who are touched only by the folks at the bottom of the pyramid. I suggest—strongly suggest—inverting the pyramid, as shown in Figure 7.2.

Now, mind you, this doesn't mean making the rank and file responsible for *all* decisions that face an organization. It's more a cultural change than an organizational change. This means two things: First, those folks who really do listen to the voice of the customer, who have the customer contact day in and day out, need a stronger voice in most organizations. They should drive the formation of customer net value propositions, and hence innovation. They are the Carpet Timers and should be recognized and treated as such.

Second, it also implies that the CEO and other members of the management team need to break down the barriers and distance that separate them from their customers. They need to be part of the customer contact mix. Bottom line: They need to do carpet time, too.

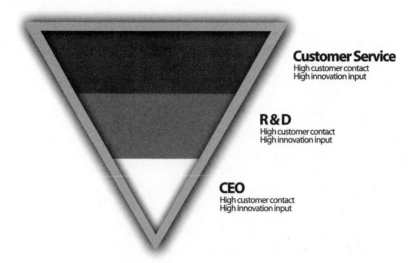

Customer Service
High customer contact
High innovation input

R&D
High customer contact
High innovation input

CEO
High customer contact
High innovation input

Figure 7.2   The Inverted Pyramid

Cyber Carpet: Keeping Face with Social Networking Tools

A five-author team of techies headed by Rick Levine predicted in their provocative book, *The Cluetrain Manifesto,* in 2000 (Levine et al., 10th anniversary ed., Basic Books, 2009) that the Internet would actually put a more human face on commerce. Customers would be able to use the power of the Internet to drive companies.

Now, ten years later, companies are getting really smart about this and using these powerful tools to stay close to their customers—worldwide—in real time. They're learning to use the Internet as a giant "wiki" and social network to advance their own products while also really listening in on the customer voice.

Increasingly, CEOs are starting to utilize social networking to get in touch with their customer base—a thing virtually unheard of in years past. One successful example of this is Blendtec's YouTube video campaign "Will it Blend?" The video series features Blendtec's CEO, Tom Dickson, comically attempting to blend all manner of objects in one of his company's appliances. Thanks to the viral effects of the series, the company's blender sales have quintupled.

(continued)

And a growing number of high profile CEOs now have their own blogs, giving daily updates on various topics and soliciting customer and industry feedback. Here are a few notables:

Craig Newmark, Craigslist founder

Mark Cuban, Owner, Dallas Mavericks

Ross Mayfield, CEO, Socialtext

Matt Blumberg, CEO, Return Path

Alan Meckler, CEO, Jupiter Media

Kevin Lynch, Chief Software Architect, Adobe Systems

Robin Hopper, CEO, founder—iUpload

Jason Calacanis, CEO, Weblogs

John Dragoon, CMO, Novell

Jonathan Schwartz, former president and CEO of tech giant Sun Microsystems, had a very active blog, but when the company was sold and absorbed by Oracle Corporation in early 2010, he published a page suggesting his followers keep up with him on Twitter until his next assignment was known. Online retailer Zappos' CEO Tony Hsieh sends tweets on his Twitter account and has thousands of followers on both Twitter and his blog. Zappos counts more than 10,000 fans on its Facebook page as well.

Times certainly have changed for some CEOs, but not all. Still today, most CEOs are cut off from their most important constituencies—employees and customers. Press conferences are carefully staged and annual meetings are rehearsed. In most cases the goal is to reveal as little as possible. But that's not the case for many of the country's most successful businesses.

The point is clear—as the Internet makes the world flatter between company and customer, smart and agile companies will not only learn to use its full capabilities just to market products, but also to listen to customers. That listening power, used right, can be used to define and refine net customer value propositions more quickly and accurately than ever.

The Cluetrain Manifesto is indeed pulling out of the station. You'd be well advised to get on board soon.

Chapter Takeaways

- Carpet time is an euphemism for really sitting down and observing and listening to your customers as they use your products or services. The purpose is to capture their true feelings about the experience and to learn more about their true needs. Carpet time feeds directly into the identification and creation of net customer value.

- Carpet time is most effective if you listen well and are open minded, perceptive, and empathetic.
- Carpet time can be done in formal or informal sessions, ranging from focus groups or formal or informal observation in the field. It can be done one-on-one, many-on-one, or one-on-many.
- Focus groups, Innovation Safaris, Idea Portals, and Listening Posts are all important carpet time tools. Surveys and other voice of the customer tools are generally *not* effective carpet time tools.
- Carpet time should be used to keep all levels of an organization tuned into the customer. The Internet and especially the advent of social networking tools and innovation social networks have stepped up the capability—and the imperative—to use technology to enhance carpet time and thus the company's real and evolving perception of the customer experience.

8

The RealOpen Innovation Framework

As I mentioned previously in the book, there are more than 170 different so-called innovation management systems—at least that I've found. The reality is, of course, most of these systems have two very basic problems. First, they're actually risk management, rather than innovation management systems; and next, they are a cookie-cutter approach that almost always results in failure.

Now it's time to examine just what I believe—and what I use—as a process in the real world to make innovation work.

I must warn you now—if you were expecting a detailed step-by-step, fill-in-the-blank recipe, you'll be disappointed. Why? Because different processes work for different organizations, industries, and technologies. As noted in Chapter 2, there is no grapefruit diet panacea solution that manages innovation. One size does not fit all.

Because of this, I've developed a framework called RealOpen, which contains conceptual steps within, which your organization will use to develop the specific processes and measures to succeed. I call it a "prescription" framework because it's like a doctor prescribing specific prescriptions to individual patients. The framework provides the diagnostic chart; the doctor applies it to the particular patient. I'll come back to this in a moment.

As the name implies, RealOpen is a holistic innovation framework and toolbox with a strong "open innovation" component. Why? Because in today's world, it is essential to utilize all sources of ideas and technologies, inside and outside, to meet the fast changing needs of the marketplace. So RealOpen starts with and manages open, external, and internal ideas, all with similar effect.

A Prescription, Not a Diet

One of the things I believe in deeply is what I call a *prescribed*, or a customized, approach to innovation management. No two organizations are alike; there are too many complex variables including technology, market environment, and organizational culture, not to mention the overall goals of the company itself. In fact, several organizations I work with have the goal of developing a range of technologies that would quickly position the company for increased likelihood of a strategic acquisition. Other companies are publicly traded companies that have a completely different goal in terms of their long-range planning.

So the first problem with most so-called innovation management systems is that they are designed with a one-size-fits-all mentality. And, as mentioned, they are almost all risk management systems disguised as innovation management systems. But what makes them even worse is that most of these systems create additional layers or barriers between you and your valued customers.

Open Innovation

At this point I'd like to take a short sidetrack to make a few comments on open innovation and how it fits into this context. Open innovation is a catchy and oft-used phrase. We've heard a lot about it, so much so that open innovation has actually become a job title. Many companies have vice presidents of open innovation. The movement towards open innovation is brilliant and has helped a lot of companies.

I recently posted some information about open innovation on several social networking sites and was surprised to see the wide variations of opinion on its benefits and usefulness. The people who sell open innovation solutions and services are, not surprisingly, widely in favor of it, whereas some organizations that have grown weary of the latest grapefruit diet seem to yawn when you mention the name.

I think there is a real benefit to open innovation. The problem is most organizations don't have the necessary infrastructure to take advantage of openness; it is poorly managed. Great concept, very bad deployment in a large number of cases.

RealOpen is designed to do three things: speed the process, provide results, and build profit. RealOpen accomplishes these things by creating an external innovation sourcing function that is manageable, which includes a filtration process to quickly decide which innovations should be acted upon.

According to recent studies, the overwhelming majority of innovation gatekeepers are not open to external innovation. One reason for the lack of openness is the fact that most organizations have 30 percent more technologies in their portfolio than they have resources to act upon.

Open innovation can be distracting and can bring with it a high resource "burn rate." Burn rate in innovation consumes fuel. It consumes people, time, and organizational bandwidth. Speed rules the day. If you can speed products forward, speed them through what I call the "Forget" and the "Forging" stages in RealOpen, you'll have the ability to build bandwidth without increasing cost.

What Is RealOpen?

Finally, the system that we developed and have recommended to our clients over the last 20 years is really not a system at all, at least not in the traditional sense. It's called RealOpen, and it's a toolbox—a toolbox full of tools that can be configured for any corporation or any industry of any size. It can also be configured to accommodate your current stage of corporate evolution.

If you were to look at RealOpen, and compare it to the PC disc operating system (DOS) of the early 1980s or to the Windows or Macintosh graphic user interface, it's obvious that straightforward, clear, easy-to-understand systems, although more complicated in background, are far simpler to the user and have a higher adoption rate and, ultimately, a higher success rate.

The RealOpen system is like a graphic user interface. It is a fluid, non-linear, and nonlegalistic system that makes it easy for companies to configure systems to help them find, filter, evaluate, and ultimately commercialize world-class innovations.

Everyone operates their system, and their computers, differently, and they use different tools based on the specific needs of their business and their organization. I wouldn't expect a computer user to be bound by a specific sequence of actions, such as being allowed to first check only e-mail before turning on the browser, and finally being allowed access to other software items. RealOpen is no different.

In the process of researching innovation superstars I was surprised to see many of them used systems similar to our RealOpen system. Without exception all of our innovation superstars used innovation management in a fluid and flexible manner, often with systems varying from department to department. Systems had one purpose and one purpose only—to speed great products to market.

The core concept of RealOpen is simple. First, with RealOpen, you pre-filter your innovations, the idea being to get highly vetted technologies that exactly meet your *developmental platform* (I'll explain this term later). Second, it is designed to move projects quickly, without spending too much time or resources on evaluating the innovations.

The term RealOpen really defines three different deliverables. First, as already described, it is a framework within which a specific process can be designed. Second, it is also a framework for innovation management training. More recently, it has also become a software tool used to manage the innovation process.

RealOpen includes fast-track methodologies to quickly move innovations forward, or to *Forget* them if they don't belong in your building. It allows you to develop the discipline needed to create comprehensive product innovation platforms that assure you're developing technologies that make sense for your business and for the target customers of your business.

At this point, a picture may be worth a thousand words (see Figure 8.1).

Figure 8.1   The RealOpen Framework

RealOpen, in a Nutshell

As you can see from the figure, RealOpen is a multi-step framework that moves you from idea stage (whether generated internally or externally) through to the launch phase for a product. As we will learn below, the *Find* and *Filter* stages—the gateways into the rest of the RealOpen process, are really the keys to making RealOpen work, and there are many tools in the RealOpen toolbox to help these two stages along. *Find* is a carefully orchestrated step that enables you to create the right ideas internally and source them externally, while the *Filter* step makes sure only the right ideas advance to the more expensive and in-depth *Forge* stage, and eventually to launch. Along the way, the transitional *Forward* and *Forget* steps help move the right innovations forward while getting rid of the failed ones with minimal pain and risk.

Once a product, technology, or idea gets to *Launch*, we move forward into what I call "layerization of value," where I lay in other features, recognizing that most new products or services aren't really finished when they leave the building. All of these processes should be constantly measured against the tenets of the Webb Triangle's three success drivers: need, build, and sell. The emphasis is on effective filtration and speed, not on bureaucracy and risk management.

What Is an Innovation Platform?

Before detailing specific RealOpen steps, one of the concepts we use to help get the right innovations into the development process easily and quickly is something I call an innovation platform. An innovation platform defines your product and customer vision precisely enough to use as a filtration model and focal point for incoming ideas and technologies. I've often said, if innovation is the answer, then what is the question? In this case, it's the innovation platform.

An innovation platform is like a conventional marketer's produce platform, except it has current and future products in mind. The following Peter Drucker-styled questions help frame an innovation platform.

- What is our business?
- Who are our customers?
- How do we create value for those customers?

I find that most organizations do not have a well-defined platform, that is, a wish list of what they want to create for their customers. Without such a platform, you cannot be really open, and you can't automate filtration. You have to know what you want!

I know that sounds ridiculously simple, but it's surprising that when I interviewed over 200 companies in researching this book, 70 percent of them did not have a formal innovation platform. It's like a personal goal—how do you achieve a goal that you don't know you have?

With a proper innovation platform you can create filters to apply to ideas and technologies. Those filters use what we call *toggles*. As the name implies, toggles are a go/no-go switch that determines whether a technology should move forward. The toggles can be applied not only to internal innovations but also external ideas. I'll explain further with an example shortly.

Innovation platforms not only keep your innovation efforts focused on the right products, they are also designed to simultaneously promote speed—a fast, fluid, smart system that is driven by time. They also take a lot of risk and wasted effort out of the initial stages of the innovation process. Innovation platforms help RealOpen move an idea from Find to Filter. If the filtering indicates a product meets your platform, the product or idea moves Forward. Then it gets Forged to the point of validation, then it goes Forward again. This process may repeat itself many, many times before it gets to Launch.

Now, finally, it's time to examine RealOpen step by step.

Find

The first item out of the toolbox is what I call *Find*. Now the idea of Find, or Fast Find, is easy to understand, easy to use, and implements tools that can be deployed in different ways by different companies. The main point is, in order for you to succeed, you must access technologies. You access technologies from two sources: the outside world, and inside your corporate walls.

There are, all told, seven ways to find new technologies and ideas for your business.

1. *External innovation portals*. External innovation portals are tools that allow outside contributors—innovators or customers—to submit or push their ideas to your

organization. Typically they contain some filtering mechanisms to capture only the most valuable ideas.

2. *Internal innovation portals.* Internal portals are like external portals except that they are for employees and others inside the walls of your organization.

3. *Captive R&D.* This is the traditional source for ideas and technologies—your own internal R&D or product development department.

4. *"Project Xs"* are stimulative simulations in the form of ersatz competitors. By creating competitive companies and observing what they would do to compete with your business, you can learn more about what you should do yourself.

5. *Frontline innovation initiatives* are campaigns that allow frontline employees—those with the most direct customer touch—to submit their ideas, from their experiences or customer knowledge, into the innovation process.

6. *Innovation safaris.* As introduced in Chapters 6 and 7, these are team voyages into the customer world usually done by product development and higher level management personnel, in order to observe customer behavior, learn needs, and eventually develop ways to address those needs through ideation sessions.

7. *Micro-crowdsourcing* campaigns are usually done in conjunction with external innovation portals, but they are specific idea-generating campaigns done with carefully selected "micro-crowds," or segments, of the external idea and technology-providing world.

All of the tools within our Find suite are designed to help you find products, both internally and externally. Figure 8.2 illustrates the components of the Find stage.

External Innovation Portals

Closed organizations have become extremely adverse to external innovation, and have developed a variety of ways to punish anyone who would like to submit an innovation to them. Great companies like Procter & Gamble have developed online submission portals that include explanatory videos that make it easy for anyone to submit an idea or technology to them. Online submission portals are a great

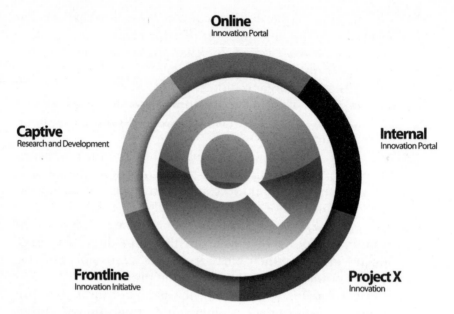

Figure 8.2   The "Find" Stage

way to not only get ideas, but also they are a great way to open up your organization to the outside world and do some "carpet time" with your customers—to learn what they're thinking and what they want.

To keep up with the available ideas and technologies of the outside world, you need to be marketing the planet looking for new innovations, but in order to manage the input of those ideas, you have to automate the process of submission. Online innovation portals are a great way to identify ideas and innovations, from within and from outside the organization using, for instance, tools like Brightidea's WebStorm, introduced in Chapter 7. We recommend the Brightidea systems widely because they do provide an easy and convenient way for your entire organization to participate in the innovation process.

If you set up an online portal that allows an outside innovator, or entrepreneur, or customer, or field representative, or anybody to submit an idea, you can filter that idea by having the person answer the 10 to 30 toggle questions, which are part of the Filter process step I'll describe further below. Ninety percent of those innovations will not qualify. But your product development and innovation folks have never had to talk to anybody, wasting resources, and you've never had to expose yourself to a third party disclosure for intellectual property. That's powerful, because it builds speed and significantly increases your access in real time to external innovation.

Internal Innovation Portals

You can use the same format internally, allowing anybody from service technicians to customer service representatives to engineering or marketing personnel to submit an idea. Any person in your organization can easily submit an innovation. And by the way, if the innovation isn't accepted, you're still giving the potential innovators something to do. Externally, you're giving them a shopping list of things that need to be done, and sometimes the resources to help do them. It is also helpful to give feedback to the outsiders, even in a standard form letter, advising them of status and why or why not their technology was or wasn't accepted. The principles of good customer relationship management apply here, too.

Captive R&D on the Fast Track

There isn't much to say here about your R&D group, which probably already has its idea generation processes. The key is to make them observant, that is, in tune and in touch with customer and organizational needs, and fast—able to interact and respond to the outside and customer world quickly and effectively. R&D needs to be hooked into the other resources in the Find wheel. The new product development or R&D function should be able to fast-track methodologies with the right facilitation. Bureaucracy must be replaced with speed and results. We recommend a wide variety of fast-track methodologies to put speed in the driver's seat. Often established corporations will tend to roll to a stop in terms of managing speed in the innovation management process. Fast-tracking does not adversely affect quality, safety, or market success, it simply collapses time lines in order to actually increase the likelihood of market success.

Project Xs

I also like Project Xs. Project Xs involve taking an external team and creating a competitive technology to the technologies already in your product offering. We've been involved in five or six of these, and I don't believe I've been involved in one of these that didn't provide substantial new revenue with minimal investment.

You have two options when using the Project X tool. First, you can use it as an internal tool where you formulate a team inside your organization that has been put together with the express purpose of competing with your company.

The idea of being your own competitor may sound unusual. But because you know your technologies and your capabilities, your strengths and your weaknesses, you get a unique perspective that allows you to develop competitive products and solutions for your own business. As a result of this new vantage point, you see your weaknesses, or threats, more clearly. This then leads to the creation of new products, services, and technologies.

The second Project X option is to hire companies like ours, and we become the competitor. We design and develop a range of technologies and solutions to specifically compete against you. You can look at those solutions to see where potential threats come from—or you may in fact, as has often been the case—*adopt* one of the competing technologies or solutions developed to compete against you.

In many ways, this is nothing but a change in vantage point, but it's one that works very well. I have watched amazing things happen both with internal and external Project Xs. In fact, a final footnote is in order. Probably the hardest part of the process for most organizations to deal with is the fact that you'll be exposing your own weaknesses. It is a true form of self-assessment and self-analysis, sort of an equivalent of an individual's self-help book, for a company. But I believe such self-assessment is not only necessary, but can produce very positive unintended consequences.

Frontline Innovation Initiatives

Another tool is what I call the "Frontline Innovation Initiative." This means training your sales reps and marketing and customer service people to become active observers. Remember that active observation is the genesis of all innovation. I always say the greatest innovators of all time were not trained in innovation, nor were they particularly good at innovating—they were good at observing the *opportunity* to innovate. Then, they got help with the innovation (including even Edison)—and that's how it got done.

Frontline innovation initiatives are critical in today's fast moving markets and shortened product life cycles.

"I'm an Observer"—Innovation Safaris

Let's talk some more about the "Innovation Safari" tool I introduced in Chapter 7 as a carpet time tool. Innovation safaris are an amazing way to connect to—or get reconnected to—your customers. You can use innovation safaris as a way to identify what is important to your customers through active observation.

Now, active observation is an important point, and I'd like to examine it further. I have found that active observation is one of the true secrets to innovation superstardom. Haven't you noticed that people who pay attention to how they impact the lives of others tend to have a more peaceful, successful existence? The same is true for companies. Companies simply need to have the ability to pay attention to how their policies, procedures, methods, packaging, pricing, delivery, and everything else affect their customer. Because there are so many dimensions of interaction between a company, its products and the customer, active observation is required.

When people ask me how I've become such a successful inventor, my answer is; "Very simple. I'm not an inventor. I'm an observer."

The same is true for all great inventors.

The ability to live consciously is a fundamentally important characteristic of the life of every individual. But it should be—and it needs to be—a matter of systematic deployment with corporations. It must become not only a habit, but part of the organizational culture.

Active Observation with the Safari

How do you become an active observer? Again, it gets back to the innovation safari tool.

Great organizations like John Deere will go out into the field and spend months *living with* their customers. They observe the impact of fuel costs and the efficiency of being able to plant, manage, and harvest crops. They will look at every single ergonomic issue. Literally, everything that affects that customer is observed, not through some focus group member with a clipboard, but by living with the customer and plowing the fields together and observing—first hand—how to add meaningful net customer value through their observations.

Now in a more controlled way, we have had clients do one-day innovation safaris. Really, they work quite well. We had the privilege of working with a great medical company, but we were discouraged to find their engineering department had spent virtually no time in the operating room. So we set up three different innovation safaris in two hospitals and one ambulatory surgical center. Immediately after the safari, we facilitated an "ideation" session. That session resulted in a multi-million-dollar technology that wouldn't have been on the R&D radar screen had we not spent time in the field discovering where the problems, needs, and opportunities were within their market space.

Every company in every business in every space is different, so we begin each innovation safari with a meeting prior to the safari to make sure we've identified the best range of customers and to make sure about what kinds of systems and measurement tools we need to take into the field with us to gather as much information in as short a period of time as possible.

Innovation safaris work with mathematical certainty. They're inexpensive to do, and they score points with customers, who typically like to be listened to and brought into the development process. Yet, most companies haven't made them part of a regular business practice, especially for the people who have the greatest decision making authority. I believe *every* organization should use the innovation safari throughout the enterprise, even to discover the needs of internal customers.

We have also used innovation safaris in customer service to help companies learn opportunities to provide exceptional value in service.

Micro-Crowdsourcing

One of the biggest problems with crowdsourcing, however, is that the crowd is very, very big. As a result of that, the crowd typically isn't "vertical" enough to solve a problem; it is hard to get to the depth necessary with any part of the crowd at any one time. Yet, you're exposing your question to a very large audience.

We recommend the use of what we call micro-crowds. Using techniques that only attract *relevant* crowds will give the greatest likelihood of providing great solutions. I'll talk more about crowdsourcing in Chapter 9.

In our program we put a lot of work into developing innovation platforms. Maybe not in the old product platform sense—real platforms are highly customer connected, so that we *know* what our wish list looks like. By developing those platforms and comparing them to our business value and our net customer value, we're able to filter those innovations quickly, so they don't sit in the building for long periods of time and consume fuel.

This is critical: With innovations, you must learn to dump them quickly if they don't fit—"bail, don't fail" or "fail early," as I discussed in the early stages of *The Innovation Playbook*. That's critical to building speed and the bandwidth to focus on the *right* innovations.

Innovation platforms are one of the key components of what I call the Filter step. Most organizations have filtration systems that identify whether an idea or project is likely to provide a profitable return on investment. Most of the filtering systems are really centered on the business-case analysis of an emerging technology. In fact, 90 percent or more of new product development systems are designed to build business cases around innovations.

For most people, that makes perfect sense. I, however, humbly disagree.

When you develop filtration systems just to define the business case around an innovation, somehow—in most cases, anyway—you've left out the customer as the principal driver. Several amazing technologies would have never made it to market if you had used the standard business-case analysis.

I believe an organization can get on the right track by having the discipline to create a comprehensive innovation platform, and that the innovation platform is what drives their product or technology platform. Many companies feel they actually have that through their planning process. But do they really? Usually they have comprehensive business planning instruments or new product planning instruments that are so complex and/or large that very few people even know what's contained in the documents.

We believe it is important to develop a platform that says: "We're in the X business, and we provide Y value to Z customers." That is the basis of your filtration system (see Figure 8.3).

Filter, Don't Evaluate

It's important to realize that, in our system, we separate *filtration* from *evaluation*. We believe strong, well-thought-out filtration significantly

Figure 8.3   The "Filter"

reduces the burden on R&D organizations to evaluate or even develop products or technologies that never should have entered the new product development process in the first place.

This is important enough to restate: *We believe that your focus should be 80 percent on filtration and 20 percent on evaluation.*

Most organizations have it backwards: They spend 80 percent of their time evaluating and 20 percent filtering, which, at the very least, leads to a lot of wasted time, and at most, to poor decisions and bad products, especially if the filtering process I just described doesn't happen at all.

The reason so many organizations focus on evaluation over filtration is that it requires a great deal of discipline—the discipline of customer focus, the discipline of innovating to customer needs, the discipline to say "no" in a way that removes risk from the idea creators. The result is a haphazard approach of dealing with what comes in the door. The wrong things get early focus and attention, and many of these things ultimately get tossed out later on in the development process, if not by the marketplace.

I believe that an idea or technology should be thoroughly vetted—at a high level—before any team or resources are used in its evaluation.

Filtration is best developed through the creation of what I call *toggles*. Toggles are the questions that go into the 20 or 30 key components of success, or at least the relevancy of an idea of technology submitted to, or within, your organization.

Toggles

Toggles are gate-keeping questions designed to vet the external source and filter out innovations (or innovators) that don't fit. To create toggles, you first need to come up with a broad and deep understanding of what you want from your outside contributors; then you want a sequence of questions and filters that get you and the inventor to that want list. The thought process might look something like this.

Suppose we have a small medical start-up company looking to build its ophthalmic surgical adjunct business. They want to create an automated innovation portal to go out and aggressively look for new technologies. But because they're small, they have limited resources to evaluate those technologies. So, in this kind of case, you would sit and look at yourself and ask, "What regulatory class am I looking for? Is it an FDA Class I? A Class II? Or a Class III?. Since it's a surgical adjunct company, they may be looking at innovations that are only Class I or a Class II. What about stage of development? Again, in this case, they may only want products that are in a mature stage of development. What about patents? Are they really looking for concepts? Products that are patent pending? Or products that have issued patents? The list goes on.

When we build an innovation portal for a client, we have anywhere between 15 and 30 simple questions a submitter can answer; the list does two very magical things. First, it provides a quick, comfortable environment for the inventor to submit an innovation, and—most important—without disclosing any intellectual property. You don't have to worry about nondisclosure agreements, nor spending hours on the phone with someone who could be a crazy inventor or a general malcontent. You simply send people to a site that honors them and gives them an easy way to submit their idea.

Now suppose you're the ophthalmic company and someone comes in and presses the "Class I" button. They're okay. Suppose they press the button for Stage of Development and they're okay. Intellectual property status—they're okay, on and on down the list.

If they hit the "go/no-go" buttons and they all say "go," then the product or enhancement has already been pre-filtered for you. So the innovations that come through this firewall are innovations that specifically connect or dovetail into your innovation platform.

For the ones who do not go through, a mail-merge response comes back: "Thank you for your submission. There were four areas that don't meet our requirements; however, we appreciate your submission and would like to give you this gift of an educational CD, or a Starbucks card, or something else as consideration." This message is to give you the reputation of treating innovators well. When an innovator honors you with a submission, you should give him or her something in return.

Great companies develop a reputation for true and genuine openness, and the beautiful part of automated innovation portals is that they do not require you to spend time on the phone. Your inventors are pre-building and pre-vetting the technology, and you don't have to worry about the legal issues associated with intellectual property disclosure.

Figure 8.4 is an example of specific toggles used in an innovation portal web site.

A focus on filtration, rather than evaluation, significantly increases your access to world technologies. It significantly reduces, if not eliminates, the cost of evaluating technologies that are fuzzy or simply not relevant.

The best way to look at filtration over evaluation is automation. If you've been hand-manufacturing a product for years, and suddenly you get a large sales increase opportunity, you would have to look at vertical integration and maybe even robotics. Unfortunately, it is a time-consuming process to go from a hand-operated factory to one that is highly automated, but that's what has to happen to modern organizations that want access to the next generation of technologies. You have to scale up in terms of volume.

What most organizations ultimately do, unfortunately, is push good innovations away because they don't have the time and bandwidth to evaluate them. What I'm saying is simply this—don't evaluate them, *filter* them—but look at more innovations, not fewer.

Now here is an extremely important point, in fact, it might be one of the most important in *The Innovation Playbook*. In order to keep up with your current market, with its short product life cycles and rapidly emerging technologies, you must look at a lot more

Thank you for contacting XYZ medical. Our goal is to connect with the world's best innovators to develop strategic partnerships to deliver world-class medical innovations. Therefore we have provided an online innovation submission portal that allows you to easily submit your innovation without disclosing the details of your idea. This process actually pre-screens innovations to verify that they comply with our innovation platform. Once you've submitted your innovation you will receive an instant response indicating that we either have no interest or would like additional information. This approach eliminates the runaround many companies put inventors through. In order to provide additional value to our external inventors, we also have a free e-book called "successfully commercializing your medical idea," which gives you valuable step-by-step information you can use to take your product to market in the event that it doesn't meet our current needs. You can also sign up for our monthly online newsletter that provides ongoing tips and market trends. On behalf of the entire XYZ medical team, we sincerely appreciate that you are considering us as your marketing partner.

1. *Type of Device.* XYZ medical is currently looking for Class I exempt, Class I and Class II medical devices. Is your product a class I or class II device?
   Yes   No
2. *Stage of development.* XYZ medical is looking for products that have proven feasibility and functionality. We are currently not accepting concepts or unproven technologies. Have you verified the products feasibility and functionality?
   Yes   No
3. *Patent status.* XYZ medical only accepts products that have a provisional or utility patent pending or issued that has been prepared by a license patent attorney or agent. Do you have a pending patent?
   Yes   No
4. Did you conduct a formal novelty search and/or market clearance search through a licensed patent attorney or patent agent?
   Yes   No
5. Are you a physician or healthcare practitioner?
   Yes   No
6. Have you conducted market and competitive research?
   Yes   No
7. Has the product been the subject of a white paper or other published article?
   Yes   No
8. What is the current stage of the technology?
   a. Concept validated
   b. Concept prototype ready for production in
   c. Production currently in the market

Figure 8.4   XYZ Medical Innovation Portal Innovation Submission Questionnaire

---

   9. Is the product a single use sterile disposable or is it reusable?
      a. Single use
      b. Reusable
   10. Do you have revenue projections for the subject technology?
         Yes   No
   11. Do you have a cost of goods sold of the subject technology?
         Yes   No
   12. Does the product have a reimbursement (CPT) code? If so what is the number?...
         and the list can and usually does go on, to perhaps 20 or 30 questions.

Figure 8.4   (*Continued*)

different technologies to make certain you're still in the game. But most organizations systematically push away inventors and entrepreneurs because they don't have the resources to evaluate the technology. Again, that's why we choose the Pareto principle of 80 percent filtration, 20 percent evaluation.

Build great filters, and you will have access to the best technologies on the planet. It's almost a self-fulfilling promise—if you're *able* to use and accept more ideas and technologies, you'll get more of them, and ultimately, more of them will make it through your filters and stick.

Forward or Forget

Another set of tools we use that falls under the heading "fast-track methodologies" is a set of transitional tools we call *Forward or Forget*.

Most people and most organizations, allow ideas or technologies to stay in the building way too long. The bad and ironic thing is they allow *both* great ideas and bad ideas to stay in the building too long. I introduced "failing early" earlier in the book in Chapter 3. We need to not "fail" but instead "bail early"—which means Forget.

You must decide—does the idea match our product platform, or not? If it doesn't, get it the heck out of there, because the technologies and ideas waiting in your building for some sort of action are consuming fuel. So the point is—when they don't fit, Forget fast.

The flip side of the Forget tool is the Forward tool. Once an idea or technology is vetted and accepted, and goes through the initial stages of development successfully, it must be put on into the Forward stage and given a detailed timeline. The reason for doing this is to keep it moving, and again, to avoid unnecessary consumption of organizational fuel—let alone, a delayed introduction into the market.

Filtration can be done almost completely automatically once you develop your business value, your customer net value, and your innovation platform. What happens after the filtration step? The answer is simple: move forward fast.

Fast Forward

Moving forward fast means taking a look at your risks and your rewards and assessing whether the innovation and its technology meet your business model and your business values. Make certain it delivers exceptional value to your customers and that you have all the requirements we've discussed earlier, including commitment, sponsorship, and support in the organization.

Once you do, get it to market as fast as possible and ahead of the competition (you should be in good position to do this if your boxes are checked).—Speed rules the day.

Fast Forward should be part of every single thing you do in your business.

If you don't move forward fast, the resulting lethargy becomes a self-fulfilling ticket for failure. I was involved with a $400 million company that was an expert at going over and over an idea forever, and it seemed their strategy was to think about the technology until it finally became irrelevant. Why? Because at that point they had mitigated the risk that the technology would fail. In other words—try nothing, fail nothing.

Forge

Once you move your technology forward, it's time to *Forge*. Forge is the investigation and decision about product or technology feasibility—that is, "Can we make it?" or "Can we do it?" "Can we do it profitably?"

Forge can happen in a variety of stages depending on the product, service, or type of technology. Figure 8.5 maps out where we are in the process.

We can go from Forward to Forge to Forget at any stage of the process, in fact, at all stages, there is an exit ramp for projects or ideas

Figure 8.5   The "Forge" Stage

that don't make sense. As individuals and organizations, we need to be free to exit when necessary, and to cut the "fibers of emotional connection" to an idea. No matter who or what department is involved, we must feel comfortable forgetting technology that doesn't make sense.

Every organization has a measure of profitability—that's obvious. The message here is: "Check it out quickly." Don't spend years trying to develop elaborate spreadsheets based on data points that are wild guesses. As I'll discuss later, you should keep it to four testable scenarios maximum.

At the Forge stage we set out not only to establish the manufacturability and deliverability of the product, but also the sale-ability and protect-ability of the product or idea. As the innovation enters the Forge stage, groups adjacent to the main development team should begin to forge the sales conduit and the intellectual property protection necessary to bring it to market. Can the product be delivered to customers with the exceptional value we think it should have? Can we gain from protecting the innovation to create a monopoly and/or licensing revenue streams down the road?

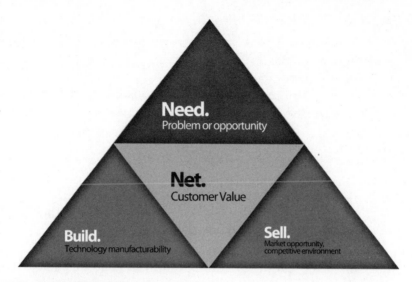

Figure 8.6   The Webb Triangle

As you enter into the Forge phase, *now* you actually start the process of evaluation. However, you do start that process with the idea that you're going to create this product or technology.

The Webb Triangle

That brings us back to a tool, briefly introduced in Chapter 6, called the Webb Triangle. The Webb Triangle is another one of those simple, yet powerful tools that focuses and drives agile decision making about an idea, a technology, or an innovation in a nonlinear, not risk-centered way. I've invented dozens of products with a tremendously high success rate, and for the past 20 years, I've used this simple formula.

The Top of the Triangle: Need

At the top of the triangle is the need, problem or, opportunity, and it asks a few important questions:

- Is there a need?
- Is the need widely recognized?
- Is the need large enough to constitute a viable market for a business?

Or,

- Is there a problem?
- Is the problem widely recognized?
- Is the problem fix large enough to constitute a viable market for a business?

Or, lastly,

- Is there an opportunity?
- Is the opportunity widely recognized?
- Is the opportunity large enough to constitute a viable market for a business?

Lots of other questions can be addressed at this stage. For instance: Can we take an existing technology and possibly cross-pollinate it into another market segment? Can other existing technologies perhaps connect to some of our other products and services?

The Left-Hand Corner: Build

The *Build* set of drivers can be found at the lower left-hand corner of the Webb Triangle. Perpetual-motion-fueled machines would be a tremendous breakthrough and energy saver; the problem is you can't make one. You can't make one because perpetual motion defies the laws of physics.

In the Build section, you ask yourself if you can actually *deliver* on the need, problem, or opportunity. Can you create, obtain, or manufacture the subject product or technology? Can you do it in such a way as to be profitable and in line with the needs and value implied by the top tiers of the net customer value strata (from Chapter 6)?

The Lower Right: Sell

Now we move into the lower right-hand corner, the *Sell* corner, which looks ahead to such questions as: Is there a market? What is the market? How do you define it? Position the product? Promote it? Sell it? What are all of the environmental factors that will determine the success of the innovation? And so forth.

Now, for many, this model is over-simplistic. But since we know our product platform extremely well, and we've already pre-filtered the idea or technology, we know that we can move it forward through more simple, nonlinear evaluation tools.

The Center: Net Customer Value

There's one final, important note. In the center of the Webb Triangle is the customer. This is where we ask ourselves the final and most important question: Can we provide net customer value? If the innovation meets the requirements, and can be manufactured and marketed with reasonable effort and cost, it forges ahead. You continue the process to get information with which to design and validate the product.

Value Layerization

Also, during the Forge process, don't assume that the product is fixed in concrete at that point. You should always look for ways to improve the innovation, even at this stage. The new ideas and refinements that can come forward at this stage always amaze me. It also amazes me how many businesses fail because they develop a technology that was "not done cooking," that is, they locked into a specific delivery and failed to evolve it during or after the initial Forge stage.

I believe a final stage of *Value Layerization* should be hard-wired into your innovation process. Of course, you should make sure the innovation met the original design requirements, but you should also look for ways the innovation can deliver additional value prior to its launch—for instance, product or product line extensions, new channels, licensing to other companies, or altogether new uses.

One way many companies do this is to use Project X teams to look at internal innovations as a competitor to see what they would do better before a new product or technology is launched.

Packaging for Launch

Another tool we talk about is what we call *Packaging for Launch*. So many—too many—technologies are launched prior to being finished. Once again, the Apple Newton—from a company proud of its innovations overall—is a great example. They identified a great need. They found some real problems to solve. Without question, they identified there was a market composed of people looking for a personal digital assistant.

The problem was they weren't able to create a technology on the Build side that met the needs of the hungry market at a reasonable cost. As a result, the technology failed.

So in this last packaging stage, you need to determine that the product has *totally* met its design requirement, not just in terms of functionality, but more important, in terms of its ability to deliver net customer value *at a high level*. Is the product *exceptional* or close to it?

Now at this point, the product may need additional layers of innovation. We may need to add additional functions in terms of value to really make it—and us—a superstar. That's what this phase of the developmental process allows us to do.

RealOpen and the Four-in-One Garlic Press

I would like to tell you more about how I used the RealOpen innovation management system in my own business. In addition to being a management consultant working for some of the best corporations and universities in the world, I also own several businesses. A few years back I started a gourmet kitchen gadget company. I started it because I wanted to combine my expertise in handheld surgical ergonomics with my love for gourmet food.

The company I started is called Van Vacter. Van Vacter was named after my grandfather, a Dutch immigrant. The idea was to create unique and special tools that allowed for improved ergonomics and to provide better ways to achieve food preparation.

In the process of developing the company, the first thing we had to do was follow the RealOpen system and create an innovation platform. Before you can begin to innovate, you have to know what it is you want to invent. So we began by looking at the market and the competitive environment, and we settled on a platform in the general area we wanted to target. Once we did that, we set up an online innovation submission portal allowing people to submit their innovations.

We then marketed the innovation portal to the micro-crowds, getting access to the experts on kitchen gadgets. We connected to gourmet chefs and other experts in the food preparation environment. Once we had a well-defined platform and an online innovation submission portal, we began the process of working on our own internal methods, using, first and foremost, Innovation Safaris. We spent a great deal of time with gourmet chefs in Napa, California. We traveled around the country to look at regional foods to identify emerging food trends. Once we'd completed our Innovation Safaris, we went back to our office and conducted "ideation" sessions. As a result, we were able to create some amazing products. Meanwhile, our innovation submission portal, which was providing pre-filtered innovations, was filling up quickly—so fast, in fact, we had to take it offline because we were getting so many great ideas we simply didn't have the resources to develop them all.

Once we began to assimilate our external ideas coupled with our internal ideas, we used our fast-track methodology to move them forward or to forget them quickly. Once we passed the ideas through we were able to quickly develop the technologies. In fact, as a result of using Project Xs, in which we looked at competitive technologies, we actually created a company called "Hanz" for the purpose of being our phantom competitor. We developed competitive technologies, some of which, not surprisingly, ended up becoming part of our product portfolio.

As a result of using these various techniques—Project Xs, Frontline Innovation, Innovation Safaris, and all of the other tools within our Find program, we were able to access hundreds of ideas and technologies in unbelievably short periods of time. Because we committed to fast-track methodologies through our Forward or Forget program, we were able to move those with lightening speed. In fact, our largest competitor was a $500 million a year company with dozens of people in its R&D department. On our side, there were only two of us—myself and an industrial designer—and in that period of time we launched a new successful product every month for the first 12 months. During that same time, our large competitor had only launched two products. So the system was working and working with mathematical certainty.

From the beginning of the process all the way to commercialization, we referenced the Webb Triangle to make sure there was a genuinely recognizable need, a problem or an opportunity we could take advantage of. We always looked at manufacturability in context of price sensitivity. And of course we had the tools in place to keep us connected to the market environment and competitive scenarios, so as we were moving products forward we were getting real time information to help us make intelligent decisions.

But even as we would move toward commercialization, we constantly tried to identify ways to layer new value. Often products were forgotten. We gave them a decent burial, grieved for a few hours, and then realized forgetting technologies at any stage of the process was fundamentally necessary in order to have the necessary resources to develop market-leading technologies.

Even as we moved towards commercialization, we also looked at ways to layer the value for launch. Our most popular creation, for example—the 4-in-1 garlic press—was a tremendous product. For years, people had been trying to create a multifunctional garlic press. We did it! Not for just two functions, but for four. However, as we began to test it with our customers before launching

(continued)

Figure 8.7   Van Vacter Four-in-One Garlic Press

it, we identified that it was hard to clean. So we immediately designed a cap that also served as a cleaner. Again, this resulted in a product that has been so popular it is sold by more than 800 retailers worldwide and is constantly in demand.

So—the process works. We didn't use all the tools, and in the beginning, we used a different set of tools. As the company began to mature, we relied more on hard-wiring the systems to our frontline people and creating ongoing ideation sessions and pasteboard programs. You'll find when you use the RealOpen system, you'll customize it in a way where it becomes truly part of your organization. You'll also find you constantly rearrange it, just like the icons on your desktop, to optimize usage.

Over the past year, we've begun to use other tools in the RealOpen framework that we have used with our other clients over the years. We're finding now that we're looking to float innovations online, and we have set up an innovation "digital command center" that allows us to manage our online reputation and access new ideas and float ideas to potential buyers before we put them to development. These topics are covered under "Digital Innovation" in the next chapter.

So as you can see, RealOpen is a system that is custom designed for your organization. Whether you are financial services company, a medical device company, a software supplier, a university, or a research organization, the bottom line is companies and their organizations are so unique they must have a configurable system that allows for a prescribed approach towards accessing, filtering, evaluating, developing, and commercializing ideas. I was excited to see that RealOpen worked as well on my kitchen gadget company as it has for micro-silicone implants and Class III medical devices.

Innovation Scenario Tactics

Innovation scenario planning is one of the most useful tools in to-day's innovation management. Not only is it exciting, but it is also fundamentally important that all organizations have an innovation scenario tactic. Innovation scenario tactics are especially important today because markets are moving more quickly than ever and prod-uct life cycles are shorter than ever before.

When things are moving very dynamically, you need to create multiple innovation scenarios so you're always moving toward the target or market goal, regardless of internal or external events.

In hockey, if a puck was always in the same place or on one trajec-tory towards the goal, the angle of your attacking hockey stick would always be the same. The problem is the puck is *never* still; today the puck is moving faster than ever before. There are technology drivers, that is, emerging technologies, and a lot of cross-pollinations of tech-nologies between one market and another that can have dramatic effects on the movement of a market (like digital cameras and cell phones, for example). The changes in needs, problems, technolo-gies, and opportunities all drive the trajectory of innovation. Pricing and other customer drivers will also move the puck quickly. Also weighing in are intellectual property drivers, regulatory drivers, and other market drivers unique to a product or industry.

If the hockey puck is moving so rapidly, how then do organiza-tions plan for the changes within their business? In the innovation scenario tactics, we recommend that you always create four possible scenarios. We break them down, simply, as Most Likely, Likely, Possi-ble and Unlikely. Those become Plan A, Plan B, Plan C, and Plan D respectively (see Figure 8.8).

The idea here is to examine two columns. One column would be known factors such as pricing trends, known technology changes, changes in consumer buying habits, competitive and emerging com-petitive factors, and so on. We look at all things known today and put them in a list in the first column. Then, next to that list, we add *unknown* factors, such as regulatory changes or other environmental changes.

Typically these lists contain from 30 to 50 items on both sides of the ledger. From these lists, and taking the listed items in combi-nation, you build your four scenarios. Under "Most Likely" you list both your knowns and your most likely unknowns. This pattern is

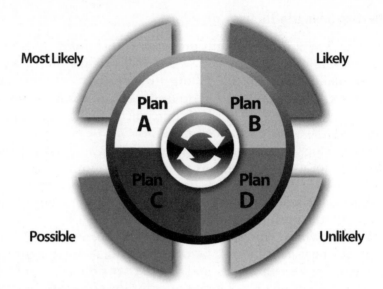

Figure 8.8   Innovation Scenario Tactics

continued through Most and Least Likely scenarios, that is, Plan A through Plan D.

A Medical Device Industry Example

Here I'll share some of the highlights of a rather elaborate scenario sketch developed for the medical products industry, and show how it might influence a company's innovation platform and ultimately drive its innovation. The content is used with permission from a study titled "Future of Medical Devices: U.S. Trends and Scenarios Through 2015," co-authored by Jim Austin, Director of Life Sciences, Decision Strategies International; Terry Fadem, Managing Director, Corporate Alliances, University of Pennsylvania School of Medicine; and Paul J. H. Schoemaker, Research Director, Mack Center for Technological Innovation, The Wharton School of Business.

This is an industry-wide study, but it serves as an example of the kinds of externally-driven scenarios you might develop for your own innovation and product platform. Each of these scenarios would in turn be used to create an adjusted version of your own product platform. There are four scenarios.

Scenario A: Necessity is Thy Mother   Driven by economic downturns and the ever-rising cost of health care, the federal government establishes universal data standards and open, medical device data bases on patient outcomes (with appropriate privacy requirements). Health care data generally flows freely, with appropriate patient controls, from devices to doctors and across networks.

Highlights

- New opportunities for informatics technology companies.
- Nascent efforts with disease prevention supported by new business models and data availability.
- Greater regulatory scrutiny of medical devices, with more emphasis on managing data and cost.
- Benefits of new products, combined with universal data standards across the system.
- CMS negotiates the rates for all drugs and medical devices (replacing private initiatives).
- Patients absorb more of the costs of health care and move towards self-care (education, online information, etc.).
- Driven by economic constraints, the general level of reimbursement for new medical devices and health care is reduced.

Scenario B: Tough Love   In this scenario, the benefits of medical devices are well recognized and their long-term cost-effectiveness proven in a series of large population, well-controlled studies. However, the federal government has imposed greater regulatory and data ownership/access constraints on private manufacturers in the effort to drive system efficiencies and business transparency.

Highlights

- Positive reimbursement rates, especially for new approaches such as disease management, lead to a growth in procedures across all segments.
- Devices increasingly are "neural networks"—not only feeding back medical and ongoing performance data, but also linking to sophisticated patient and cost-benefit outcome databases.
- As the number of procedures performed increases, some question the cost/benefit of more aggressive cases (orthopedic implants for 90-year-olds, etc.) supporting increased

patient/provider emphasis on prevention rather than ever-more-sophisticated interventions.

- With heightened competition, many suppliers face declining margins in this world of "resource plenty."
- Universities create multi-specialty disciplines combining informatics, biologics, material science, and engineering.

Scenario C: Stagnation   Low reimbursement levels, technology snafus, and a lack of data standards slow the growth of the medical device sector.

Highlights

- Health care cost containment, increasingly by rationing care and raising patient contributions, of primary concern to most stakeholders.
- Patient privacy a major issue for patients, effectively halting national database and registry initiatives.
- The potential of medical devices limited due to information sharing constraints and lengthening new product development cycles.
- Patients bear an increasing proportion of medical device costs, yet struggle to obtain information on the full range of options open to them.
- Investment in R&D declines from both private and public funding sources.

Less skilled workers are more typical of those who must install, calibrate, and manage *ex vivo* medical devices (such as diagnostic equipment and IV pumps) in patient care settings.

Scenario D: Isolated Islands   While reimbursement is readily available and innovation continues, medical devices have not fulfilled their potential in reducing health care system costs or improving life quality—in large part because of public data management and informatics limitations. Devices stand alone and do not benefit from being linked to broader networks.

Highlights

- Reimbursement for medical devices is strong, supported by a growing economy and the aging of America.

- National or regional data management standards and protocols are lacking.
- Privacy concerns and increasing data security problems have further delayed data sharing networks' role in medical device therapy or product selection decision.
- With lack of data sharing networks and increased privacy legislation, devices focus more on disease-specific treatments than on broader disease prevention.
- Medical device companies are growing, but within defined niches and established competencies.

The scenarios are summarized as shown in Table 8.1.

From each scenario, an innovation, or product platform is developed, with an assessment of the likelihood of the scenario. As an innovation organization, you would innovate to the most likely scenario, watching for external environment changes even daily that might change the likelihood of each scenario.

Companies that have not deployed the innovation scenario planning tactic in the past aren't usually familiar with the idea that the market is speeding up with shortening life cycles. Yet, one of the biggest problems we see is the time it takes most organizations to adopt innovation scenario tactics. I see innovation scenario planning as an idea that truly separates the mature, successful innovation organization from one with years of growth still left.

Table 8.1   Scenario Blueprint Summary—Key Uncertainties and How They Vary by Scenario

	Scenario A	Scenario B	Scenario C	Scenario D
Level of Reimbursement	Tightened	Expanded	Tightened	Expanded
Legal/Regulatory Environment	Restricted	Restricted	Unfettered	Unfettered
Role of Consumer in Selection	Large Role	Moderate Role	Moderate Role	Minimal
Level of Private Investment	Medium	High	Low	Medium
Availability and Utilization of Information	High	High	Low	Low

Source: "Future of Medical Devices: U.S. Trends and Scenarios Through 2015," by Austin et al.

Chapter Takeaways

- RealOpen is a framework for managing innovation with special emphasis on finding ideas and technologies from the inside and outside worlds, and filtering them quickly and effectively. The RealOpen process is not one-size-fits-all but rather a framework, which creates specific processes that should be developed for your organization.
- The Find step makes use of seven different processes to diversify and speed up your ideation processes.
- The Filter step makes use of a predefined innovation platform, a clearly stated vision of your business, customers, and products, both present and future.
- Innovation-platform-based filtration is preferable to case-by-case "business case" innovation evaluation.
- Forward or Forget stages help to move the process along quickly.
- The Forge process takes the product or idea into its first real stages of development; using the Webb Triangle to fine-tune the realism and viability of the project.
- Innovation scenario planning is a way to keep a few different irons in the innovation fire, and to be flexible according to the most recent "where the puck is going" market and technology changes.

CHAPTER

9

Creating a (Digital) Innovation Culture

As I pointed out in Chapter 5, the term *culture* is difficult to define, almost as elusive as the term *love*. Regarding love, we all know we need it, crave it, and cherish it, and we all know it gives necessary oxygen to our inner beings to help us effectively carry out other aspects of our lives. Yet we don't always know how to give it or receive it. What we think is the right kind of love may at times be dysfunctional or even destructive.

And so it is with organizational culture. So it is with the support and "oxygen" that the right kind of culture gives to an organization so that it can function, and most particularly, innovate. Yet, many organizations ignore culture, or implement cultures that are dysfunctional or even destructive to the execution of good innovation. This chapter's aim is to give some pointers on how to build a successful cultural base to support innovation. It also examines how to best incorporate what we're now coming to call "digital innovation" as a tool to sustain not only the innovation process, but also the innovation culture.

Recall our model in Chapter 5, *The Anatomy of an Innovation Superstar*. In that chapter we defined three essential parts of the anatomy of the body of innovation: Customer, Process, and Culture. The Customer part was analogous to the head—containing the information and brains to decide what needs to be done in the interest of the customer. Process was compared to the torso, containing the vital parts necessary to keep the organization alive and functioning, while Culture was the legs, supporting the rest of the being and propelling it forward.

Culture, we said then, was how the organization thinks, feels, and works as a whole to achieve excellence. It is about pride, passion, and environment. It's about whether the company provides a functional environment for employees to succeed, and thus, for innovation to succeed. It's about having the right empathy and focus on customers that allow their input and needs to get into the company brains in the first place; an organization that doesn't listen to customers won't make the right customer-focused decisions, and will thus be doomed to fail.

You may have recognized that love requires the same essential ingredients: a functional environment, a passion to think, feel, and work together, a consistent empathy, and, above all, the right focus. So consider this a chapter about love, only in this case, it is a love of customers that translates into a loving organizational culture that allows other great things to happen.

Focus Upon Others, Not Thyself

The starting place for both love and culture is focus. Without the right focus, all other efforts will be misdirected or misguided, and the best intentions will miss the mark or go unnoticed. As a result, I believe the organization must start out focused in the right place, and as I also introduced in Chapter 5, that place is *external* focus.

External focus for an individual is simply focus on the other, not on oneself, and focus on listening with unfettered attention to the other person, with empathy, compassion, validation, and a top-to-bottom satisfaction of that other person's needs. In an organization, external focus is an unfettered focus on the customer, which *also* entails listening, empathy, and especially a top-to-bottom satisfaction of the customer's needs.

Beyond satisfying these needs, in culture as in love, delivering above expectations brings delight and substantial reward to both parties involved. In the case of both individuals and organizations, love and culture bring about the right decisions—in the former case personal and the latter business decisions—to bring mutual reward and beyond that, the visceral connections and loyalty that, if managed properly, can last forever.

External Focus Is a Lack of Internal Focus

We hear this question all the time: What is external focus and how do we, as an organization, get there?

It's a great question. If you give a PowerPoint presentation in a conference room about external focus, or wander up and down the organizational halls whispering "external focus" in the ears of the occupant of each and every cube, will external focus happen? Maybe, for a while. But will it be sustained? Will there be a permanent commitment to external focus? Will it be ingrained and behavioral?

Probably only until the next set of forms arrives that accomplish some mundane organizational task, or worse, that control the risk of the project or process you're working on.

What's Wrong with Innovation: Internal Focus . . .

Further, it turns out that almost everything we find wrong with innovation in an organization has, at its roots, internal focus as a cause. Excessive risk management, delayed or slow launches (or no launches at all), inadequate resources, solutions that don't meet or exceed customer needs and thus fail in the marketplace—all can be attributed to internal focus.

So the Solution . . .

The solution to creating external focus is simply to eliminate internal focus. Leadership that avoids internal focus creates external focus. Employees are more likely to become devotees and enthusiasts, which self-perpetuates into more external focus, and you have an oxygen-giving positive spiral of good feeling and external focus that satisfies customer and organizational needs alike.

Again, the solution is pretty simple but bears repeating: To achieve external focus, get rid of internal focus.

The Innovation Focus Model

One diagram and model I like to pin on the wall to keep myself reminded of what I just talked about is what I call the Innovation Focus Model. See Figure 9.1.

In the model you can plainly see two wheels, one of internal, one of external focus. The internal focus wheel features such components as Process Focus, Risk Focus, Blame Focus, Tech-Centered Focus, and a Reactive Mindset; none of these features of internal focus should be of any surprise to readers who have followed along. And the negative effects of these features on innovation, similarly, do not need to be explained again.

Innovation
Socialists

Innovation
Capitalists

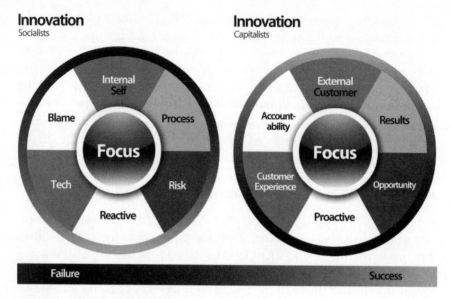

Figure 9.1   The Innovation Focus Model

On the external focus wheel one sees Results in lieu of Process, Opportunity in lieu of Risk, Accountability in lieu of Blame, Customer-Centered in lieu of Tech-Centered, and most of all, Proactive in lieu of Reactive. As a manager and leader, you must try to keep your organization on the right side of this chart.

Socialists and Capitalists

At the top of the chart there are the terms *Innovation Socialists* and *Innovation Capitalists*, which correspond to internal and external focus, respectively. Recall from Chapter 2 that I named No. 9 of Nick's 10 Reasons Why Innovations Fail: Innovation Socialism. Here I describe the fact that many organizations, especially in the not-for-profit space do not reward their innovators for the successful commercialization of their technology; the technology becomes an end in itself. Activity, not results. Many of these innovators aren't punished—or even measured—for—their lack of results. The end result is often—nothing.

My point here is that internal focus can lead to this end. Start and kill ten innovations because of adversity to risk, and the internally focused organization still feels like it accomplished something, because it did start the innovations, and because it did go through the motion of killing them. But these false starts do nothing for the customers; they do nothing for the external world. So while the process was executed and it worked, it ultimately sucked resources away from things the outside world, and thus the organization, really needed.

So I refer to external focus as Innovation Capitalism. In Innovation Capitalism, innovation must start, grow, and launch based upon its own merits. That means it must be externally focused and externally driven to the point of generating the return on investment and income necessary to sustain it. To do that, in a capitalist society, it must offer something *better than the competition* and *better than before*. To do *that*, coming full circle, it must be sufficiently focused on the outside world to know what better than the competition and better than before *really is*.

It's so simple: A culture existing on the right side of the model is aligned for success; one on the left side will eventually collapse under its own weight.

Revisiting the Pyramids

While reflecting on external focus, I'd also recommend revisiting the Innovation Pyramid or Inverted Pyramid model first offered in Chapter 7. This model shows a traditional framework where lower levels of the organization are the ones in contact with customers, and thus these employees can see, hear, and feel customer acceptance and delight—or the lack thereof—with a company's products.

The external focus model requires the pyramid to be turned upside-down; so that the top layers of the organization are closer to, or even in contact with, the customer. This contact can take many forms, as described in earlier chapters, everything from watching listening posts and electronic customer feedback to full-blown innovation safaris. The point is that an organization running in the traditional pyramid is more likely to stay internally focused because leaders and key decision makers are insulated from the customer—and thus from the outside world.

Turning the pyramid upside down is thus an important tactic towards achieving enduring external focus.

Focus, Leadership, Communication, and Eating Your Own Cooking

External focus may be the proper cultural foundation for doing innovation right, but it isn't the entire story. An organization that is externally focused, but still dysfunctional, still won't get there.

The best way I can expand on external focus is to summarize a lengthy interview I had with Art Beckman, Director of the Innovation Program Office for Hewlett-Packard's Software and Solutions operations. This session went into considerable detail about HP's innovation culture, methods, and processes. One of the simpler, but more profound takeaways from the discussion was their definition of "innovation culture." "Innovation culture" in HP's words is, "a combination of leadership and communication."

Champions of Innovation

For HP, leadership is all about the fundamentals of leadership that I will describe later in this chapter. But it's also about having a designated innovation champion within the organization to foster the right focus and climate for change, whether acting as an internal cheerleader, mentor, consultant, or "process engineer" for the various processes and tools an innovating organization might put into place.

HP has created the Innovation Program Office within the Software & Solutions organization, which has a largely unconstrained charter for making innovation happen throughout the organization. Some companies actually have a VP of Innovation. However it might be set up, the idea is that innovation gets the right kind of dedicated, flexible leadership; the position also validates the organization's commitment to innovation in the first place.

The Garage

The small Palo Alto garage where HP was born in 1939 has become an enduring symbol of grassroots innovation ever since. HP now not only uses the "Garage" metaphor as a historical reference to its innovative roots, but also as a name for the Software and Solutions business innovation portal bearing that name.

The Garage, based on a Brightidea platform, is set up as a source of internal information, collaboration, and feedback to guide innovation and its innovators. In HP's words, the garage ". . . was opened to systematically gather, organize and allow collaboration on ideas to improve our business . . . it manages open idea submission, brainstorming, collaboration and "idea campaigns." The idea campaign is billed and designed as an intense two-week campaign to tease any and all ideas about a topic out of the organization. The Garage is a part of a framework that has been established called the Elements of Innovation Success from HP Software & Solutions. These elements and The Garage tool can be applied by each organization in a manner best suited to match the individual business unit's innovation objectives.

The Garage serves as the "daily news" of what's going on with innovation in the organization, product launches, competitive products and so forth. It's also a path for innovators, non-innovators and management in the organization to share and communicate with each other in a way that doesn't consume much time bandwidth and organizational fuel. The Garage has worked wonders for keeping innovators and their innovations on track in the rather large and complex organization known as HP.

You Cook It, You Eat It

On of HP's strongest cultural strategies for success may have been somewhat inadvertent. Under CIO Randy Moss, the company embarked on a massive data center and software consolidation project in the mid-2000s. The goal was to save billions (yes, with a "b") by consolidating some 85 data centers at individual divisions in the United States into three data centers, and making similar cuts in the number of software programs that were run at these locations.

Now quite clearly HP is a technology company that sells just this sort of enterprise IT solutions to its customers, so why shouldn't their customers benefit from the same tactics HP was employing internally? The Moss initiative required many of the same software and solution innovations as HP's customers needed. The fact that HP was using and benefiting from the same technologies it was selling to customers was a big plus for the organization's innovators—much as the opportunity to share the beer experience being created for customers is a motivator for the employees of Sierra Nevada brewery.

Before and After

You can almost tell a good innovation culture from the moment you walk in the door. There's a certain buzz in the building. There are examples of products in the lobby, often with pictures of customers using them. The products—or videos or facsimiles thereof—are displayed with such pride, as though the CEO of the company were giving a one-on-one presentation. There are written customer testimonials, industry awards for excellence on the walls. People look relaxed, content, even casual, but they're obviously working hard. They look, feel, act, and decorate their offices like entrepreneurs. The environment is conducive to work, but it is also relaxing; tastefully decorated with a warm atmosphere, plenty of open space, exercise facilities, and an attractive cafeteria. It is focused on employees, and more importantly, externally focused to the hilt.

In the words of Beckman at HP, many companies that "get it" like today's HP, made the switch from a "before" that could be described as "pure innovation," not customer focused, risk adverse, top-down, internally focused. The "after," with the right culture can be described as "more organic," where risk is not punished, where as a result there are earlier starts, better starts, and earlier failures. The innovations are more grassroots, collaborative, open, co-created, and more "customer focused."

Success Referencing

Companies with strong innovation cultures also tend to *success reference* rather than *failure reference*. You can see it in the language the company uses in meetings. You can even see it in the body language.

Success referencing occurs when a company talks about its successes and measures new products or ideas against its successes. A new idea is assumed successful until proven otherwise, and there's an almost childishly excited hope that the new idea will have the same success as the old one. The idea gets a champion, gets sponsorship, and gets resources almost right off the bat. People buzz about what the new product and its adjuncts could really become.

Failure referencing, on the other hand, occurs when a company always looks back on failures and uses those as a model for what might happen to a new idea. "We can't do this because . . ." It becomes the mind-set I introduced in Chapter 3, in which everyone in the room plays "find the flaw" with the idea, because that's the way they can look smart and avoid personal risk at the same time. It's also easier. It is easier to "failure reference" than to "success reference."

So again, if a company holds up its own innovations with pride, and tries to fit new ideas into something resembling a success, the culture is right. If a company lives constantly in a world of fear, risk, and doubt about a new idea, especially based on some past experience, the innovation culture needs some work.

So, to develop the innovation culture—think positive—and reference success.

Chuck the Techies and Bean Counters

Well—not altogether—techies can bring brilliance in the design and adoption of a new idea, while the bean counters can supply invaluable wisdom about its viability as a stand-alone product. But when an organization's innovation centers on tech ("techno-centric") or on finances ("finance-centric") you'll have problems. Few customers have ever been satisfied, even fewer delighted, by cost cutting measures. And technology gimmicks present for their own interest and because they're cool rather than because they're solving a customer issue will also lead to problems. If your culture is techno-centric or finance-centric, long story short, it needs to become customer-centric.

Culture and the Innovation Superstar

In Chapter 5, I introduced four characteristics and checklists that define a company's cultural excellence: collective passion, craftsmanship, "fear no more," and "the right team." Each of these attributes flies a bit below the radar of the overall external focus mantra, but they're all part of the equation.

We defined each of these areas in Chapter 5. The question is: "How do you get there?"

Achieving Collective Passion

In assessing collective passion, the first question is whether or not a company really embraces or internalizes the importance of successful innovation as part of its long-term success. If it doesn't—that's big trouble. The answer, of course, is a long-term view of success, and a thorough understanding of the company's customers and what value they might want over the long term. To get to these places, a company must adopt—you guessed it—an external focus.

Aside from that, passion is really all about whether the company and its employees truly have passion for their customers and their products. Do they understand the customers? Empathize with them? Feel good when the customer feels good and feel bad when a customer feels bad? Really good, smart, people with balanced personalities and good training do these things. These concepts are hard to teach, but again, it's about putting oneself in other people's shoes. It's about external focus.

To get there, it's important to hire the right kind of people in the first place—positive, enthusiastic, energetic, and so forth. But it is also important to stress the importance of the customer, and provide a reward and internal social system that fosters these feelings. Let people talk openly about customer successes and failures. Allow them the time to find out for themselves whether customers are having good or bad experiences. Send them on innovation safaris. Make each employee feel like every customer is both their friend and their responsibility. Reward them for doing so.

And finally, do away with the dry, dull, corporate-speak in visions, mission statements, and strategic and tactical plans. Make them fun and active.

It's hard to instill passion in a person, but if you create the right environment for passion, whether with corporate culture or personal love, great things can happen.

Achieving Craftsmanship

Craftsmanship is like passion, but it is more specifically directed at the product, not so much at the customer. The idea is to produce products that not only meet but exceed customer expectations or, more colloquially, to make the customer say "wow."

How you get there, of course, starts with external focus. A company or an individual within the company will craft the best products or customer experiences when he or she can feel that experience personally. When a customer says "thank you" or gives pleasant compliments about the product or service, you're there; when they come back (loyalty) or refer others (evangelism), it's even better.

A culture of craftsmanship comes about when management has a get-it-right mentality—and gives employees the time, resources, and recognition to do it. When employees are treated like entrepreneurs, and they feel that the company is their own personal small business, they will naturally deliver a higher standard of quality and take more responsibility for their products. So giving employees the time and empowering them to get things right goes a long way towards craftsmanship.

Further, in my opinion, one of the best ways to instill the idea of craftsmanship and entrepreneurship in an organization is to give employees an ownership share or a share of the profits. In large companies, of course, this can mean shares of stock or options or profit-sharing bonuses. In smaller companies it can also mean bonuses and shares of profits, and it may also be ownership depending on how the business is set up. Either way, when employees have skin in the game, better results almost always follow, especially in the area of craftsmanship but also in the area of passion just described.

Achieving "Fear No More"

The fear factor has been addressed so many times in this book that to say much about it here would be repetitive. Simply, you must create a culture where employees can take smart risks. They can start—and end—projects when it makes sense. It's a culture where failure is rewarded and sometimes even celebrated as a necessary step to success.

Psychologists sometimes group people into two types: people who live in fear and dispense fear all their lives, and people who live in love and dispense love all their lives. We all know the types. And to get the right culture, management needs to do the latter (that love thing again). Positive reinforcement, and even delivering bad news with a soft touch and a "here's how things can work better next time" can help. Managing fear properly in an organization is a lot like providing a positive environment for children, where they can make mistakes, learn from them, and not feel like they have to lie or work around you to get what they want.

Also—recall the discussion in the Chapter 3 sidebar, *Seeing the . . . Benefits of Failure?* A healthy organizational culture recognizes the new health that failure—tried, recognized, and learned from—can bring to an organization. Such an organization has a smart-risk culture. Remember, a tree, pruned of its dead branches, comes back healthier for the experience. Have a failure? Take the team out for drinks, talk about it, and celebrate it.

Getting the Team Right

Some businesses may be small enough to carry on as one-man bands, but it's not likely to be the case for long, especially if a business is destined for success.

So I say that successful innovation is highly dependent on having a good team, and the right team, in place, with the right mind-set. The right team has energy, collective enthusiasm, and diverse skills and personalities. They are interesting people, and they interest each other. And they can all put their own interests and rewards aside to honor one common bond: the interests of the customer. They are externally focused individuals, other-centric individuals who interact easily with others and realize that in many situations, one-plus-one equals three.

Selecting such people isn't easy because these attributes are almost indiscernible on a resume. It's all about finding out what kinds of experiences these people have had with others, and with helping others—whether in a business or rock climbing on a 1,000-foot granite face. Signs of customer involvement and team involvement in the past should be observed. And of course, positive, forward verbal language (we, us instead of I, me, they, and them) and body language are all plusses.

A successful team culture shouldn't rely 100 percent on the individuals in the team. Of course, the environment created by management is extremely important. People need the chance to act and interact in positive team settings—at work and at play. Team oriented organizations have group functions, basketball courts, gyms, and organized after-work events. Teamwork is encouraged—and teams are built through team-building events. Team-oriented organizations consider these items as investments, not expenses, and they are all part of the investment an organization makes in keeping ahead of the game.

The Critical Role of Leadership

It wouldn't be surprising if, by now, you've concluded that a lot of what we're talking about with respect to culture is really a matter of leadership. External focus, passion, craftsmanship, creating a safe environment in which to innovate, and building the right team are all outcomes of smart, properly focused, compassionate, and effective leadership. Specifically, I like to see the following characteristics of leaders and the leadership style they deploy in the innovation space.

Keep—and share—the focus.
We've made much of the external focus that gives oxygen and direction to innovations. Leaders must get focused, stay focused, and show that focus to their teams.

Keep a long-term perspective.

This one's easy: A leader focused exclusively on short-term results will get just that—and a company that runs out of ideas fails in the marketplace longer term. Keep your eyes on the prize—the prize is almost always long term.

Really understand the customer.

Sounds simple, but how many leaders really understand their customers. All of their customers, not just the biggest ones? How many have taken the inverted pyramid to heart? How many take the time to really get into the heads and into the experiences of their customers? How many of them innovate by walking around? Do top management presentations, or company annual reports, reflect ideas taken straight from a customer's experience? Well, there are a few such leaders, like Howard Schultz of Starbucks, perhaps. But most rely on cumbersome market intelligence, or worse, try to dictate what the customer needs, as Microsoft does. These processes are seldom fast enough; they miss market opportunities—or worse, tick customers off.

Understand innovation—and innovators.

Leaders are simply more effective when they understand who and what they're leading. Do leaders in your organization really understand how innovation works? Or do they let their "innovation program leads," where they exist at all, do that for them? Leaders who have "been there, done that," or leaders who take the time to work in the kitchen, so to speak, will gain a better understanding of what's eventually served up.

Passion, patience, and perseverance.

Here I combine an assortment of leadership qualities into a single bullet—for a reason. Passion without perseverance doesn't work, and without at least some patience, the organization will go into stop-start mode and overreact to every new input. Leadership is really about a combination of good elements and traits without too much emphasis on one trait; otherwise it looks false or contrived.

Always think win-win.

Good leaders look for scenarios where everyone can win—the customer, the organization, the employees, the shareholders, the leaders themselves. Out the window go such examples as Merrill Lynch's John Thain, who had the gall to complain about not receiving a year-end bonus from his firm—which had lost billions. His argument that he prevented more severe losses rings hollow when considering the "win-win" principle. And GM CEO Rick Wagoner—as justified as he might have felt in taking the corporate jet to Washington, hat in hand, to ask for a bailout—clearly sent the wrong leadership message to everyone inside and out.

Be quick and patient.

These seemingly opposing traits actually do work well when worked together in the right way. I just mentioned General Motors CEO Rick Wagoner as an example of poor win-win thinking; now I'll call his number as an example of an executive who failed via paralysis, by leaving a failed business model of too many brands and too many dealers unchanged as the Detroit-based corporation hemorrhaged shares and cash. Something needed to be done faster, and the organization would have responded well (I believe) to an executive who really had a clear vision and took charge. At the same time, I have a big problem with impatience overdone—leaders who don't appreciate that good strategy may take some time to implement and that initiatives need room to develop and mature. Such leaders will create frustration and stress in those beneath them. I need to also stress that good leaders don't have to be an expert in the field to lead well. Take Andrew Carnegie as an example. His management team knew more about steel than he did, and honest admission of that fact not only motivated his team but reflected his own culture of respect.

Be truthful.

People—both customers and employees—are smarter than you think. They want honesty, and can generally see through the alternatives. Employees will respond better when a CEO admits a mistake or a hard truth about their organization or its innovations. Jeff Bezos, founder and CEO of Amazon.com has often been quoted as saying one of the key elements of being a good business leader is the capacity to tell hard truths, not run away from reality. And we all know what troubles can be caused when a company tries to hide its failures from its customers, as the recent Toyota debacle clearly illustrates.

Have fun.

Too often I see way too much seriousness and dryness in corporate environments. I believe the best work is fun work; that is, when I'm having fun, I put more energy and thought into my work; I think frankly most people do. You may not have always observed it, for when the straight-laced, dark-suited bunch get together for an off-site all forms of productivity melt away into silliness—but I think it's because these people don't have much fun during normal work life, so they overcompensate. Fun leadership begets happy employees and expansive thinking.

Even Mistakes Can Be Fun

The results at Southwest Airlines, which has led its industry in innovation and clearly in fun, speak for themselves. Even more specific examples arise, such as another in the airline industry. Recently, Eric Brinker, JetBlue Airways Corp.'s director of brand management and customer experience, admitted to making a little mistake. His team decided to replace a popular, but hardly healthy, mix of Doritos chips called Munchie Mix. The junk food fans revolted. It was soon clear; the customers wanted the junk food. Brinker realized they needed to reverse the action, but he didn't want his team to become dispirited. So he launched the "Save the Munchie Mix!" campaign that read: "Some pinhead in marketing decided to get rid of the Munchie Mix!" He invited employees to write poems and stories about why the snacks should return to JetBlue. He kept things fun, in hopes that the experience wouldn't cause employees to hesitate when making their own creative decisions.

That such a leadership style stimulates passion, craftsmanship, teamwork and a positive innovative spirit should by now be obvious.

Towards a Digital Culture: Digital Innovation

It may seem odd to incorporate a section on digital innovation in a chapter on culture. But the way I see it, not only has the world as a whole gone digital, but so has innovation. As in other aspects of business—marketing, operations, customer service—digital media will open the doors to effective innovation—, and close doors to those who choose to lag or ignore it altogether.

My point is that today there is a tremendous opportunity to speed customer input and innovation efficiency by using digital media as your platform. In fact, in our practice, we continue to recommend that clients set up what we call a *digital command center*. The idea of a digital command center is to be able to acquire great information quickly to aid in the innovation process, and to link innovation and other marketing and image activities in such a way as to improve your company's reputation and even to manage the brand.

We've developed a holistic Digital Innovation model that incorporates several digital platforms in and around innovation. Some of these activities, such as listening posts, have been discussed in earlier chapters, but I will examine them again here just as parts of a whole. Figure 9.2 illustrates the Digital Innovation Model:

Here are the key components of digital innovation:

Listening Posts

Listening Posts were introduced in Chapter 7 as a Carpet Time method to capture the buzz in the marketplace and media about

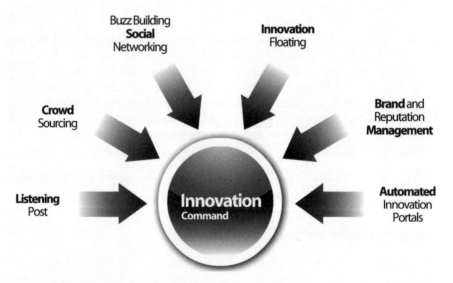

Figure 9.2   The Digital Innovation Model

your products and product concepts. Listening posts are easy to set up as keyword selectors for various media. For example, you can set up a listening post by entering a keyword—your product or your brand—on Yahoo! News or Google Alerts. It's a great way to quickly, and in real time, identify what people think about product concepts, service concepts, brands, and so on. You can also set up posts and questions on social networking sites and other new media to capture buzz and get more specific answers to questions you might pose. Listening posts are a great way to get real time feedback— *for free*.

Crowdsourcing

I've also said a fair amount about "crowdsourcing" already. Crowdsourcing is the process of sending out questions, or problems, to problem solvers, and providing rewards for people who deliver solutions to specific problems. Crowdsourcing can be done easily and cheaply on innovation portals like Brightidea's WebStorm. I've also advocated (as described in Chapter 8) managing the size of the crowd to get the kind of relevant feedback you want with micro-crowds.

Getting the Best from the Madness of Crowds

Early triumphs like the Linux operating system and the Wikipedia Web encyclopedias brought the ideas of crowdsourcing and open innovation forward as emerging disciplines, but they aren't magic idea factories. A look at recent cases and research suggests open innovation models work best when carefully designed for a particular task and when incentives are tailored to attract the most effective collaborators.

In a February, 2009, paper, "Harnessing Crowds: Mapping the Genome of Collective Intelligence," by Thomas Malone and Robert Laubacher, both of MIT Center for Collective Intelligence, and Chysanthos Dellarocas of the Massachusetts Institute of Technology, the authors call this phenomenon "collective intelligence." You may have heard it called crowdsourcing, wisdom of crowds, peer production, or wikinomics.

Over the past decade, the rise of the Internet has shaped a variety of forms of collective intelligence.

(continued)

Wikipedia, which has been developed with almost no centralized control, is probably the best example. It has thousands of volunteer contributors from around the world that produce articles of remarkably high quality—and the contributions are from people who aren't getting paid.

Threadless—a T-shirt company—asks site visitors to submit to a weekly design contest and then vote for favorites. The entries receiving the most votes get sent into production and designers get royalties and prizes. In doing this, the company utilizes the collective intelligence of more than 500,000 people to design and then select its T-shirts.

In the 2009 paper, it is suggested that there's much more to this ideal of crowd intelligence that just a "fuzzy collection of cool ideas." To unlock the true potential, managers need a deeper understanding of how these systems work and what motivates contributors to contribute. The MIT Center for Collective Intelligence gathered almost 250 examples of Web-enabled collective intelligence. They looked at who participated in the organization and among the crowd, and the motivation behind the participation. Sometimes it's money, but it can also be love or enjoyment, glory or a competitive drive. Money talks—for example, InnoCentive is a company that offers cash rewards, typically totaling in the five or even six figures, to researchers anywhere in the world who can solve challenging scientific problems such as how to synthesize a particular chemical compound.

They also looked at "what and how" behind the average project. This is the same as the project's mission or goal. It may be to create something new, it may be to decide or answer a question. Companies like Threadless both create and decide. The company found there is a difference between situations in which contributions are received or evaluated independently or in which there is a dependency between the contributions. Collaboration, which occurs when participants are working together to create something and must depend on one another to some extent, can be motivating. Wikipedia articles are a good example of independence but also collaboration—articles are created independently, but additions or editorial changes made within an article are strongly interdependent.

It was found that the crowd mentality was most useful in situations where "the resources and skills needed to perform an activity are distributed widely or reside in places that are not known in advance."

It was also found that, for this to work successfully, you must be able to divide an activity into pieces that can be performed by different members of the crowd. There should also be safety mechanisms in place that prevent people from sabotaging the system. In many cases the final decision is left to a specific internal group in charge of the crowd's task, even if some of the intermediate decisions are made by the crowd.

Not mentioned explicitly in this paper—but pertaining to culture—is the idea that to succeed, a company must have a culture open to outside ideas and a system for vetting and acting on them—as stated by Henry Chesbrough, one of the original champions of open innovation and the executive director of the Center for Open Innovation at the University of California, Berkeley, in a recent *New York Times* article.

These thoughts will help guide you through the maze of crowdsourcing and the cultural characteristics important to pull it off.

Buzz-Building

Digital innovation also includes what I call buzz-building. Now, historically, if you were a national company, building buzz historically could be an extremely expensive task. If you were a local company, it was slightly easier, because you had a local market and presence, and it was easier to "go viral" in such a market.

But now, with the Internet, you can build buzzes and get your products and services noticed by crafting intelligent blogs, posting on social networking sites, and the list goes on. In fact, most marketing departments and marketing agencies have created a digital media section, and in some companies, the marketing department has transitioned into a digital media department altogether. It's *that* important. So buzz-building through social networking and other digital marketing modalities is a powerful way to sell and to be successful in any market.

That buzz, of course, can generate feedback useful to the innovation process, and more generally, to the development and strengthening of your innovation culture.

Innovation Floating

Another concept that I call *innovation floating* is also very powerful. In fact, my company has created special and powerful web sites and photo-realistic imagery on technologies that didn't even exist to send images out to the digital universe. Such images can also be presented as film clips for YouTube or other media. Floating can occur not just for the consumer space but also for the distribution and channel space. The purpose is to get feedback on the product, and learn whether people would buy it if it was in the marketplace. We recently tested online a new product color for one of our clients that manufactures canes. We found that customers preferred black to chrome 90 percent of the time. This saved the company tens of thousands of dollars when compared to the non-digital approach. One issue with innovation floating is that unless it is done right, it can negatively impact future patent rights.

Prior to engaging in innovation floating, particularly with people outside of your company, it is highly recommended that you consult with a registered patent attorney to ensure that your innovation floating program does not invite problems down the road. According to patent attorney Robert Siminski, one major risk of poorly structured innovation floating programs involves "public disclosure" of an invention, which can serve as the basis for invalidating any resulting patents. Another risk is that if not properly controlled, "feedback" can find its way into patent applications, thereby calling into question who should own any resulting patents.

The bottom line is this; properly structured innovation floating programs can provide significant value while poorly structured programs can have serious ramifications.

Online Brand Reputation Management

Another important area that can be addressed digitally with ultimate benefits to the innovation process is brand reputation management. Reputation management is the observance of online feedback from your customers about your products and services—and the corrective action you might take to turn the buzz positive. It's extremely important—whether you're a corner liquor store or a multinational company, your reputation online *is* your reputation. Naturally your brand reputation, in turn, serves to nourish your innovation culture.

In fact, many in the corporate world today keep track of online feedback just like a credit score; when there's a "ding" against it, you act. New firms have been set up to specialize in online reputation management. Sometimes the information is erroneous or laden with bad assumptions, but still it's important to keep track. Online brand reputation management provides a significant proactive opportunity to really *build* a brand, by creating your own Internet footprint that speaks favorably about your company and its products and services. But also, don't forget what people are saying, feeling, and experiencing becomes input to your innovation process.

Automated Innovation Portals

Again, covered earlier, but really important, are the automated innovation portals that capture both external and internal ideas and feedback; they are the key to soliciting, acquiring, managing, and reviewing ideas on the open innovation front. The key is the automation, through the filtering and toggle questions I laid out in Chapter 8.

To reinforce the idea, remember that to make open innovation work through such portals, you need to clearly state your needs (remember the innovation platform?). Developing a platform not only gives the necessary structure to filter out unwanted ideas, but it also helps you as an organization to focus externally and to get your culture aligned to a set of products and product characteristics that really meet the needs of your customers. A well-defined wish list, to me, is a sign of a company with a well-developed innovation culture.

So, in summary, digital innovation is centric to almost all businesses today. You should be using listening posts, micro-crowd sources, buzz-building, innovation floating, brand reputation management, and most importantly, automated innovation portals.

Chapter Takeaways

- Above all else, external focus is the cultural lifeblood that keeps innovation flowing in the right direction. Without external focus, the remaining cultural elements of good innovation will be difficult if not impossible to achieve.
- Almost all things that go wrong with innovation can be attributed to internal focus. Therefore, creating the right culture for innovation really starts with getting rid of the manifestations of internal focus—excessive risk aversion and process focus, bureaucracy, blaming, reactivity, failure referencing.

- Beyond external and customer focus, effective innovation cultures exude passion, craftsmanship, safety for risk takers, and good teamwork.
- Today's effective innovation culture must also be digital in order to keep up with the pace of change and to properly augment customer knowledge and ultimately the innovation process itself.

CHAPTER

10

Dancing with the Innovation Superstars

At last, we approach the endgame, the final chapter, of *The Innovation Playbook*. It's time for a lighter chapter to digest and synthesize the plays of the playbook, to demonstrate how they are put into practice by selected Innovation Superstar companies, and to show how you yourself can put them into practice in your organization.

As such, Chapter 10 is divided into two parts. In the first part I will briefly summarize the excellence I've found in four Innovation Superstars, not as top-to-bottom case studies but as a brief overview of the outstanding elements of their innovation activities and thought processes—the takeaways—I think you can best put to use. Next, I will share with you some of the details for the Innovation Superstar certification program. This is platform created to help you continue to refine your knowledge of what it takes to achieve excellence in innovation, and attain a valuable credential.

Warming Up on the Dance Floor

Before I begin the process of introducing some of my Innovation Superstars, I'd like to point out something that you'll notice throughout this chapter: Innovation Superstars are completely alike, yet they are totally different. They are completely alike in that, through their daily focus on adding meaningful net value to their customers, they have created an organizational culture that drives innovation. They are completely different in that they use different technology platforms; they live in different markets, and serve different customers. They're often different in all ways, with the exception of their organizational culture.

From that culture, which is a byproduct of daily organizational focus, they are able to create systems and methods that are unique to them, that allow them to easily find, filter, evaluate, and quickly commercialize world-class innovations.

The point I'm trying to make is this: All Innovation Superstars have a culture of delivering value. They use innovation as the delivery mode. It doesn't matter whether you're a restaurant, a high-tech software company, a tool manufacturer, a physician, or anything in between, developing a daily focus that is centered on delivering meaningful net customer value creates the culture necessary that will ultimately drive the systems and methods that will allow you to rule the world.

Here are my four Superstars, and the characteristics that I think make them outstanding:

1. *Snap-On Tools* makes it through passion, customer connectivity, and consistently successful innovation.
2. *Sierra Nevada Brewery* exudes a similar passion plus a unique and genuine focus on employee satisfaction and involvement.
3. *Hewlett-Packard* is an excellent example of how to overcome some of the obstacles to innovation often found in very large corporations.
4. *The Nielsen Company* takes a balanced approach, covering all the plays of superstardom with strong, passionate, and centralized leadership.

Finally, we can't forget Adobe, already covered in Chapter 7, a true case study in effective customer connectivity, open innovation, streamlined processes, and aligned corporate culture.

So let's get started.

Snap-On Tools

As a person who has spent his entire life in computer and medical technologies, it may surprise you that my first Innovation Superstar is a tool company. But my interest in Snap-On Tools began when I was only six years old. My father was a commercial refrigeration mechanic, and he had a toolbox, like most mechanics do. But in his toolbox was a top drawer, and in that top drawer was a beautiful felt liner, and that drawer was where he kept his Snap-On tools.

They were expensive, so he didn't have very many of them, but his tools were clearly his most cherished possession. So how could my father be so highly connected to something as mundane as a hand tool? Well, if you remember back in Chapter 5 of *The Innovation Playbook,* I talk a lot about the anatomical features of an Innovation Superstar.

One of the catch-all cultural criteria for a superstar is what I called *craftsmanship.* Snap-On Tools are beautifully made. They are comfortable in your hand, and their quality, look, and feel are absolutely exquisite. But there is more to it than that. Their customer connectivity has allowed them to create innovations that are simply world-class. How do they do it?

Referring again back to Chapter 5, there's another dynamic in play here, again part of culture, that I call *collective passion.* They're tool guys who love tools, who are creating tools for other people who love tools. It's what they live; it's what they breathe—they get *excited* about it. They have the collective passion I find in every Innovation Superstar. From their Vice President of Innovation to their VP of Worldwide Sales, I could hear that excitement in their voices; I could feel the passion they had for this amazing line of products. Collective passion isn't something you can create through a new innovation management system. You have to have a team that gets it. You have to have a team that really loves the customer and has the passion to create world-class innovations that blow their customer away.

Another important component of Snap-On's success is the company's ability to keep its eyes on the proverbial prize—in this case, on customer value. They know that you can't focus on risk management in an environment surrounded by fear of product failure and still do amazing things. What's incredible about Snap-On Tools is that they produce more than 200 new inventions every single year! The overwhelming majority of these new products succeed in the marketplace. That's incredible—the ability to create a system, essentially an invention assembly line, that allows them to develop technologies that "nail it" 90 percent of the time is pretty incredible.

Sierra Nevada Brewing Co.

At the beginning of this chapter, I said that Innovation Superstars are very much alike yet completely different. I meant that they are in a variety of markets and deliver a variety of different services and technologies. That's why I decided to take superstars from a variety of different industries, so I could illustrate that anybody, in any organization, can achieve innovation stardom, and as a result, lead their marketplace.

So, with that in mind, I'd like to introduce my next Innovation Superstar: Sierra Nevada Brewing Co, located in the college town of Chico, California. Actually, for those of you who have been reading along, I already introduced Sierra Nevada way back in Chapter 1.

You might be wondering why I feature a beer company as an Innovation Superstar. After all, it's not exactly high technology—which of course, is exactly my point. Sierra Nevada is not in the technology business, they're not even in the product business, they're not even in the service business. Successful companies are in the *customer value* business. In this case, beer is the value.

What's interesting about Sierra Nevada is that, in an industry that's almost completely driven by how much you spend on advertising; they spend virtually no money on advertising or promoting their product. That's pretty incredible, considering they are the sixth largest brewer in the United States.

Again, I'd like to overlay the anatomical features of Chapter 5 onto Sierra Nevada. One point I'd like to reiterate from the early pages of *The Innovation Playbook* is that great companies deliver great products and services, while bad or sick companies deliver bad products or services. Sierra Nevada is a great company. They understand that in order to deliver the best product in the world, they must create an environment that fosters innovation and quality.

What I've consistently found in Innovation Superstars is that they're systemically value-centered. What do I mean by that? They care about their community. They care about their employees and their product. They care about the world they live in—for example, Sierra Nevada Brewing Co. has one of the largest solar arrays in the state of California, second only to Google. Their goal was energy independence, and in fact they are able to produce 80 percent of their own electricity. In addition, they are extremely conscientious about all things related to the environment. Their president, Ken Grossman, is committed to delivering a product that is environmentally conscious.

Sierra Nevada cares about its employees. If you're lucky enough to work there, you have access to the company's own medical clinic, which operates four hours a day, six days a week, only for Sierra

Nevada employees and their families. You also have access to a massage therapist—because the company decided that was a way to provide additional value free of charge to its employees. And, if you're a beer lover—and the folks who work at Sierra Nevada are definitely beer lovers—you get a "beer buck" redeemable for one case of beer with every paycheck.

I must admit that I love great beer, and I think I know what great beer is. While touring their amazingly pristine factory, I saw a bunch of people just like me working there—beer lovers. They were talking about beer, they were enthusiastic about it. As I talked to various people on the floor in the production area, there was a tremendous pride and enthusiasm that they were part of something "so cool." When their friends find out they work at Sierra Nevada, they're treated almost like royalty—that's a great company, one that produces amazing products.

When I interviewed Grossman, I asked one very important question: "Do you still love this?" He smiled, and said, "Absolutely." You could see the sincerity in his eyes and his smile. Even though he has been in the business for 30 years, he still wakes up every morning with a tremendous amount of pride and passion—and that's what makes an Innovation Superstar.

Hewlett-Packard

One of my favorite Innovation Superstars is HP, and in particular, I'm impressed with the "HP Garage" initiative I introduced in Chapter 9.

I'll never forget my first "dot.com" consulting engagement at the very beginning of the dot.com boom. The first day of that engagement I sat in on one of their ideation sessions. They were developing an online messaging system, an idea somewhat new at the time. It was interesting to listen to some smart "kids" with some big ideas. As it turned out, basically my role was one of "adult supervision" to help them create systems that would likely result in a scalable product that could provide a return on investment for themselves and their investors.

Even though this company created some extremely cool technologies, the fact of the matter was—it was easy! They didn't have a legal department, a human resource department; they didn't have a new product development system in play—they had no idea what risk management *was*. They had no infrastructure whatsoever.

It was a group of very smart people getting together to do something very cool.

That is easy, and that is why I love HP. Why? Because it is extremely hard to create a complete cycle of innovation while confronted with all of the issues and structure of a colossal multinational corporation.

So HP created what they call the "HP Garage" initiative starting with the HP Software & Solutions organization, referencing to the physical garage where the company was born in 1939. What I really liked about HP from the beginning was discovering how much they care about what employees think about the quality of their work life and the variety of processes and methods they're required to use each day. They know that their most important asset is their employees, so they are extremely conscientious about making sure they understand how their employees feel about the various systems that they are forced to use. That's not easy in the bureaucracy of large corporations.

The other thing that's amazing about HP is that, like Adobe (see Chapter 7), they allow each one of their organizations to use variations on innovation management systems in order to meet the specific and unique needs of their product or business in each division. That is really hard for corporations to do. Most love to be legalistic; most love to find a one-size-fits-all solution to all of their businesses—and HP has systematically resisted that.

HP Software & Solutions has created the Elements of Innovation Success that provides a framework for each organization to implement as they best match their organization. The elements cover how each organization should get leadership commitment to innovation, how they set their specific innovation objectives, what processes and tools should be considered, and the importance of communications, celebrating success, and measuring results. There is also a focus on how to enable an innovative culture, to support risk taking for innovation success, and how the customer must help shape innovations that touch them.

The HP Garage initiative allows people at the front end, who deal with customers every day to post ideas and to comment on ideas that are currently in development. That is so important Innovation Superstars know that they need to listen to front-line personnel to make sure they understand how customers are using and accepting different technologies and where there are opportunities to improve. They also have the opportunity for service technicians to be able to chime in and post comments regarding certain opportunities to increase the quality and reliability of a technology or to add new innovations.

I've discussed the difference between "innovation capitalism" and "innovation socialism" in Chapter 4 and again in Chapter 9. One of the biggest challenges with large corporations as it relates to the innovation function is to avoid becoming "socialistic," that is, to demand that there be rigid and legalistic tools that their departments must comply with. HP is an innovation capitalist; each one of their innovation champions is like an individual entrepreneur. They're given the freedom, and they have the enthusiasm to create technologies.

Also, HP is still in love with its customers, and cares about what the customer experience is all about. Unfortunately, most corporations have lost that customer connectivity, something that is indeed very hard to keep up when you're a colossally large company like HP. HP stays committed to its customer communities through user groups and annual symposiums to hear what their customers are thinking, are experiencing, and want, and then they take that information and do something about it. That takes commitment, and that's what makes HP an Innovation Superstar.

The Nielsen Company

Most of you have heard of the "Nielsen ratings" used to measure the popularity of television programs and other media. These ratings are only a small part of today's Nielsen Company's world-leading offering of marketing and media information and measurement.

I get bored with the mission statements of a lot of companies, but that of Nielsen is so focused and descriptive that I had to take a second look: "In a world increasingly defined by global markets, connected consumers and volumes of digital information, The Nielsen Company employs advanced data collection methodologies and measurement science to help businesses turn new and traditional sources of data into customer intelligence to better manage their brands, launch and grow product portfolios, optimize their media mix and establish meaningful customer relationships."

But innovation superstardom isn't just about mission statements, is it? In fact, it's no accident that Nielsen has achieved such market leadership in a space requiring clever uses of technology to deliver customer solutions. How can you know what viewers are watching? How can you connect the effect of an ad to the piece of programming or even the medium or combination of media being deployed? How do you learn more about the habits and desires of the viewers? These questions all demand creative, effective, and in today's fast moving media environment, very rapid solutions.

So I talked to the Senior VP of New Product Introductions (NPI) and Innovation at Nielsen (aha—a true innovation champion in high places!), Anne Marie Dumais. She had an interesting story to tell. And—the passion she exuded while telling it came through loud and clear.

Dumais' first principle, like the one we lay out in the superstar anatomy—is to "stay connected with clients." Now for her, and the some 30,000-plus people in her organization involved directly or indirectly with innovation, this means "walking in their shoes." She says every person involved with a client or a project needs to "go to the street with their client" early on to walk in their shoes. Individuals and teams visit clients to find out needs and to observe situations where they "may not know they have the need." They become "really good at understanding value propositions." It is carpet time, often done by innovation safari, done and done well.

Dumais has been implementing a cross-channel, common cross-business innovation platform to manage innovations across the company's many businesses and 100-plus worldwide locations. Now when I first heard this I was a bit concerned—remember prescriptive systems, which are adapted to the individual needs of every business. That's not what's happening here—but Dumais has been so passionate about communicating the vision and so inclusive about getting everyone's "fingerprints on the system" that it's working. She gave it the internal code name "Square Watermelons," to gain internal interest and to convey the idea that it was nothing conventional. I like the official name even better—BPQ or Better Products Quicker. According to Dumais, this name was carefully chosen not only to convey the importance of speed but also to be inclusive of all types of innovation, not just new products or some such.

Like the Real Open platform we recommend, BPQ is a common-sense framework with a heavy dose of openness at the front end. An innovation portal based on Brightidea's WebStorm is used to harvest inputs from all levels internally, plus outside where it makes sense. Nielsen will post a challenge, or a problem to be solved, and carry on contests internally to get solutions, offering contestants value points, gold, silver, and bronze medals, and opportunities to attend senior leadership meetings to discuss the winning ideas. Ideas are evaluated quickly and apolitically, with rapid decisions, results, and feedback. What I heard about and saw was a great example of "find" and "filter" processes done democratically and done right. You will not find here organizational divisions having their own independent ideation sections, rather, quite the opposite. Dumais insists on the company-wide best practice of "open, simple, and integrated" as a rule for driving ideation from anywhere and anyone in the company.

Dumais also added some best-practice principles I really liked and that serve them well. First, they set up challenges and solicit inputs in such a way as to eliminate any solutions that will take more than a year to do. It keeps solutions simpler and avoids the risk of missing the market. Secondly, they really embrace the 80-20 rule, sticking to the 20 percent of the innovation that achieves 80 percent of the customer value. According to Dumais: "Perfection is unsustainable in a business driven by fast changing customer needs" as it gobbles up resources and flexibility. Fulfilling the core and relevant needs of a customer base is paramount, and includes the distinction between filtering out the "nice to have" versus "must-have."

In short, I was quite impressed with Nielsen's approach to all three elements of Innovation Superstardom—Customer, Process, and Culture. They're a great example of balance and effectiveness—and also what can happen when you have a dynamic, respected, and empowered leader in charge.

Now You, Too, Can Be a Superstar

I have found over the years that to learn a valuable professional discipline it helps tremendously to have a more-or-less-formal training and certification program around it. It brings focus, and the end result is that you have a certification and credential that you can build on and apply in a variety of work environments. So in conjunction with *The Innovation Playbook*, I, along with my organization, Lassen Scientific, Inc., have created a certification called, not surprisingly, the Innovation Superstar Certification. Further, we have developed two levels of training tools as part of an Innovation Superstar Certification Program to help you and others in your organization get certified.

The Innovation Superstar Certification Programs

The Innovation Superstar Certification Programs Level 1 and Level 2 were developed to fill a real market gap (see Figure 10.1). There

Figure 10.1   The Innovation Superstar Certification

are several programs already in the marketplace that are centered on creativity; there are several more centered on conventional new product development or NPD training. There are also workshops and training programs that provide direction on small segments of the innovation process.

The ideology behind the Innovation Superstar training program is to provide holistic training in all areas of innovation management but not to create a program that mandates that users utilize a sequential and completely pre-structured process but rather a process that was designed to be prescribed to the unique needs of their organization. We developed both the RealOpen Innovation System (discussed at the end of this chapter) and the Innovation Superstar Certification Program to provide specific training for two classifications.

Our Superstar L1 program is designed for engineers, product managers, and people who are involved in the day-in, day-out activities of evaluating, developing, and commercializing new technologies and innovations. Our Superstar L2 program is designed for innovation leaders, typically the CEO, the VP of Innovation, or the VP of Research and Development. In the university research space, it's typically the technology transfer officer. The goal with L2 is to develop strategic innovation at the leadership level.

Thus, the programs are designed in two special ways. First, they are highly targeted to job function. Second, they are designed in a non-legalistic way that allows the participant to select a variety of tools and to configure those tools to meet the needs of their organization. Another goal of the Innovation Superstar training program is to make it holistic. By that I mean it covers everything from accessing innovations to filtering innovations to developing digital command centers to creating innovation submission portals to developing your innovation platform. It shows how to use the Webb Triangle to quickly evaluate innovations in a nonlinear fashion. It also uses fast-track methodology throughout the process to help companies increase speed and throughput. This is extremely important in the current economy.

The program provides a wide range of tools, so whether you are working in a new product development department or a new organization needing all of the skill sets, from accessing to commercialization, it is all included in the L1 and L2 Innovation Superstar training programs.

There is also an online certification program to be released in fall of 2010, as well as on-site certification for participants in the L1 Superstar program. The Innovation Superstar L2 program does require on-site training, testing, and oral interviews.

Once the participant completes the program, he or she can petition for certification. To get certified, participants are required to take a 50-question multiple-choice test and achieve a grade of 85 percent to complete the certification process. Participants in both of the Innovation Superstar training programs receive a tremendous amount of resources. The program requires the purchase of this book, *The Innovation Playbook*, which includes all material covered in the training program. In additional, participants receive free online resources so that they can study and pretest prior to the certification test.

Next is some additional detail on the two certification levels.

L1 Certification

L1 Certification is designed for all professionals in an organization dealing with innovation or product development, either in its entirety or certain segments of the process. After studying more than 200 of the most innovative companies in the world, we incorporated the best of the best. In this program you will learn:

- The basics of the state of the art RealOpen innovation management system.
- How to automate innovation filtration.
- How to develop world-class innovation platforms.
- How to develop real VOC by developing systematic Carpet Time.
- How to out-invent the competition with Innovation Safaris.
- Value layering your innovations with Project X.
- Fast-track innovation assessments with the Webb Triangle.
- How to hard-wire internal and external innovation to your corporate culture.
- How to replace risk management with opportunity management.
- How to build a systemic culture of innovation.
- How to lead your market with customer and market driven innovations.
- How to use the state of the art RealOpen innovation management system.

Additional considerations:

Program prerequisites: Participants should have a minimum of two to four years of direct experience in the area of product and project management. Most participants have a bachelor's degree or further education.

Training material: Program textbook is this book—*The Innovation Playbook: A Revolution in Business Excellence.*

Training methods: ICL L1 is available as an online certification program or as an on-site workshop. A score of 85 percent or above on a 50-question multiple-choice test is required for certification. Program fees do not include certification.

Certification: Certification is issued to program participants that complete an on-site or online training program and who have completed the test questions with an 85 percent or better score (see Figure 10.2). The purpose of the certification is to validate satisfactory course completion. No certification accreditation is expressed or implied.

Figure 10.2   Innovation Superstar L1 Certification

L2 Certification

Level II is our strategic innovation level. This program is specifically designed for organizational leadership including CEOs, CIOs, and vice presidents of new business development and research and development. The program includes:

- Comprehensive orientation of the RealOpen innovation management system.
- The must-have tool for innovation-scenario tactics.
- The five leadership skills of innovation.
- How to structure innovation teams.
- Developing a digital command center.
- How to increase access to market-leading innovations.
- How to improve innovation filtration and throughput.
- The role of innovation across the enterprise.
- The latest tools, and techniques and methods for increasing speed and profitability through innovation.
- How to configure an innovation-driven organization.
- How to create innovation champions within your organization.

Additional considerations:

Program prerequisites: Participants should have a minimum of four to six years of direct experience in the area of product and project management. Most participants have a graduate degree.

Training material: Program textbook is this book, *The Innovation Playbook: A Revolution in Business Excellence.*

Training methods: ICL L2 is available as an online certification program or as an on-site workshop. A score of 85 percent or higher on a 50-question multiple-choice test is required for certification. Program fees do not include certification.

Certification: Certification is issued to program participants that complete an on-site or online training program and who have completed the test questions with an 85 percent or better score (see Figure 10.3). The purpose of the certification is to validate satisfactory course completion. No certification accreditation is expressed or implied.

The RealOpen Service and Software Offering

Finally, in addition to the Innovation Superstar Certification L1 and L2 programs, we also make RealOpen available in a couple of forms.

Figure 10.3   Innovation Superstar L2 Certification

speed.results.profit

Figure 10.4   The RealOpen System

RealOpen is a service and software offering that assists clients in developing innovation platforms and customized submission portals. The RealOpen system frees companies from the burden of managing innovation submissions through the development of customized innovation submission portals. These portals also provide our proprietary toggle system that pre-filters the innovation, thereby providing the client pre-vetted technologies. The RealOpen system also includes a range of consulting and training services to assist the clients in developing their own innovation management systems. This provides a convenient way for clients to choose from a turnkey solution of accessing external innovations or the training and consulting services to create their own.

The system guides you through:

- The creation of a comprehensive innovation platform.
- The development of a comprehensive internal and external submission portal connected to the platform.
- The development of a digital strategy to solicit external innovation submissions.
- The creation of custom innovation measurement tools.
- Installation of fast-track methodologies to quickly move the innovation from filtration to the find/forget phase.
- Fast-track innovation assessment through the Webb Triangle.
- Creation of a multi-front innovation procurement plan.
- The development of a digital command center.
- Access to all other RealOpen tools.

For more information on RealOpen training and software, visit www.theinnovationplaybook.com (see Figure 10.4).

Chapter Takeaways

- The fundamental principles of *The Innovation Playbook* apply to you, wherever you are. Although most associate Innovation

Superstars work with technology and in the high tech industry, Innovation Superstars can be found in a variety of businesses, including tools, beer brewing, and financial services, among so many others.

- As a reader of *The Innovation Playbook*, you are already well on your way towards achieving our Innovation Superstar Certification. As an individual, or as an organization, you can take a few short steps to complete the certification and to round out your knowledge and become prepared to apply our principles to your organization. You, too, can dance with the Innovation Superstars.

- To receive your free online training program, a $150 value, go to www.theinnovationplaybook.com, select register my book, and then enter offer code: book. Someday, you'll be glad you did.

About the Author

Nicholas J. Webb is a successful inventor, entrepreneur, author, and management consultant in the field of innovation and innovation management. He has served as the CEO of several successful technology firms including Myocure, Inc. a pioneer in refractive ophthalmic surgery. He is the founder of Nupak Medical, LLC, a medical product manufacturing firm. He has also served as a CEO with several other technology-related companies. He is a successful inventor, having been awarded more than 35 patents from the U.S. Patent and Trademark Office. His technologies range from one of the world's smallest medical implants to industrial and computer technologies. He currently serves as the CEO of Lassen Innovation, Inc., which provides strategic innovation and management consulting services, and he has attained certification as a Certified Management Consultant. His client list represents some of the best companies and research organizations in the world. Nicholas is a frequent speaker and workshop leader at vertical industry conferences as well as innovation, licensing, and technology forums around the world. Nick combines his own personal experience of "having been there" with a proven strategy for increasing profits and market share through a combination of the use of leading-edge innovation methods and general business best practices. He lives in Northern California with his wife and four children.

About *The Innovation Playbook* Web Site

Special Book Offer $149 Value

With the purchase of your Innovation Playbook, you are entitled to our introductory training program called The Innovation Superstar Level I. This program is an interactive innovation-management training program. It provides a series of audio and video lessons and allows you to test your innovation skills. The program includes the following features:

Innovation Superstar Certified* (ISC) Level I

- Introduction to the state-of-the-art RealOpen innovation management system.
- How to automate innovation filtration.
- Developed world-class innovation platforms.
- Value layering your innovations with Project X.
- Fast-track innovation assessments with the Webb triangle.
- Hard-wire internal and external innovation to your corporate culture.
- Replace risk management with opportunity management.
- Build a systemic culture of innovation.
- Lead your market with customer and market-driven innovations.

236

Certification is available at an additional cost.

The free offer does not include the certification fee. Certification is issued to program participants who complete an online training program and have completed the test questions with an 85 percent or better score and paid the certification fee. The purpose of certification is to validate satisfactory course completion. No certification accreditation is expressed or implied. Innovation Superstar and RealOpen are pending trademarks of Lassen Scientific, Inc. a California corporation.

Visit the web site at: www.wiley.com/go/webbinnovation.

Index